The
Programming Language
Landscape

$24 95

The Programming Language Landscape

Henry Ledgard

Human Factors Limited
Leverett, Massachusetts

Michael Marcotty

General Motors
Research Laboratories
and
Wayne State University

SCIENCE RESEARCH ASSOCIATES, INC.
Chicago, Palo Alto, Toronto, Henley-on-Thames, Sydney

A Subsidiary of IBM

The SRA Computer Science Series

William A. Barrett and John D. Couch, *Compiler Construction: Theory and Practice*
Marilyn Bohl and Arline Walter, *Introduction to PL/1 Programming and PL/C*
Mark Elson, *Concepts of Programming Languages*
Mark Elson, *Data Structures*
Peter Freeman, *Software Systems Principles: A Survey*
C. W. Gear, *Introduction to Computer Science*
C. W. Gear, *Introduction to Computer Science: Short Edition*
A. N. Habermann, *Introduction to Operating System Design*
Harry Katzan, Jr., *Computer Systems Organization and Programming*
Henry Ledgard and Michael Marcotty, *The Programming Language Landscape*
James L. Parker and Marilyn Bohl, *FORTRAN Programming and WATFIV*
Stephen M. Pizer, *Numerical Computing and Mathematical Analysis*
Harold S. Stone, *Discrete Mathematical Structures and Their Applications*
Harold S. Stone, *Introduction to Computer Architecture, Second Edition*

Acquisition Editor	Alan W. Lowe
Project Editor	James C. Budd
Production and Composition	Human Factors Limited
Illustrator	Drake Maher
Cover Photo	Foto Saporetti

Library of Congress Cataloging in Publication Data

Ledgard, Henry   1943
  The programming language landscape.

  Bibliography: p.
  Includes index.
  1. Programming languages (Electronic computers)
I. Marcotty, Michael, 1931-   joint author.
II. Title.
QA76.L44   001.64'24   80-25219
ISBN 0-574-21340-6

© 1981 Science Research Associates, Inc. All rights reserved.

Printed in the United States of America.

10 9 8 7 6 5 4 3 2

Acknowledgments

Cover   Background detail from the painting of Il Moro meeting the Emperor, from Grammatica di Donato. Photograph by Foto Saporetti, Milan, Italy.

Chapter 1   Aerial photograph of the Alps near Freiburg, Switzerland. Photo by Swissair A.G.

Chapter 2   Enlarged portion of a U.S. Geological Survey topographic map of the Grand Canyon, Arizona.

Chapter 3   Photograph taken in Grand Canyon showing Sumner Butte. Photo by Don Hart.

Chapter 4   Photograph taken at Guam by United Press International.

Chapter 5   Highway crisscross near Frankfurt, Germany. From "The World from Above" by Hanns Reich. Photo by Aero Exploration.

Chapter 6   Monument Valley, Arizona. Photo by David Muench.

Chapter 7   Factory Chimneys in England. From "The World from Above" by Hanns Reich. Photo by Aerofilms.

Chapter 8   The Souf Oasis. Photo by Georg Gerster.

Chapter 9   American Superhighway. From "The World from Above" by Hanns Reich. Photo by Instituto Geografico di Agostini.

Chapter 10   Balancing rock in Chiricahua National Monument, Arizona. Photo by Ed Cooper.

Chapter 11   Zagros Mountains, Western Iran. From "The World from Above" by Hanns Reich. Photo by Aerofilms.

Chapter 12   Battersea Power Station, London. Photo by Robert Estall.

Chapter 13   Volcano. Photo by Eliot Elisofon, Life Magazine, © 1951, Time Inc.

Chapter 14   Landslide. Photo by Nat Farbman, Life Magazine, © 1959, Time Inc.

Chapter 15   Flock of sheep on highway. From "The World from Above" by Hanns Reich. Photo by Bayer Flugdienst.

Chapter 16   Mangrove Swamp, Everglades. Photo by Dan McCoy.

Stronicę tę Poswięcamy Wirtuozce Wielu Dziedzin,
Pani Lindzie Skrzypek-Strzegowskiej

Contents

A Closer Look

Enhancement

The Landscape Re-examined

Preface

There are several approaches to the study of programming languages. One is to examine several existing languages in detail, compare and contrast their salient features, and attempt to draw conclusions about underlying design principles. Another path starts with the design principles, studies them in relative isolation, and then seeks examples of the implementation of these principles in real languages. This text follows the second approach because we believe that it is only by understanding the basic concepts that meaningful comparisons may be drawn between various languages.

Central to our approach is the use of mini-languages, each of which has been designed around some key language feature. The mini-languages allow a concept to be studied without the need to understand the wealth of detail and complexity found in real programming languages. One of the first uses of this technique was in Ledgard's paper, "Ten Mini-Languages: A Study of Topical Issues in Programming Languages," Computing Surveys, September 1971.

The chapters are self-contained. Each has its own mini-language, with a small number of constructs designed to illustrate the concept under discussion. Most of the mini-languages are built on a common core described in Chapters 2 and 3. An overriding theme of all of the chapters is the need for much greater simplicity in language design.

The reader is expected to have experience with one (perhaps more) high-level languages. The concepts discussed here are drawn mainly from Ada, Algol 60, Algol 68, Cobol, Fortran, Lisp, Pascal, and PL/I. Between these languages, almost any programming language principle, good or bad, can be found. Other languages referenced include APL, Basic, Bliss, and Simula 67. Obviously, there can be no attempt to present a description of all these languages. However, the reader, even if unfamiliar with these languages, should have no difficulty in under-standing this text. It is expected that the reader will wish to refer to detailed manuals to obtain a deeper understanding of some of the languages mentioned. Reference material for all languages mentioned is cited in the bibliography under the name of the language. Suggestions for further reading are contained at the end of each chapter.

There is no firmly established convention for the style of writing the names of programming languages. Usage varies, with no obvious criterion, between use of upper case only and just capitalizing the initial letters — for example, between FORTRAN and Fortran. In this text, we have adopted the rule that, if the name is pronounced as a sequence of letters, all the letters will be written in upper case, otherwise the name is treated as a normal proper noun. Examples of the application of this rule are: AED, Ada, Algol 60, APL, BCPL, Fortran, and PL/I.

For teaching, this book follows the guidelines of course CS 8, "Organization of Programming Languages," given in Curriculum '78, Communications of the ACM, March 1979. As such, it may be useful for undergraduate and early graduate courses, as well as for anyone seeking a perspective of the programming language area.

Although each chapter in this book is self-contained, we treat programming languages in four successively deeper levels. The first level, Chapters 1 through 3, introduces the area of programming language, discusses a number of broad issues, and generally set the landscape for the remainder of the book. The second level, Chapters 4 through 8, discusses five dominant features of most contemporary languages: assignment, control structures, data types, procedures, and nesting.

The third level, Chapters 9 through 12, elaborate on these and other related concepts. Chapters 13 through 15 treat three specialized but important areas: dynamically varying data structures, exception handling, and concurrent processing. The last chapter, Chapter 16, presents some views on the complexity of programming languages. Some suggested term projects are given at the end of this chapter.

The design of translators is not discussed specifically. However, implementation is not forgotten and the reader can see how language design, translation processes, and execution environment interact. Of particular interest throughout is the clarity and naturalness of expres-sion that can be obtained from differing language constructs.

This book owes its inception to a mixed graduate, undergraduate course that Marcotty has been teaching at Wayne State and Oakland Universities. We are particularly grateful for the excellent proofreading done by the 1980 fall semester Principles of Programming Languages class at Wayne State University, especially by Elizabeth LaCharité, Karen Schaefer, Madea Jones, Dan Cecchini, and Louis Paine.

The book has gained much of its breadth from the work done by Ledgard on the design of Ada. The syntax of many of the mini-languages has also benefited from this work. Andrew Singer provided thoughtful comments throughout the development of this text. Finally, we are grateful to J.A.N. Lee, who for many years has promoted the use of mini-languages in teaching.

Henry Ledgard
Michael Marcotty

The Landscape

1
Introduction

thru pg. 20

1.1 THE BUILDING OF THE TOWER OF BABEL

Before 1954 almost all programming was done in machine language. Solving a problem on a computer required the detailed encoding of long sequences of instructions into numbers in binary or octal form. Sometimes, some mnemonic help was provided by the written form of the machine language, and letter codes were used for operations, for example, MPY in place of 021 for multiply. This help was later augmented by the use of symbolic names instead of numeric addresses to refer to values. The nature of the work is illustrated by the fact that the actual writing of the instructions was called *coding* rather than *programming* — programming implies the more difficult task of designing algorithms.

The problems with this method of expressing algorithms were:

■ The programs had to be tailored to the particular characteristics of the available computer. Much effort was devoted to overcoming deficiencies of the computer's architecture, for example, no index registers, lack of built-in floating point operations, and restricted instruction sets.

■ When a new computer replaced the old one, all this inventiveness was for nought; the old programs had to be thrown away and the process of building a new library started again.

- The close association between a program and a particular machine design not only permitted but actively encouraged the invention of all kinds of tricks to wring maximum performance from the computer. The correctness of programs constructed in this way was very difficult to verify, and it was practically impossible to discover the algorithm behind a program coded by a colleague.

- The language in which the program was written contained practically no textual redundancy that could be used to detect errors. Almost any combination of characters could be executed. To tie the execution errors back to the faulty code was difficult and time consuming.

These shortcomings led to the development of so-called *automatic programming systems.* These systems generally provided operations such as floating point addition and trigonometric functions, together with either fixed or variable operands. Usually, the programmer had to write statements in a fixed format that did not allow mathematical expressions to be written in anything resembling natural notation.

Automatic programming systems gave the programmer a synthetic "computer" with an instruction set that was different from that of a real machine. In particular, the synthetic machine generally had floating point operations, index registers, and improved input and output commands. It was thus much easier to program than its real counterpart. The programmer was able to think of a floating point addition as just that, and forget the details of carrying it out in the hardware. The synthetic machine was thus an *abstract machine.*

The early automatic programming systems were costly to use since they slowed the actual machine down by a factor of five or more, most of the time being spent in floating point subroutines. Experience with these systems, coupled with their familiarity with cunning programming tricks, convinced programmers that any mechanical coding method would fail to apply the versatile ingenuity that all programmers believed they used constantly in their work.

The advent of computers with built-in floating point and indexing further increased the skepticism. By speeding up the floating point computations by a factor of ten, a common source of inefficiency in handwritten programs was removed. Consequently, the automatic generation of programs that were efficient, by comparison with handwritten ones, became an order of magnitude more difficult. Those who wanted to simplify programming could only gain acceptance for their system if they could demonstrate that it could produce programs that were almost as efficient as handcoded ones in practically every case.

In this atmosphere John Backus formed a group in 1954 to develop the Fortran (FORmula TRANslator) compiler aimed at the automatic translation of mathematical formulas into machine instructions. The group hoped to bring about a radical change in the economics of scientific computing by making programming much cheaper through a drastic reduction in the time it took for a working program to be prepared. Because of the atmosphere of skepticism, the group's emphasis was on the efficiency of the translated program rather than on language design.

It was thought that, once the ideas of an assignment statement, subscripted variables, and the DO statement had been adopted, the remaining problems of language design would be trivial! Their solution would be dictated either by the need to provide some machine facility or by some programming task that could not be done with existing structures.

At that time, nothing was known of many issues that were later thought to be important: block and control structures, nested subprograms, and type declarations — issues that are addressed in detail in this book. The Fortran programming system was viewed as applying to just one machine and very little thought was given to the implications of making a machine-independent programming language. As a result, certain characteristics of the machine on which Fortran was first implemented became part of the language; for example, the naming of output channels was determined by the numbering of the tape units on the IBM 704 computer.

Fortran was just one of several programming languages that appeared in 1956 and 1957. This period was the beginning of a programming revolution; it almost seemed that each new computer, and even each programming group, was spawning its own algebraic language or favorite dialect of an existing one. Most of these languages were aimed at helping the scientific programmer and were restricted to a particular machine. Their designers were generally a small group of implementors, rather than users, drawn from a single company. A primary design objective was to produce efficient machine code, even if it meant sacrificing some clarity of expression in the language.

The objectives of the designers of Cobol (Common Business Oriented Language) were different. In 1959, a committee of representatives from several organizations was established to design a machine independent programming language suitable for use by the business community. The committee decided that the language should make the maximum use of simple English so that managers who had no programming experience would be able to understand the programs. It was felt by many committee members that arithmetic operations should be specified by words like ADD and MULTIPLY rather than by the symbols + and * because these words would be more readily understood. The important thing is not whether the committee was right, but that a serious effort was being made to design a language for communication between people and computers.

Fortran and Cobol are only two examples of the many languages that have been developed for programming computers. In many cases, however, little thought has been put into their design. This is demonstrated in two major ways:

■ The external form of the language has often been designed according to what was thought to be the easiest form for computer analysis rather than what was most natural as a means of expression.

■ Economy of design and simplicity of structure are rarely seen.

The profusion of programming languages and their design weaknesses severely hinders valuable communication between programmers. We are still in the state ascribed in Genesis as leading to the failure of the Tower of Babel project. This is despite the efforts of many very talented people working individually, in groups, in small and large committees, and even in international committees. Some have attempted to design a "universal" language. There have been several candidates for this position but none has achieved widespread acceptance and use.

If programming languages are examined carefully, they are found to resemble each other more than their external forms would lead us to suppose. They are built on a number of basic concepts; it is the object of this book to study these concepts so that we can have a better understanding of these languages.

1.2 WHAT IS A PROGRAMMING LANGUAGE?

The computer was conceived as a device that would speed up complicated and time consuming computations. Despite this, it is not its ability to perform arithmetic that is important in the majority of applications, but the fact that it can store and access large amounts of data. These data form an *abstraction* of some part of the real world.

Consider the master file used in a payroll application. Each employee is represented by the data needed for the accounting procedures involved in preparing the payroll. These will probably include such items as the employee's name, social security number, and salary. Other data, such as hair color, shoe size, and name of a favorite breakfast cereal, will probably not be included. These, while very much part of a full description of the employee, are irrelevent to the paycheck computation and do not form part of the abstraction that represents the employee in the master payroll file.   *data items = abstract objects*

efinitions The data stored in the computer are thus a representation of real world objects. We speak of the data items as *abstract objects.* Associated with an abstract object is a set of operations that transforms it into other abstract objects. The computation consists of applying these operations to an initial set of abstract objects, the input data, so as to transform them into new abstract objects that represent the result of the computation.

We define an *algorithm* as a specification of the sequence of operations to be performed on the initial set of objects to produce the resulting set of objects. This algorithm must be represented in a form that can be communicated both to the computer and to other programmers. A *programming language* is a set of conventions for communicating algorithms. An algorithm expressed in a programming language is a *program.*

Although all programming languages share a number of common principles that we shall study later, the languages are of different varieties. These may be very loosely classified according to the area of application or mode of use.

A *commercial language* is one that is particularly concerned with the manipulation of files of alphanumeric data and with the production of reports. Cobol is the best known commercial language.

A *scientific language* is one that is used mainly for the manipulation of numeric data. Fortran is the best known scientific language.

An *interactive language* is one that is designed to allow a programmer to make changes and corrections from a terminal during execution. For example, both Lisp and APL are designed to be used interactively.

A *procedural language* is one that allows the user to specify a set of imperative statements that are to be performed in a particular sequence. Most contemporary programming languages are procedural.

A *nonprocedural language* is one in which the user does not specify the sequence of operations that are to be performed to obtain a problem's solution. Only the problem is defined; the emphasis is on what is to be done rather than how it is to be done. Well-known examples of nonprocedural languages (although some may dispute that they are, in fact, programming languages) are sort and report generators, in which the user specifies the forms of the input and the output without any description of the detailed steps required to transform the former into the latter.

An *applicative language* is one in which the program consists of the evaluation of a function that uses the input data as arguments and whose value is the result of the computation. "Pure" Lisp is an example of an applicative language.

A *real-time language* is one that allows the programming of procedures that can be executed concurrently and can be activated in response to external signals as required. Concurrent Pascal and Ada are examples of real-time programming languages.

A *special purpose language* is one that is designed with a limited objective, such as ease of use in a particular application area. For example, the language Apt is used to write programs to control machine tools.

You should recognize of course that these classifications are very informal, and that certain languages will fall into more than one category.

Implementation Schemes

The realization of a programming language in a computer system is called the *implementation.* Programming languages may be implemented in one of two ways: *compilation* or *interpretation.*

Compilation: The program written in the programming language, the *source program*, is translated into an equivalent program, the *object program*, in the machine language of the computer on which it is to be executed, the *target machine.* The object program is then executed by the target machine.

The translation from source program to object program is performed by a program generally referred to as a *translator* or *compiler.* The translator is itself usually executed on the target machine. However, if this is not feasible, for example, if the target machine is too small for the compiler to run, then the translator is executed on a larger machine, possibly of an entirely different architecture. In this case, the translator is known as a *cross compiler.* Much of the programming for minicomputers is done through cross compilers.

Interpretation: The source program is translated into an object program that cannot be executed directly by an actual computer. Instead, the execution of the object program is achieved by an *interpreter.* This is a program that is executed on the target machine performing the operations specified in the object program by means of subroutines.

The use of an interpreter allows for greater flexibility than can be achieved by direct execution. However, the penalty is that interpretation is generally much slower than direct execution. Examples of languages that are often implemented in this way are APL, Basic, and Lisp.

There is no hard line of differentiation between compilation and interpretation. Even in systems where the compiler produces machine code for a real machine, an extensive support library of subroutines is usually required for execution of the object program. As the system design moves more in the direction of interpretation, the library becomes bigger and less is done by execution of compiled codes.

Interpretation and execution merge at the point where the object program consists of a sequence of machine code subroutine invocations, and the interpreter consists of the subroutines that are invoked during execution. The amount of processing performed by the translator ranges from doing nothing, in which case the character string representation of the source program is interpreted directly, through complete translation into target machine code. An implementation of a programming language includes the translator, interpreter, and supporting subroutines.

There is, of course, a relationship between a language and its implementation. While there may be several different ways of realizing the facilities of a language, some are inherently more difficult and expensive than others. The ability to manipulate strings that do not have a predetermined upper bound for their length, for example, offers great flexibility to the programmer; at the same time, such a facility requires expensive storage management techniques. Awareness of the associated implementation complexities allows a choice to be made between utility and cost.

1.3   WHY STUDY PROGRAMMING LANGUAGES?

Although they are all natural languages, an ability to speak English does not automatically confer the ability to understand French and German. Nevertheless, the three languages are based on very similar principles due to their common Indo-European origin. English is blessed (or cursed) with a very tolerant grammar; many students whose mother tongue is English have problems with languages with more rigid grammars. This is because grammatical concepts that are only vestigially present in English are important in other languages and need to be understood. Although the subjunctive exists in English, its use is vanishing fast and most English-speaking people are unaware of it. In French, however, it has a very important place and must be understood before the language can be mastered. An understanding of the common grammatical basis of English and French clearly helps the student. Both languages, however, allow the same basic ideas to be communicated.

The situation is very much the same with programming languages; they differ widely in their external forms and range of facilities, yet they are based on a relatively small group of basic concepts. Whether you are learning a new language or increasing your knowledge of a large language, an understanding of these underlying concepts will make this task simpler. You will be able to see beyond the external format of the language to some principles that you can understand.

Of all the aspects of programming, the design of a language requires the greatest skill and judgment. The linguist Benjamin Whorf [1956] has hypothesized that one's language has a considerable effect on the way that one thinks; indeed on *what* one *can* think. The language designer's task transcends programming itself and concerns itself with the symbolism that is used to express computations. Thus, if Whorf's hypothesis is correct, the skill of the designer will have a considerable effect on the range of problems that can be solved in a language. The designer must survey the many attractive features that are available for inclusion in a language and choose the most powerful set of facilities that will constitute a harmoneous assembly. The objective is sufficient power with *minimal* complexity.

Of course, most programmers and computer scientists do not become language designers, which is a good thing since there are already too many languages. However a proper understanding of the concepts of programming languages will help make the design of programs considerably easier. Success will be indicated by a program that is a pleasure to use.

1.4 WHAT SHOULD WE LOOK FOR IN A LANGUAGE?

A programming language is the programmer's most important tool. A good language can lead the programmer to the correct solution of a problem in a natural and easy manner. Conversely, a poor language may add so much complexity to finding the solution that the programmer will abandon the attempt at solving the problem in favor of an easier one. A programming language thus serves a programmer in the same way that a notation serves a mathematician. As said in [Whitehead 1911]:

> By relieving the brain of all unnecessary work, a good notation sets it free to concentrate on more advanced problems, and in effect increases the mental power of the race. Before the introduction of the Arabic notation, multiplication was difficult, and the division even of integers called into play the highest mathematical faculties. Probably nothing in the modern world would have more astonished a Greek mathematician than to learn that . . . a large proportion of the population of Western Europe could perform the operation of division for the largest numbers. This fact would have seemed to him a sheer impossibility. . . . Our modern power of easy reckoning with decimal fractions is the almost miraculous result of the gradual discovery of a perfect notation.

The primary purpose of a programming language is to help in the task of programming. Thus it must aid in those areas that are the most difficult:

Program design: deciding and specifying what must be done and how the data are to be represented.

Understanding: explaining the working of the program to a human reader.

Verification: establishing the correctness of the program.

We turn then to some of the characteristics of a programming language that will make it useful in these areas. It will become evident that the areas are not independent and that some desirable characteristics are helpful in all three.

Program Design

In program design, the language must assist the programmer in specifying the process and the data clearly and naturally. It must be possible to construct abstractions that match the characteristics of the problem. This means that it must be possible to avoid extraneous detail that will clutter up the solution.

A common deficiency in this area is the inability of a language to manipulate abstract data objects other than the few primitive types supplied by the language. For example, in Fortran, Cobol, and to a large extent PL/I, all data must be mapped into a few basic elements. The details of this representation are likely to obtrude into the algorithm, making it more difficult to understand.

For example, a date, if it is to be manipulated in these languages, must be represented as a number. A programmer may use operations, like division, that are valid for numbers but that have no meaning when applied to dates. Thus, it is most important for the ease and clarity of programming that the language be able to treat abstract objects that match the problem data.

Understanding

All too often documentation is added to a program as a chore after the program has been made to work. As a result, either too little or too much detail is supplied. If there is not enough, the programmer who wishes to modify the program later will not be able to do the job reliably. If there is too much detail, it usually repeats what is written in the code and serves to obscure rather than enlighten.

A well-designed language will encourage the programmer to write so clearly that the program will be *self-documenting*, with only modest need for additional comments. Making the documentation an integral part of the program avoids the well-known trap of misleading documentation that occurs when a program is modified without corresponding changes in the separate documentation. For self-documentation to be possible, the language must allow the specification of operations and data to be made clearly and naturally.

A frequently applied criterion in the design of languages is the minimization of keystrokes on the grounds that this will help the programmer. Shopping lists are usually constructed this way, with terse phrases based on a great deal of contextual information in the writer's mind. Six months later, a shopping list is often too cryptic to be understood because the contextual information has been forgotten.

Readability is thus a much more important criterion than writability; after all, the program will probably only be written once, but read many times. It must be recognized, however, that, even though a language may be designed with the goal of program clarity, it does not follow that all programs written in that language will be clear. It is impossible to design a language in which an obscure program cannot be written.

Verification

To help with verification, the programming language must give the programmer confidence that the program is correct. Thus, it must aid the programmer to obtain either formal or informal verification. Again, one of the best ways of achieving this is for the program to have been written with such crystal clarity that it is obviously correct. Since it is probable that careless errors will always be made, the notation of the programming language should be designed so that the scope of such errors will be reduced and the bulk of them detected by the compiler.

1.5 LANGUAGE DESIGN ISSUES

PL/I has a rule allowing implicit declaration of variables, that is, the translator allows the use of variables that have not been explicitly declared to be used. The designers argued that this would save the programmer trouble in cases where the attributes assumed by the translator matched those required by the programmer. The penalty for this convenience is that the compiler can no longer detect simple spelling errors in the names of variables. The occurrence of a misspelled name constitutes an implicit declaration of that name as a new identifier.

More importantly, the explicit declaration of variables does a great deal to establish the intent of the program in the reader's mind. The declarations may then be viewed as "definitions" of program objects, and the executable statements as steps in the process of computing the result.

Not all programming errors can be detected by the compiler. The language must be designed so that the effects of these errors can all be explained through the language without recourse to details of the implementation or the underlying real machine. To require knowledge of the real machine is to shatter the abstract machine provided by the language. The Fortran error message

```
STATE--ABEND CODE IS: SYSTEM0200, USER 0000
IO-NONE, SCB=0F10C0, PSW IS 078D2000000A98B2E
```

has no meaning in the language; the Fortran machine does not have an SCB or PSW.

Sometimes implementors attempt to provide security without exacting a large execution time penalty by providing two compilers: a debugging compiler and an optimizing compiler for use when the program has graduated from debugging to production. This provides an added difficulty by introducing the possibility that the abstract machines represented by the two compilers may not be identical. Furthermore, it also implies that, once the program is in production and its results have become important, many of the safeguards on correctness will be removed.

Underlying all of the needed language characteristics is simplicity. The programmer must be able to understand the tool completely. How many Fortran or PL/I programmers can claim that they know the language completely? Understanding a language often represents such a large investment in time that programmers find it impossible to change to a new language despite the acknowledged weaknesses of an old one.

An important part of a simple design is that there should not be more than one way of expressing any action in the language, that is, each component of the language should be independent of the other components. The design is then said to be *orthogonal.* In a truly orthogonal design, there are a small number of separate, basic constructions and these are combined according to regular and systematic rules without arbitrary restrictions.

Many programming languages include composite data types, such as structures and arrays. They also allow functions, processes that map arguments into a result. A proper combination of these two orthogonal concepts, data types and functions, would permit functions to return results of any data type that is allowed as an argument.

An arbitrary restriction, for example, would allow arguments to be of composite data type but permit only scalar results. This type of restriction is seen in Fortran, Algol 60, and some versions of PL/I. However, there is a danger in removing all restrictions; the complexity of the language will be increased without a corresponding gain in facility.

The provision of more than one form to denote a concept always increases the size of a language. The additional complexity introduced by such features must be carefully weighed against their usefulness.

Cobol provides an example of questionable duplicate forms. The sequence of arithmetic statements

```
COMPUTE  TOTAL-HOURS      = OVERTIME-HOURS + REGULAR-HOURS.
COMPUTE  NUM-ON-PAYROLL  = NUM-EMPLOYEES   - NUM-ON-VACATION
                                           - NUM-ON-LEAVE.
```

performs the same computation as the sequence of statements

```
ADD      OVERTIME-HOURS TO REGULAR-HOURS GIVING TOTAL-HOURS.
SUBTRACT NUM-ON-VACATION, NUM-ON-LEAVE FROM NUM-EMPLOYEES
         GIVING NUM-ON-PAYROLL.
```

and both sequences are homogeneous to the eye. However, when both notations are combined as in

```
COMPUTE  TOTAL-HOURS = OVERTIME-HOURS + REGULAR-HOURS.
SUBTRACT NUM-ON-VACATION, NUM-ON-LEAVE FROM NUM-EMPLOYEES
         GIVING NUM-ON-PAYROLL.
```

the symmetry of like operations becomes less visible. A designer may prefer the concise mathematical form of the first sequence or the English-like notation of the second. In any case, it would be simpler to retain a single notation in the language. We prefer the arithmetic version in this case.

PL/I provides another ready example of questionable duplicate forms. For instance, fully qualified names for composite structures are often cumbersome to read and write, especially when the same element is referenced often in a short span of text. Consider the PL/I declaration:

```
DECLARE 1 A(1 : 10,  1 : 12),
          2 B(1 : 5),
            3 C(1 : 7)  CHARACTER(5),
            3 D         CHARACTER(1);
```

There are many different forms that can be used to reference the same component of the structure. For example, the fully qualified references

```
A(9, 11).B(4).C(7)
A(9).B(11, 4).C(7)
A(9).B(11).C(4, 7)
A.B.C(9, 11, 4, 7)
A(9, 11, 4, 7).B.C
```

and, in certain contexts, the partially qualified references

```
B(9, 11, 4).C(7)
A.C(9, 11, 4, 7)
C(9, 11, 4, 7)
```

can all be used to reference the same component in the structure. In each of these cases, any potential gain in brevity may be offset by a loss in clarity.

In some languages that attempt to provide everything for everybody, the problem of maintaining simplicity is attacked by so-called *modularity* of design. The idea is that an individual user will only be concerned with a particular part of the language and will not need to know anything about the other parts of the language. Thus the language is designed so that there are a number of, generally overlapping, subsets. In principle, this appears acceptable.

There are many problems with this approach however. The user will still be intimidated by the whole language, and separate texts may need to be written for the individual users. The compiler, which is written for the union of all the subsets, does not take account of the fact that the user only knows part of the language. There is even the danger that a user may write something that is meaningless in the particular subset being used but valid in another subset that is not known to the programmer. When the program is executed, an unintended action will take place, one that cannot be explained in terms of the original subset.

The properties that we have discussed so far have been characteristics of the *design* of a language. There are also some general questions of *implementation* that must be considered. Among these are:

Availability: Are there compilers available for the language on a wide range of machines?

External support: Are the standard processes, such as sorting, solution of differential equations, and graphic display, available for use or must they be written specially?

Implementation: Is the compiler easy to use and does it produce clear diagnostics?

Efficiency: Is the compiler efficient both in the compilation process and in the object code that it produces?

Documentation: Are the language and its compiler well documented? Are the supporting documents written clearly and unambiguously?

1.6   ELEMENTS OF A PROGRAMMING LANGUAGE

Before we can use a language, there are certain things that we need to know about it. This information must be contained in any proper description of the language.

First of all, we must know what type of objects can be manipulated in the language. Historically, programming languages have been designed to deal principally, though not exclusively, with some specific type of object. For example:

Fortran and Algol programs manipulate *numbers.*
Snobol programs manipulate *strings.*
Setl programs manipulate *sets.*
Lisp programs manipulate *lists.*

There are also attempts at "universal" languages, such as PL/I, that can manipulate many types of objects.

A more recent trend is to permit the programmer to define new abstract objects. For example, the Pascal declaration

```
type SUIT = (CLUBS, DIAMONDS, HEARTS, SPADES);
```

defines a type of abstract object, the suit, which can have one of four values. The identifiers CLUBS, DIAMONDS, HEARTS, and SPADES name these values. These are the names of *constants* of this type of abstract object, just as the numerals 0, 1, and so on, are the names of constants of the type of abstract objects called numbers.

The next thing we need to know about a language is what kind of algorithms it can be used to specify. In principle, almost any programming language, even the simplest, can be used to specify any algorithm. It can be shown that a very simple machine consisting only of a store and the single instruction

Change the contents of location A by subtracting the contents of location B from it; branch to location C if the result is negative, and otherwise proceed sequentially to the next instruction

can evaluate any computable function. However, such a machine will not be easy to program and its programs will not be easy to understand. Thus while any programming language can be used for anything (Fortran has been used for payrolls and Cobol for solving differential equations), it is important to know whether a particular kind of algorithm can be reasonably written in a language. Fortran and Cobol, for example, are not suitable for writing recursively defined functions (ones that can invoke themselves), but Algol and Pascal are.

Most real applications are so complex that they must be built from a number of smaller algorithms so that the programs do not become complicated to understand. It is therefore important to know how larger operations on objects can be constructed from smaller ones. In general, this means knowing what subroutine mechanism the language supplies.

Finally, we must know how a program in the language is to be written; that is, we must know what must be entered through the terminal or punched on the card, and what the program does. We discuss these issues next.

1.7   THE STUDY OF PROGRAMMING LANGUAGES

Generally the study of programming languages is divided into two distinct parts, the *syntax* and the *semantics*. Broadly speaking, the syntax of a language is concerned with the way that a program is written and the semantics with what happens when the program is executed, that is, with its *meaning*.

A program in a language is represented outside the computer as a string composed of symbols drawn from a finite set of symbols. Commonly, the symbols comprise the character set of a keypunch or terminal, but other sets of symbols are possible. Most of the strings of symbols are not programs in the language, they are meaningless gibberish. The syntax of the language consists of rules that define strings of symbols constructed in a particular way. These strings are called *syntactically legal programs*. The syntax rules of Fortran, for example, specify that the sequence of characters

```
2 + 3 = I + 1
```

is not a valid Fortran statement and thus no string containing this sequence of symbols outside a comment or string will be a legal Fortran program.

Only a small fraction of the legal programs will execute correctly. The rules of syntax govern only the construction of programs from the symbols and have no concern with what happens when the programs are executed. The semantic rules of the language define a subset of legal programs that have a meaning. In a similar way, there are many grammatical sentences in English, like:

```
THE SPHERICAL WALL GARGLED THE BUS
```

The semantics of English tells us that this sentence is nonsense. To return to Fortran, the sequence of statements

```
J = 0
K = 3 / J
```

results in division by zero. A program that contains such a sequence of symbols is said to contain a *semantic* error and to be meaningless.

The boundary between syntax and semantics is not well defined; different authors may define it differently. For example, the association of an identifier with a declaration is regarded by some as being syntactic and by others as semantic. There is a temptation to become over-involved with syntactic questions, and many textbooks succumb to this. The reason for this is primarily due to the fact that there is some well-developed mathematics connected with the syntax of languages. Consequently, a much tidier presentation is possible in this area. In most programming languages, the syntax is the only part defined with any degree of formalism. Usually, the semantic rules are only expressed informally. However, the semantic questions are much more difficult.

All too often, an intuitive understanding of the semantics turns out to be woefully superficial. When an attempt at implementation (which is, after all, a kind of formal definition) is made, ramifications and discrepancies appear. What was thought to have been fully understood is discovered to have been differently perceived by various readers of the same informal description. By then, it is frequently too late to change and incompatibilities have been cast in code. There is thus a great need for formalism that would remove the ambiguities and vagueness from semantic definitions. However, despite a great deal of work in this area, there is still little known about how to define semantics clearly. We return to this question in Chapter 3.

In Chapters 2 and 3, we discuss the general issues in syntax and semantics. The following chapters treat particularly important language issues common to several currently used languages.

We introduce mini-languages at appropriate points to provide vehicles for the discussion. The idea of a mini-language is that it contains only those features that are being currently discussed. Thus it is small enough to be easily described and understood, and the particular area of interest can be studied without worrying about interactions with other features in the language. Although heavy use of mini-languages provides a focus for discussion, examples of well-known programming languages are also cited frequently.

FURTHER READING

There are a number of books in the general area of programming languages, and most of them are textbooks. However, there are also a number of shorter works.

One of the more cleverly written of these is [Wirth 1976]. This paper discusses a number of language issues, and then presents an amusing script describing the design of a hypothetical computer language. Other short papers in the general area of language design are [Hoare 1973], [Richard and Ledgard 1977], and [Wirth 1974].

In 1978, a conference was held on the history of programming languages. This conference discussed the early development of a number of languages, including Fortran, Cobol, PL/I, and Basic. The proceedings of this conference appear in the August 1978 issue of ACM Sigplan Notices. This document is certainly relevant to this text. An earlier and comprehensive work in this area is [Sammet 1969].

There are other texts similar in intent to this one. Some of these are [Barron 1977], [Elson 1973], [Nicholls 1975], [Organick et al. 1978], and [Pratt 1975].

EXERCISES

Exercise 1.1   Language Complexity

It has been the fate of languages to get larger and larger as time passes. For instance, the original version of Fortran developed in the 1950's was quite small, although admittedly with some severe limitations. Then came Fortran II, Fortran IV, and Fortran 77; each larger and more complex than its predecessor. *No* language that we know of has become smaller over time.

Choose one of the languages, Ada, Basic, Fortran, Pascal, or PL/I, and two features that you would remove from the language. Give a rationale for each deletion. This rationale should include consideration of the effects of the deletion on the remainder of the language.

Note: Do not be misled by this exercise. The design of language features is often so interconnected that removal is extremely difficult. The key to smaller and less complex languages is not simply a matter of deletion. The key is the initial underlying design.

Exercise 1.2   Areas of Application

In Section 1.2 we give a loose classification of languages according to their area of application or mode of use. Choose three such areas and an appropriate language for each area, and then describe why the language is suited to the area. For example, what is it that makes Cobol such a popular language for data processing? Illustrate the points you make with examples.

Exercise 1.3 Machine Independence

What does it mean to say that a programming language is machine independent? Why is machine independence thought to be an important language design consideration? Describe some of the points that must be kept in mind when designing a machine independent language. Illustrate your answers with examples showing both machine independence and dependence from existing languages.

Exercise 1.4 Language Description

What are the important concepts used in describing a programming language and what are the criteria that should be used in judging the design of the language? Illustrate your answer with examples from an existing language description showing:

1. The application of your description concepts.

2. How your design criteria are both satisfied and violated by different languages.

Exercise 1.5 Abstract Machines

An operating system defines an abstract machine that differs from the actual host hardware. Choose an operating system with which you are familiar and determine the structure of the abstract machine that it defines. In what way does the abstract machine differ from the actual hardware? Give examples of restrictions (for example, features of the hardware that are not available to users of the operating system) and of extensions (that is, facilities that are directly available in the abstract machine but that can only be obtained by software simulation on the actual hardware).

Exercise 1.6 Language Design for Human Use

Based on your experience and drawing on examples taken from existing programming languages, list some things the language designers might do to make the programming process as difficult as possible. (This exercise is from Richard L. Wexelblat.) You might wish to have a look at [Ledgard et al. 1981].

Exercise 1.7   Programming in Two Languages

On most interactive systems you must enter a "password" in order to start programming. This helps ensure that someone else does not have access to your files of information or does not charge you for using the computer facilities.

Write a program in *two* different computer languages (your choice) to prompt a user for a password. If the password is not given correctly within three tries, the program should inform the user that the passwords given are incorrect and then terminate; otherwise, the user should be informed of a successful entry, and then, at least for this exercise, terminate. Your program will define the correct password.

a. *Successful entry*

```
Computer:  PLEASE ENTER YOUR PASSWORD
User    :  SHERLOCK
Computer:  OF COURSE, GO RIGHT AHEAD
```

b. *Unsuccessful entry*

```
Computer:  PLEASE ENTER YOUR PASSWORD
User    :  MYCROFT
Computer:  WHO?
User    :  WATSON
Computer:  WHO?
User    :  HOLMES
Computer:  FORGET IT.
```

When you are done, comment on the most significant differences between the two languages, as expressed by your two programs.

Note: The two programs should have identical behavior.

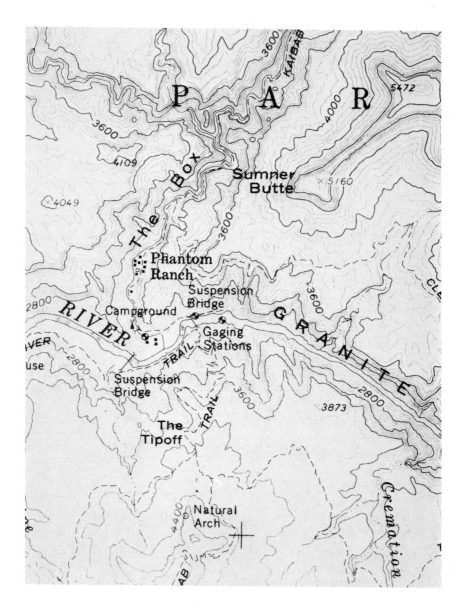

2
Syntax

Thru page 60

In this chapter we describe the outward appearance of a programming language, that is, its syntax. To help us in our discussions we will begin by describing a mini-language in an informal way. From this informal view of the syntax, we will be able to identify the syntactic components of the language. The way in which these syntactic components are designed and fitted together to form the fabric of the complete language greatly influences the ease of using the language.

This description of the syntax of the mini-language is informal. It is thus subject to the vagaries of English prose. We will discuss more formal techniques for the description of syntax and show how the example mini-language would be described with these techniques. This will lead us to the choice of a particular method that we will use throughout the rest of this book.

As we saw in the previous chapter, a program written in a programming language must be translated before it can be executed. This translation consists of two main processes, analysis and synthesis. The analysis phase converts the source program into an internal form from which the equivalent object program can be synthesized. The analysis phase is thus closely connected to the syntax of the source language. We will give an overview of this phase and see its connection to formal descriptions of the language syntax.

2.1 INFORMAL DESCRIPTION OF MINI-LANGUAGE CORE

A Mini-language Core program is introduced by the symbol program. Despite the fact that program is written with several letters, it is considered to be a unique symbol of the language. The language has several such symbols and these will be shown in lowercase letters. The program consists of two sections: a declaration section, which follows immediately after the program symbol, and a statement section. The statement section follows the declaration section; it is introduced by the begin symbol and terminated by the end symbol and a semicolon. The declaration section is formed of declarations consisting of the symbol declare followed by a list of identifiers separated by commas and terminated by a semicolon, as in:

```
declare A, B;
declare X, Y, Z;
```

The statement section consists of a sequence of statements. There are five kinds of statements: assignment, if, loop, input, and output statements. Each is terminated by a semicolon.

The assignment statement consists of an identifier, the symbol :=, and an expression, in that order. The following are examples of assignment statements:

assignment

```
X := B;
X := X + 1;
```

The if statement has two forms

If

```
if comparison then
    statement...
end if;
```

Symbols

and

```
if comparison then
    statement...
else
    statement...
end if;
```

where "statement..." represents a sequence of statements, and if, then, else, and end are symbols. Two examples of the if statement are

```
if (X = 2) then
    A := B;
    X := X + 1;
end if;
```

and

```
if (A ≠ B) then
    X := X - 1;
else
    X := X + 1;
end if;
```

A loop statement has the form

```
while comparison loop
    statement...
end loop;
```

where while, loop, and end are symbols. An example of a loop statement is:

```
while (Z < X) loop
    Z := Z + 1;
    Y := Y + Z;
end loop;
```

The input and output statements are similar to each other. The input statement consists of the symbol input followed by a list of identifiers separated by commas. The output statement consists of the symbol output followed by a similar list of identifiers. Examples of these statements are:

```
input A;
output X, Y, Z;
```

Expressions are built from operands consisting of identifiers, integers, and parenthesized expressions separated by operators. The operators are the symbols +, -, and *. The following are examples of Core expressions:

```
A + B * 3
(A + B) * 3
```

Order of evaluation

If several operators occur in an expression, the <u>parenthesized expressions are evaluated first, followed by the operator * and then the operators + and -.</u> The operator * is said to have a higher *precedence* than the + and - operators. The + and - operators have equal precedence. <u>Sequences of operators of equal precedence are evaluated in order from left to right.</u> Thus

        A + B * 3

is equivalent to

        A + (B * 3)

and

        A - B - C

is equivalent to

        (A - B) - C

Comparison

<u>Comparisons consist of parentheses enclosing a pair of operands, each an identifier or integer, separated by one of the comparison operators =, ≠, <, and >.</u> For example,

        (A = 3)
        (X ≠ Y)
        (5 > Y)

are comparisons.

Identifier

<u>An identifier consists of a sequence of letters A through Z, with any two adjacent letters possibly separated by an underscore.</u> Thus

        A
        ALPHA
        SUM_OF_SQUARES

are all examples of identifiers.

Integer

<u>An integer consists of a sequence of the digits 0 through 9.</u> Particular implementations of Mini-language Core may impose limitations on the lengths of identifiers and integers.

In addition to the rules given for the construction of a program in Core, there are two constraints:

Two Constraints

1. *All identifiers used in the statements of the program must be declared.*

Thus, for example, the program

```
program
   declare A;
begin
   input  A, B;
   output A, B;
end;
```

is illegal because the identifier B has not been declared.

Constraint 2

2. *No identifier may be declared more than once.*

That is, no identifier may appear more than once in the declaration section of the program. For example, the declaration section

```
declare A, B;
declare B, C, C;
```

is illegal since both the identifiers B and C are declared more than once.

Example 2.1 gives a complete example of a program in Mini-language Core.

```
program
   declare COUNT, LIMIT;
   declare LAST_TERM, THIS_TERM, NEXT_TERM;
begin
   COUNT     := 0;
   LAST_TERM := 1;
   THIS_TERM := 1;
   input LIMIT;

   while (COUNT < LIMIT) loop
      output LAST_TERM;
      NEXT_TERM := LAST_TERM + THIS_TERM;
      LAST_TERM := THIS_TERM;
      THIS_TERM := NEXT_TERM;
      COUNT     := COUNT + 1;
   end loop;
end;
```

Example 2.1 A program in Mini-language Core

2.2   THE SYNTACTIC COMPONENTS OF PROGRAMMING LANGUAGES

A program consists of a hierarchy of *syntactic units.* At the highest level we have the complete program. In Mini-language Core, the complete program consists of the three symbols, program, begin, and end, together with everything contained within the framework they provide. In other programming languages there may be other large structural units. For example, in PL/I, a program may consist of several separate "external" procedures that have been individually translated and subsequently linked together for execution.

At the next level of syntactic structure there are statements and declarations. Each of these units is one of a number of specific forms. Some statements contain expressions: these are syntactic units of arbitrary size built according to certain rules, with subunits separated from each other by operators.

At the bottom of the syntactic scale are the *lexical* elements, the symbols from which programs in the language are constructed. In the case of Core, the lexical elements are

```
program  begin  end  declare  if  then  else  while  loop
input  output

0 1 2 3 4 5 6 7 8 9

A B C D E F G H I J K L M N O P Q R S T U V W X Y Z

_  ,  ;  +  -  *  <  >  =  ≠  (  )  :=
```

and the blank character, which, when we need to represent it explicitly, will be denoted by the letter ♭.

The set of symbols from which a language is constructed is its *vocabulary.* Some of these symbols are always used by themselves, for example, begin, end, +, and *. Others are used to construct larger syntactic units like identifiers and integers. Identifiers and integers are always terminated by one of the special symbols, shown in the last row of the lexical elements above, or by blanks. The symbols used to terminate identifiers and integers are known as *delimiters.* In all the mini-languages used in this book, at any point where a delimiter can occur in a program, an arbitrary number of blanks may be inserted.

If the purpose of a programming language is to communicate algorithms to programmers as well as computers, then the programmer will sometimes need to annotate the program. Annotations, generally called *comments,* can provide the human reader with explanations at a higher level of abstraction than is possible in the actual programming language. From the point of view of the translator, comments do not change the program in any way; it is as if the comments were not there. The compiler's only action is to copy the comment into the listing of the source code. No vestige of the comment appears in the object program.

In the mini-languages in this book we shall use a single convention for comments:

Convention for comments

> A comment is introduced by two contiguous hyphen symbols (that is, --). These two symbols and the remaining characters on the same line are treated as the text of the comment and have no effect on program execution. A comment can occur in the program at any point where a blank may appear.

For example, we may have

```
INCHES  :=  FEET * 12;    -- make conversion to inches
```

Since this convention is uniform throughout the mini-languages in this book, it will not be mentioned when describing them. Comments will, however, be used frequently in examples.

Get not se inline ments.

A comment on comments. You may notice that the above comment is quite superfluous in describing the program's meaning. Generally, we believe that such inline (as distinct from header) program comments should be rare. Good mnemonic names and other programming conventions can make the use of inline comments virtually nonexistent. In this text our major use of inline comments will be to make points about the language (not the program).

2.3   SYNTAX AND THE PROGRAMMING PROCESS

Impacts 1. clarity 2. Number of errors made during writing

The importance of program clarity has been discussed in Chapter 1. In a large measure, the syntax of a language controls the clarity of programs. This does not mean that programs written in a language with a perfectly designed syntax, assuming that such a thing were possible, would necessarily be easy to read. It is always possible to write obscure programs, whatever the language.

A second effect of the design of the syntax is the number of errors that can be made during the writing of the program. These syntax errors are not due to incorrect thinking, but occur because the syntax does not conform to the programmer's intuition. For example, both from their experience with natural language and from mathematics, people are used to certain ways of using spaces and punctuation. Programming languages that vary from these "normal" uses will guarantee errors where none need be made.

Were frequency counts of the types of syntax errors committed available, they would provide an interesting way of comparing languages. Each language would have its own set of characteristic errors, which would generally reflect the weak spots in its design.

There have been several experimental studies of the relationship between programming language design and programming errors [see for example, Gannon and Horning 1975].

In the remainder of this section, we will discuss particular aspects of syntax and the considerations that must be borne in mind during language design. It must be emphasized that this is only representative of the questions that need to be weighed during the design process.

Free Form versus Fixed Form

Some programming languages have rigid requirements on the form in which statements in the program are to be written. Originally, all statements in Fortran had to start in column 7 and the programmer was unable to indicate the structure of the program through indentation of the statements. Such rigid requirements remain true to this day in some Fortran and Basic implementations. If we consider the way in which we normally use blanks, indentation, and other layout techniques when we write prose, it is remarkable that this convention has survived so long. It is very important that the programmer be allowed to use white space to enhance the overall readability of the program.

One of the design considerations of Fortran was that blanks could be ignored at all points in a program, and the compiler would rely on other delimiters to analyze the program. For example, the two statements

```
DO 13 K = 1.3
```

and

```
DO 13 K = 1,3
```

are both valid statements. The first is an assignment statement that assigns 1.3 to the variable DO13K, and the second is the start of an iterative statement that loops with the variable K having the successive values 1, 2, and 3. It has been said that just such a confusion led to the loss of a Venus probe. One of the arguments for this philosophy is that, when Fortran first came out, there were no Fortran coding sheets and programmers wrote their programs on blank paper; as a consequence, it was feared that keypunchers would find it too difficult to count blanks accurately. A result of this convention is that we still see Fortran programs written without any blank characters at all.

Just as free form encourages the use of horizontal white space, it should also encourage the use of vertical white space. The language and the compiler should allow empty lines to appear in the source program. In addition, there should be some way of controlling the layout of the listing of the source program produced by the compiler. This would allow separate sections of a program to be started on separate pages.

Comments

There are various conventions for comments:

■ Start the comment in a specific column and continue to the end of the line. This is often used in low level languages like assemblers. The use of free format in higher level languages prevents the use of this convention.

■ Use a symbol to make a complete line into a comment. Fortran uses a letter C in column 1 for this purpose. The main disadvantage is that it does not permit comments to be put on the same line as the statement being annotated.

■ Start the comment with a special symbol and terminate it with a special symbol. This is a common convention. Algol 60 uses the keyword *comment* to mark the start and continues to a semicolon. Pascal uses { to mark the beginning and } as a terminator. With this method, it is possible to put a comment into the middle of a statement and continue the comment on the same line, as in

```
if BASE_PTR = nil  { the list is empty } then
```

which is not possible with the other two conventions. This advantage is, however, offset by the danger that, since the end of line plays no part in marking comments, the omission of the terminator can cause part of the program to be treated as a comment by the compiler — generally with bad consequences.

■   Start the comment with a special symbol and continue to the end of the line. This is the convention used in Ada and is the one we have adopted for the mini-languages used in this book. This method seems to have advantages in readability, convenience of use, and reliability.

for this text

Semicolons

It has become common practice to use semicolons as punctuation in programs. There are, however, two views on their usage. They can be used either to terminate or to separate statements. In the Mini-language Core fragment,

```
while (LIMIT > COUNT) loop
    NEXT_TERM := LAST_TERM + THIS_TERM;
    LAST_TERM := THIS_TERM;
    THIS_TERM := NEXT_TERM;
    COUNT     := COUNT + 1;
end loop;
```

the semicolon is used to terminate the four assignments and the one loop statement.

If the semicolon had been used as a separator, there would be no semicolon after the fourth assignment since that statement does not need separating from the next statement in the sequence. Instead, the end of the sequence would be marked by the symbols end loop. PL/I has adopted the convention of using the semicolon as a terminator, while Algol 60, Pascal, Bliss, and several others use it as a statement separator. Pascal makes things even worse by effectively using the semicolon as a terminator and a separator in the declarative part, thus making the placement of the semicolons very confusing.

Pascal shortcoming

In an experiment reported in [Gannon and Horning 1975], errors with separators were ten times more likely than errors with terminators. It seems that the rule where a statement is always terminated by a punctuation mark is easier to understand and remember than the rule that a punctuation mark is required whenever one statement is being separated from another. Such a rule reflects usage in normal prose.

Reserved Words

Mini-language Core uses symbols like while, loop, and if in the construction of the statements. These serve the dual purpose of differentiating one kind of statement from another and of making the programs easy to read. We have used lowercase to distinguish these

symbols from the identifiers that can be constructed by the programmer. In some languages, the luxury of upper- and lowercase is not
possible. Moreover, keypunches and terminals are often limited to a
single case, generally upper. In such cases, the fixed symbols of a
language are called *keywords* and have the same representation as
identifiers.

There are three main techniques used to distinguish keywords
from identifiers:

■ Precede them by a special symbol, for example, $.

A loop statement in the Mini-language Core might then
become:

```
$WHILE (A < B) $LOOP
A := A + X;
$END $LOOP;
```

The special symbol here is obtrusive and seriously affects the
readability of the program.

The other two techniques are really antithetical and will be
discussed together.

■ Define the keywords to be *reserved words*, that is, forbid
the programmer from using these keywords as identifiers.

■ Rely on context to make the distinction. That is, to say

```
WHILE := LOOP;
```

is an assignment statement because of the symbol   :=.

These last two conventions are heavily debated. Ada, Pascal, and
Cobol have opted for reserved words, while PL/I has no reserved
words. The arguments may be summarized as follows:

*Keyword
Summary*

■ If keywords are reserved then there is no danger of a
loss of readability due to the programmer choosing identifiers that clash with keywords. While it is true that a perverse
PL/I programmer could write

```
IF IF = THEN THEN
THEN = ELSE;
```

it is likely that the programmer would soon tire of this.
There is neither evidence that unreserved keywords actually

presents a readability problem in PL/I programs nor that programs are more readable with reserved keywords.

■   A language that has reserved words requires the programmer to memorize all the keywords of the language — even for parts of the language that have no bearing on the problem being solved.

■   If a reserved word language is extended, it is quite likely that new keywords will be required. This will extend the list of reserved words and render illegal existing programs that have used these new keywords as identifiers before they were made keywords.

■   In a reserved word language, the keywords provide fixed markers in the syntax that allow the compiler to make better recovery in the face of syntax errors and give more meaningful error messages.

This matter is not fully resolved.

2.4   THE DESCRIPTION OF SYNTAX

In our informal description of Mini-language Core in Section 2.1, we gave what appeared to be a complete description of the rules for writing a program in Core. However, the description suffers from the imprecision of English and its possible ambiguities. It is difficult to know whether the description is complete.

For example, consider the following questions:

1. Does the begin symbol need a semicolon after it?
2. Is it legal to have a program without a declaration?
3. Is it legal to have a program without statements?

Of course, once these questions have been thought of, it is possible to amplify the informal description to include their answers. However, what about all the other possible questions?

There is thus a need for a more formal way of describing the syntax of programming languages. In this section we will describe the most common approaches to this problem.

Some Basic Notions

■   A *grammar* defines a set, generally infinite, of the sentences that can be written in a language.

■ A *sentence* of a language is a finite sequence of symbols from a vocabulary constructed according to the rules of the language's grammar.

■ A *vocabulary* or *alphabet* is a finite set of symbols.

■ A *symbol* is an atomic entity represented by a graphic, for example, +, (, a letter, or a digit.

In some languages like Mini-language Core, complete words, for example, begin, may be treated as symbols. Such symbols can be distinguished from identifiers, which are also constructed from letters, by using a different typeface, making them reserved words, or some other device, such as introducing them with a special symbol, as discussed above.

The following are examples of languages:

L1. The set of strings of length greater than zero composed of the symbols 0 and 1. These two symbols constitute the vocabulary of L1.

L2. The set of strings consisting of *n* occurrences of the symbol A followed by *n* occurrences of the symbol B. The vocabulary of this language consists of the symbols A and B. The grammar states that there are equal numbers of occurrences of the symbol A and of the symbol B. The strings

```
AAAABBBB
AB
```

are examples of sentences in L2.

L3. The set of grammatical sentences in English. The vocabulary here consists of the words of the English language; the grammar is the grammar of English, which requires that the form of a verb match the subject of the verb. Thus HE IS A MAN is legal, while HE ARE A MAN is not.

In describing these languages, the sentences were defined by giving rules for constructing them from the vocabulary of the language. These rules form the grammar or the *rules of syntax* (often referred to as simply the *syntax* of the language). In the languages L1 and L2, the rules are quite specific; L1 and L2 are very simple languages. In the case of L3, use was made of the vague term "grammatical sentences." The rules of English grammar are very complex and ill-defined in many places. Luckily, programming languages are not nearly as complex as English, and we are able to produce reasonably simple and precise grammars for them.

Grammar defined bottom pg. 36 ¶ 2.4

2.5   GRAMMARS FOR DESCRIBING SYNTAX

In the analysis or parsing of English sentences, the words in a sentence are placed in different categories according to their functions in the sentence. In the simple sentence THE MAN EATS THE APPLE, THE MAN is the subject and EATS THE APPLE is the predicate. The subject consists of an article followed by the noun MAN. The predicate consists of the verb EATS followed by the direct object THE APPLE, which is an article and a noun.

We can represent this analysis by a tree-like structure known as a *parse tree:*

or derivation tree - pg. 41

Nonterminal nodes

{ Nodes { Level

Root - No parent node

} Syntactic categories

} Parent node to apple

```
                          sentence
                    _____|_____
                   |                   |
                subject             predicate
              ____|____          _____|_____
             |         |        |             |
          article    noun     verb       direct-object
             |         |        |          ____|____
             |         |        |         |         |
             |         |        |      article     noun
             |         |        |         |         |
            THE       MAN     EATS       THE      APPLE
```

Terminal nodes in Capitals

In this parse tree there are two kinds of objects named points, generally called *nodes*. One type of node represents of the words of the original sentence. These appear at the ends of the branches of the tree and are called *terminals*. They appear in uppercase, as they do in the original sentence. The terminals taken in left-to-right order form the original sentence. The other type of node, written here in lowercase, are *nonterminals* and bear the names of the grammatical categories they represent. These are often called *syntactic categories*.

Each nonterminal of the parse tree has one or more *subnodes* connected by a line drawn from the bottom of the node. Each subnode is either a terminal or a nonterminal. Except for one nonterminal (the *root* of the tree), each symbol has exactly one *parent* node. The grammar of a language consists of a set of rules that specify for each nonterminal precisely what subnodes it may have.

For our example sentence, we can write a grammar as:

sentence	::=	subject predicate
subject	::=	article noun
predicate	::=	verb direct-object
direct-object	::=	article noun
article	::=	THE
noun	::=	MAN
noun	::=	APPLE
verb	::=	EATS

consist Subnodes

Can't handle context sensitive

see pg 42 BNF

consists of

The ::= symbol indicates that the item to the left has the items on the right as subnodes. This symbol is not part of the language being defined by the grammar but is part of yet another language, one used to describe languages. Such a language is called a *syntax meta-language*. In this grammar there is precisely one symbol that does not appear on the right of a rule, this is the *goal* of the grammar and will be the root of the parse tree.

The rules of a grammar can be used to generate all the sentences of a language. If we use our simple grammar, starting with the syntactic category sentence, we can see that the only possible subnodes are subject and predicate. Indeed, there is no choice possible until we come to noun, at which point we can choose between MAN and APPLE. There are thus only four possible trees that we can draw with this grammar. They correspond to the sentences:

analytically see pg 40

```
THE MAN EATS THE APPLE
THE MAN EATS THE MAN
THE APPLE EATS THE APPLE
THE APPLE EATS THE MAN
```

These are the four sentences that constitute the language defined by this grammar. Because of this use of a grammar to produce sentences, the rules are often known as *productions*.

An alternative way of using a grammar is to analyze a given sentence to see if it is a syntactically correct sentence of the language. This is done by using the rules of the grammar to attempt to construct a tree whose terminals, taken in left-to-right order, form the given sentence. If it is possible to construct such a tree, then the sentence is in the language. The analysis of a sentence in this way is called *parsing*.

Grammars are thus used in two ways:

1. *Generatively* to construct all possible sentences in the language.

2. *Analytically* to determine whether a given string is a sentence in the language.

Context Free Grammars   *Context sensitive opposited free*

In our use of the grammar to construct the four sentences, when it came to choosing a subnode for noun the second time, no account was taken of our first choice. That is, whenever we make a choice, we are not able to allow our choice to be affected by any of the categories and terminal symbols that already exist in the partial derivation tree. Our choice is made without *context.*

A rule of a grammar where context is considered would have the form

Context sensitive

$$w \; x \; y \quad ::= \quad w \; z \; y$$

where w, y, and z are sequences of terminals and nonterminals and x is a nonterminal. The sequences w and y provide the context that defines where the nonterminal x can be replaced by the sequence z.

A grammar where no account of context is taken when making a substitution is a *context free language.* Context sensitive grammars are more complex than context free grammars because the fact that a substitution in one part of the derivation tree can influence the structure in another part must be expressed in the grammar. Almost all languages, both natural and artificial, have context sensitivities. Programming languages generally have some context sensitive rules. As we shall explain later, the rule in Mini-language Core that an identifier may not be declared more than once in a program is an example of a context sensitive rule.

Programming Languages

In order to avoid the added complexity of context, the syntax of programming languages is generally defined in a context free form with additional, usually informal, rules describing the context sensitivities.

A context free grammar requires the specification of four items:

Context Free Grammar Requires:

1. A vocabulary of nonterminal symbols.

2. A vocabulary of terminal symbols.

3. A set of productions of the form

$$x \quad ::= \quad y$$

where x is a nonterminal drawn from the nonterminal vocabulary and y is a combination of symbols drawn from the combined terminal and nonterminal vocabularies.

4. A goal symbol that does not appear on the right side of any production.

Derivations

In general, the repeated application of the productions gives sequences of symbols, both terminal and nonterminal, that can be *derived* from the goal symbol. These sequences are the *sentential forms* of the language defined by the grammar G. Any string that contains only terminal symbols and that can be derived from the goal symbol is a *sentence* of the language defined by G.

We would show the derivation of the sentence

THE MAN EATS THE APPLE

as a sequence of pictures that show the parse tree growing:

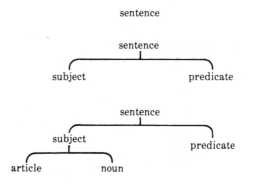

and so on. An alternative method is to show the entire derivation as

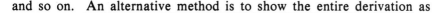

sentence
→ subject predicate
→ article noun predicate
→ THE noun predicate
→ THE MAN predicate
→ THE MAN verb direct-object
→ THE MAN EATS direct-object
→ THE MAN EATS article noun
→ THE MAN EATS THE noun
→ THE MAN EATS THE APPLE

Is derived from

where each line represents the terminal nodes of the parse tree in its current state of development. The arrow at the beginning of the lines means "is derived from the previous line by the application of a single rule." At each application of a rule, a single nonterminal is replaced by one or more symbols. Thus this representation shows the order in which the substitutions are made. The last line of the derivation contains only terminal symbols of the grammar and no further substitutions can be made.

2.6   THE BACKUS-NAUR FORM   *language to talk about a language*

Probably the most common meta-language for specifying the context free syntax of programming languages is the Backus-Naur Form, sometimes called Backus Normal Form, generally abbreviated to BNF. This was introduced in 1959 by John Backus as a method for the definition of the syntax of Algol 60. The first version of the meta-language was improved shortly thereafter by Peter Naur.

The meta-symbols of BNF are:

::=   meaning "is defined as"

| meaning "or"

< >   angle brackets used to surround category names

The angle brackets distinguish category names from terminal symbols, which are written exactly as they are to be represented.

A BNF rule defining a nonterminal has the form:

1. The nonterminal being defined,

2. The meta-symbol   ::=

3. Then a sequence of alternatives consisting of strings of terminals and nonterminals, where the alternatives are separated by the meta-symbol | .   *pg. 39 - produce sentences*

For example, the BNF production for a Mini-language Core program is:

```
<program>   ::=   program
                      <declaration-sequence>
                  begin
                      <statement-sequence>
                  end;
```

This shows that a Mini-language Core program consists of the keyword program followed by the declaration sequence, then the keyword begin and the statement sequence, finally the keyword end and a semi-colon. The nonterminal symbol <program> is the goal symbol.

The statements of the Mini-language Core can be specified in BNF as a set of productions:

IS DEFINED AS

```
<statement>  ::= <assignment-statement>
<statement>  ::= <if-statement>
<statement>  ::= <loop-statement>
<statement>  ::= <input-statement>
<statement>  ::= <output-statement>
```

This may be abbreviated

```
<statement>  ::= <assignment-statement>
             |   <if-statement>
             |   <loop-statement>
             |   <input-statement>
             |   <output-statement>
```

In the BNF definition of Mini-language Core there is a clash between the greater-than and less-than symbols used in the comparison and the printed brackets of the BNF notation. In order to avoid the clash, the symbols that are part of the Mini-language are underlined in the definition. Thus:

```
<comparison> ::= (<operand> < <operand>)
```

Recursive Productions

The informal definition of Mini-language Core specifies an integer to be an arbitrary sequence of digits. Thus, we might think that this would be represented in BNF as

```
<integer>  ::=  <digit>
           |    <digit>  <digit>
           |    <digit>  <digit>  <digit>
```

and so on, with an arbitrary number of alternatives corresponding to all possible lengths of integers.

However, each of the alternatives, after the first, really consists of an <integer> followed by a single <digit>. Thus, in order to avoid the need for an arbitrary number of alternatives, we write:

Recursive Definition

```
<integer>    ::=    <digit>
             |      <integer>  <digit>
```

This type of definition, where the defined nonterminal is part of the definition itself, is called a *recursive definition.*

A recursive definition can only be used provided that there is some way of terminating it. The single production

```
<a>    ::=    <a>  A
```

is useless since it is impossible to produce a line containing only terminal symbols. In our definition of <integer>, the alternative

```
<integer>    ::=    <digit>
```

provides the means for terminating the recursion.

Canonical Derivations

The definition for <integer> given in the last section requires a rule for <digit>. By adding this, we can define integers in Mini-language Core by the small grammar:

```
<goal>       ::=    <integer>

<integer>    ::=    <digit>
             |      <integer>  <digit>

<digit>      ::=    0 | 1 | 2 | 3 | 4 | 5 | 6 | 7 | 8 | 9
```

This small grammar allows us to derive all legal integers. For example, abbreviating <integer> by i and <digit> by d, we have two possible derivations of the integer 193:

Usually used   *Canonical derivation*

```
<goal>                      <goal>
  → i                         → i
  → i d                       → i d
  → i d d                     → i 3
  → d d d                     → i d 3
  → 1 d d                     → i 9 3
  → 1 9 d                     → d 9 3
  → 1 9 3                     → 1 9 3
```

There are many possible derivations, depending on the order in which the nonterminals are chosen for replacement. It is convenient to be able to single out a particular derivation as being *the* derivation. This is generally called the *canonical derivation.* The choice of canonical derivation is essentially arbitrary; the usual choice is the one where, at each stage in the derivation the left-most nonterminal is the one that is replaced. This corresponds to the derivation of 193 on the left.

Ambiguous Grammars

One possible grammar for simple expressions involving only multiplication and addition is:

```
<goal>          ::=   <expression>

<expression>  ::=   <expression>  +  <expression>
              |     <expression>  *  <expression>
              |     <identifier>

<identifier>   ::=   X  |  Y  |  Z
```

In this grammar, the sentence

```
X + Y * Z
```

has two distinct canonical derivations.
    The first is:

```
⊢  <goal>
    →  <expression>
       →  <expression>  +  <expression>
          →  <identifier>  +  <expression>
             →  X  +  <expression>
                →  X  +  <expression>  *  <expression>
                   →  X  +  <identifier>  *  <expression>
                      →  X  +  Y  *  <expression>
                         →  X  +  Y  *  <identifier>
                            →  X  +  Y  *  Z
```

Its corresponding parse tree is:

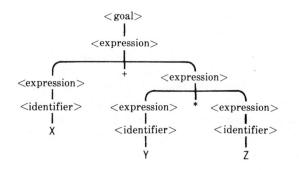

The second derivation is:

2.   <goal>
       →   <expression>
           →   <expression> * <expression>
               →   <expression> + <expression> * <expression>
                   →   <identifier> + <expression> * <expression>
                       →   X + <expression> * <expression>
                           →   X + <identifier> * <expression>
                               →   X + Y * <expression>
                                   →   X + Y * <identifier>
                                       →   X + Y * Z

Its corresponding parse tree is:

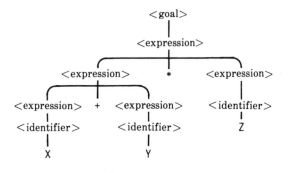

If, as in this case, the rules of a grammar permit more than one canonical derivation of a sentence of the language, the grammar is said to be *ambiguous.*

    If the only use for grammars were to determine whether a string belongs to the language, this ambiguity would be of little importance. The number of ways of generating a string would not be relevant. However, for programming languages, part of the meaning of a program is sometimes specified in terms of the corresponding syntactic structure. The existence of more than one structure could imply more than one meaning for the program.

    In the example that we have just shown, the two trees correspond to two different evaluation sequences for the operators * and +. In the first tree, the Y and the Z are bound together by the * operator and it is the result of this operation that is added to X. If we take * to mean multiplication, this derivation corresponds to the precedence specified in the informal definition of Mini-language Core. Note that the ambiguity is syntactic and has severe consequences when meaning is ascribed to the symbols.

The second derivation shows that X and Y are added together and the result is multiplied by Z. It is as if the expression had been written:

```
(X + Y) * Z
```

If we are to avoid this ambiguity, we must restructure our grammar and ensure that it defines a single correct meaning for the sentences representing expressions. The following grammar does this:

<goal>	::=	<expression>
<expression>	::=	<factor>
	|	<expression> + <factor>
<factor>	::=	<identifier>
	|	<factor> * <identifier>
<identifier>	::=	X | Y | Z

The corresponding parse tree is:

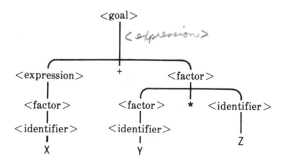

Although it is possible to determine whether certain grammars are ambiguous, it is not possible to do this in general. Similarly, although there are arbitrarily many context free grammars for any context free language, it is not always possible to determine whether two grammars define the same language.

Programming languages, including the higher level ones, differ fundamentally from natural languages. Programming languages have a smaller vocabulary and a simpler grammar. More importantly, they are formal languages; that is, every grammatical statement has one and only one meaning and that meaning can be abstracted by a simple procedure from the structure of the statement. In a natural language, on the other hand, ambiguity is common and statements that are grammatically impeccable can often be understood only from the meaning of the words.

Compare, for example, the two sentences:

```
TIME FLIES LIKE AN ARROW
FRUIT FLIES LIKE A BANANA
```

They both have the same structure, yet they are parsed differently. In one, FLIES is a verb and in the other a noun.

The if statement in PL/I has an optional else part just as it does in Mini-language Core. Consider the form of a nested if statement in PL/I.

```
IF boolean-expression-1 THEN
IF boolean-expression-2 THEN
statement-1;
ELSE
statement-2;
```

To which if statement does the else clause belong? PL/I has solved this potential ambiguity by defining the syntax so that the else clause is associated with the last uncompleted if statement, that is, with the second one. Mini-language Core avoids the problem through the use of the end if symbols.

Some problems cannot be resolved so easily. Consider, for example, the Ada assignment statement:

```
I := F(J);
```

Is the reference to F an invocation of a function procedure or to an element of an array F? In Algol 60 this problem is solved by writing the two kinds of reference as F(J) and F[J] respectively. In Ada, information from the declaration of F must be used to make the differentiation. This is called *contextual information.*

Context Sensitivity Again

It must be recognized that there are certain things that cannot be represented in BNF. Consider, for example, the Mini-language Core rule that an identifier may not be declared more than once in a program. This rule cannot be defined in BNF.

Suppose there were only three possible identifiers allowed in Core and only one declaration were allowed in a program. The declaration statement could then be defined in BNF as;

```
declaration   ::=   declare A;      |   declare B;
                |   declare C;      |   declare A, B;
                |   declare A, C;   |   declare B, C;
                |   declare B, A;   |   declare C, A;
                |   declare C, B;   |   declare A, B, C;
                |   declare B, A, C; |  declare B, C, A;
                |   declare A, C, B; |  declare C, A, B;
                |   declare C, B, A;
```

that is, all legal possibilities are specified. In the actual Mini-language Core, there is an infinite number of possible identifiers. Thus, there would have to be an infinite number of alternatives to show the set of legal declarations.

The problem is one of context. In Mini-language Core, the declaration

```
declare A;
```

is legal if it does not occur in the same program as another declaration of A. That is, in the context of another declaration of A, BNF is a context free grammar and can only show a *context sensitive* rule with an infinite number of productions. Thus, in any BNF description of the syntax of a programming language, the context sensitive rules must be given separately.

[handwritten margin note: Context sensitive rules must be given separately]

Context Free Syntax of Mini-language Core in BNF

Table 2.1 shows a BNF definition of the context free syntax of the Mini-language Core. In the form shown there, some of the structure of programs and statements has been indicated by the use of indentation on the right side of a production. This indentation is not part of the definition and has been added for clarity.

Even with the indentation, the BNF definition presents some readability problems. These are mainly concerned with the specification of optional parts and sequences. Consider, for example, the production for the <if statement> shown in Table 2.1.

```
<if-statement>   ::=   if <comparison> then
                           <statement-sequence>
                       end if;
                   |   if <comparison> then
                           <statement-sequence>
                       else
                           <statement-sequence>
                       end if;
```

Table 2.1 Context Free Syntax of Mini-Language Core in BNF

```
<program>                ::=   program
                                   <declaration-sequence>
                               begin
                                   <statement-sequence>
                               end;

<declaration-sequence>   ::=   <declaration>
                           |   <declaration> <declaration-sequence>

<statement-sequence>     ::=   <statement>
                           |   <statement> <statement-sequence>


<declaration>            ::=   declare  <identifier-list>;

<identifier-list>        ::=   <identifier>
                           |   <identifier>, <identifier-list>

<statement>              ::=   <assignment-statement>
                           |   <if-statement>
                           |   <loop-statement>
                           |   <input-statement>
                           |   <output-statement>


<assignment-statement>   ::=   <identifier> := <expression> ;


<if-statement>           ::=   if  <comparison> then
                                   <statement-sequence>
                               end if;
                           |   if <comparison> then
                                   <statement-sequence>
                               else
                                   <statement-sequence>
                               end if;


<loop-statement>         ::=   while <comparison> loop
                                   <statement-sequence>
                               end loop;


<input-statement>        ::=   input  <identifier-list> ;

<output-statement>       ::=   output <identifier-list> ;
```

Table 2.1 continued

\<comparison\>	::=	(\<operand\> = \<operand\>)
	|	(\<operand\> ≠ \<operand\>)
	|	(\<operand\> < \<operand\>)
	|	(\<operand\> > \<operand\>)
\<expression\>	::=	\<factor\>
	|	\<expression\> + \<factor\>
	|	\<expression\> − \<factor\>
\<factor\>	::=	\<operand\>
	|	\<factor\> * \<operand\>
\<operand\>	::=	\<integer\>
	|	\<identifier\>
	|	(\<expression\>)
\<identifier\>	::=	\<letter\>
	|	\<identifier\> \<letter\>
	|	\<identifier\> _ \<letter\>
\<integer\>	::=	\<digit\> | \<integer\> \<digit\>
\<letter\>	::=	A | B | C | D | E | F | G | H | I
	|	J | K | L | M | N | O | P | Q | R
	|	S | T | U | V | W | X | Y | Z
\<digit\>	::=	0 | 1 | 2 | 3 | 4 | 5 | 6 | 7 | 8 | 9

(handwritten annotations in margin:
::= \<term\>
\| \<exp\> + \<term\>
\<term\> ::= \<operand\>
*\| \<term\> * \<operand\>)*

This requires two productions to specify that the else part is optional. In order to see exactly which parts are optional, the two alternatives must be examined closely.

The production for \<statement-sequence\> in Table 2.1 is:

\<statement-sequence\>	::=	\<statement\>
	|	\<statement\> \<statement-sequence\>

In order to represent the sequence as being of arbitrary length, a recursive production must be used. Finally, the use of the < and > symbols to enclose the names of syntactic categories makes the definition less readable.

The three problems can be solved with the following extensions to BNF:

1.   ■   *Optional Items:* These are enclosed in brackets, thus introducing the additional meta-symbols [and] .

2.   ■   *Sequences:* The ellipsis symbol (...) is introduced as another meta-symbol to indicate the repetition of the preceding category or group of categories contained in brackets an arbitrary number of times.

3.   ■   *Type faces:* The names of BNF categories will be written without < and > but in a typeface different from that of the language being defined.

Using these extensions, the production for the if statement becomes:

```
if-statement::=     if comparison then
                        statement...
                [ else
                        statement... ]
                    end if;
```

Table 2.2 shows the definition of the context free syntax of Mini-language Core using these extensions to BNF. We will use this extended form of BNF to define the mini-languages used in the later chapters.

As with BNF, where there is a clash between a meta-symbol and a symbol of the Mini-language, the symbol that is part of the Mini-language will be underlined. For example,

```
variable   ::=   identifier
             |    identifier [expression]
```

The definitions of identifier and integer are the same in all of the mini-languages and, for simplicity, their productions will be omitted from future syntax definitions.

Table 2.2   Mini-language Core *Used in later chapters.*

program	::=	program
		    declaration...
		begin
		    statement...
		end;

declaration	::=	declare identifier [, identifier]... ;
statement	::=	assignment-statement | if-statement | loop-statement | input-statement | output-statement
assignment-statement	::=	identifier := expression ;

if-statement	::=	if comparison then
		    statement...
		[else
		    statement...]
		end if;

loop-statement	::=	while comparison loop statement... end loop;
input-statement	::=	input identifier [, identifier]... ;
output-statement	::=	output identifier [, identifier]... ;
comparison	::=	(operand comparison-operator operand)
expression	::=	[expression +] factor | [expression -] factor
factor	::=	[factor *] operand
operand	::=	integer | identifier | (expression)
identifier	::=	letter [[_] letter]...
integer	::=	digit...
comparison-operator	::=	< | = | ≠ | >
letter	::=	A | B | C | D | E | F | G | H | I | J | K | L | M | N | O | P | Q | R | S | T | U | V | W | X | Y | Z
digit	::=	0 | 1 | 2 | 3 | 4 | 5 | 6 | 7 | 8 | 9

2.7   OTHER CONTEXT FREE SYNTAX DEFINITIONS

Although BNF is the best known method for defining the context free syntax of a programming language, several other techniques are in use.

The Cobol Notation

The Cobol syntax notation was developed by the Short-Range Subcommittee commissioned by CODASYL (the Committee on Data Systems Languages) to develop a business-oriented programming language. As described in [Sammet 1978], although there are many similarities between BNF and the Cobol notation, the development of these two meta-languages was parallel and independent. This notation has been used, in addition to defining standard Cobol, for the description of PL/I.

Unlike BNF, which is used to define complete programs, the Cobol meta-language is used to define only small parts of the language, particularly statements. Some basic elements of the notation are:

■ *Vertical bar:* separates alternatives. Alternatives may also be listed vertically within brackets or braces.

■ *Brackets:* enclose an optional syntactical unit.

■ *Braces:* group elements of a syntactical unit or a vertically listed choice.

■ *Ellipsis:* indicates repetition of the immediately preceding syntactical unit one or more times.

Table 2.3   Syntax of Mini-language Core If Statement using the Cobol Notation

```
    if    comparison    then
            statement...
  [ else
          statement... ]
        end if;
```

where "comparison" is

$$\left(\begin{cases} \text{integer} \\ \text{identifier} \\ \text{(expression)} \end{cases} \begin{cases} < \mid = \mid \neq \mid > \end{cases} \begin{cases} \text{integer} \\ \text{identifier} \\ \text{(expression)} \end{cases} \right)$$

As an example of this notation, Table 2.3 shows the definition of Mini-language Core if statement.

Syntax Diagrams

An entirely different method of syntax definition is the graphic representation known as *syntax diagrams* or charts. This method has been used to define the syntax of Pascal in [Wirth 1973] and Fortran 77.

The rules take the form of flow diagrams. The possible paths represent the possible sequences of symbols. Starting at the beginning of a diagram, a path is followed either by transfering to another diagram if a rectangle is reached or by reading a basic symbol contained in a circle or box with rounded ends. For example, an identifier in Mini-language Core is defined by the diagram.

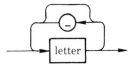

Table 2.4 shows the definition of the context free syntax of Mini-language Core by syntax charts.

2.8   OVERVIEW OF THE TRANSLATION PROCESS

A translator is a program that is used to transform a program, the *source program*, from the source language into an equivalent *object program* in the target language. Frequently, but by no means universally, the source language is a high level language and the target language is some form of machine language.

An implementation can be looked upon as a sequence of two processes:

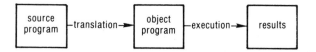

Usually these two processes are separate, but the dividing line can vary considerably. The translation phase may merely transform the source

Table 2.4 Syntax of Mini-language Core Defined by Syntax Charts

PROGRAM

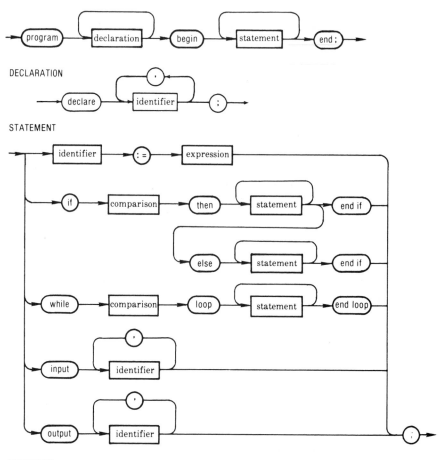

DECLARATION

STATEMENT

EXPRESSION

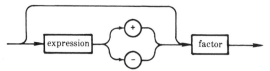

FACTOR

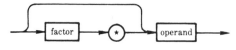

Table 2.4 continued

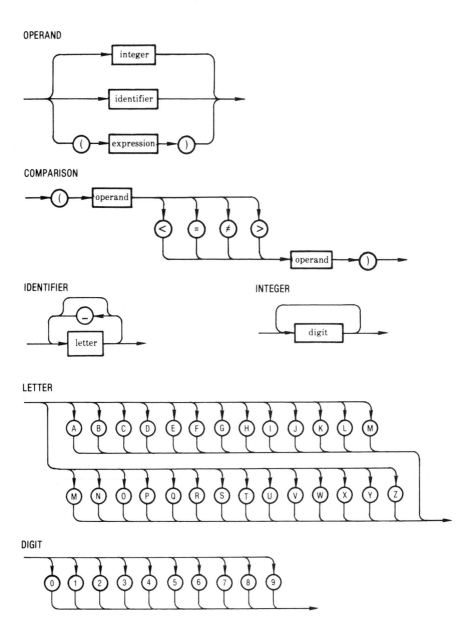

OPERAND

COMPARISON

IDENTIFIER

INTEGER

LETTER

DIGIT

program into some internal form that does not correspond to the architecture of any real machine. As described in Section 1.2, the execution may be an interpretation of this by another part of the translator. Some languages are implemented in this way so as to achieve extra flexibility, for example, APL and Lisp.

The translation process may be divided into two subprocesses: *analysis* and *generation.* We will discuss only the analysis part here; generation will be treated in the next chapter.

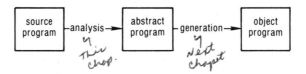

During the analysis phase, the source program is parsed and an abstract representation of the program is built. The abstract representation of the program can take a number of forms depending on the design of the translator. It can be in the form of a tree having a similar construction to the parse tree. Another alternative is for it to consist of a sequence of instructions for a hypothetical machine, typically one where each instruction has an operator, two operands, and a result.

In the original source form, the program is represented as a character string with only a single dimension, although a program really has two dimensions. In order to achieve this, the source program contains a number of syntactic symbols whose sole function is to indicate the two-dimensional structure of the program, for example, semicolons to separate the statements and symbols or keywords like begin to show the major structure of the program. In the abstract form, the program does not contain these syntactic symbols because it is represented as a two-dimensional structure and has no need for them. While the abstract representation of the program is being built during analysis, some equivalent of the derivation tree is constructed. Generally, only a part of the derivation tree is present in the translator at any one time, since it is too big to exist in its entirety.

An abstract program really represents many equivalent source programs. For instance, in PL/I, the keyword PROCEDURE may be used or, equivalently, the abbreviation PROC. Two source programs that differ only in their use of abbreviations for keywords will have identical abstract representations.

During the generation phase of the compiler, the abstract program is converted into the equivalent object program. This part is sometimes known as the *code generation* phase. Although we have shown the code generation to be a separate phase from the analysis, this is not always the case and the part of the object program corresponding to the beginning of the source program may be generated before the end of the source program has been parsed.

If the parsing and code generation are combined, the translator is frequently known as a "single pass" compiler. Most translators for large languages require several passes over the program being translated. Often the actual number of passes depends on the parts of the language that are used in a particular source program. The decision that a single pass compiler will be used imposes certain constraints on the source language. These constraints are required to ensure that sufficient information is available to generate code before the source program has been completely parsed. This means that, for example, variables must be declared before they are referenced so that their type is known at the time the code is to be generated to manipulate their values.

The analysis phase may itself be divided into three subprocesses: scanning, parsing, and completion.

analysis phase

During the scanning phase, the source program is divided into *tokens*, the basic syntactic units from which a program can be constructed. Each token represents a sequence of characters that can be treated as a single logical entity. Identifiers, numbers, operators, language symbols like begin and semicolons are typical tokens of the Mini-language Core. There are two kinds of tokens: those that represent fixed sequences of characters like :=, begin, or a comma, and those that represent classes of character strings like identifiers or numbers.

All tokens have a type, and those that represent classes have a value as well, for example, an identifier token might have the value COUNT.

It is the function of the parsing part to take the tokens and build the derivation tree whose root is the goal symbol of the grammar and whose terminals are the tokens.

There are two classes of parsing techniques: *top-down* and *bottom-up.* Each class is characterized by the order in which the productions of the derivation tree are recognized. The top-down parser builds the tree by starting with the root, the goal symbol, and by working down to produce a tree whose terminal nodes match the sequence of tokens in the source program. The bottom-up technique replaces right sides of productions by the corresponding left side symbol until only the goal symbol remains. These two strategies for parsing have been extensively studied.

Somewhat greater attention has been given to bottom-up techniques since they are more efficient and the research was conducted at a time when parsing efficiency was thought to be very important. It turns out that parsing is a relatively small part of the whole translation process; the generation of the object program takes the larger part of the time. Another attraction of the bottom-up technique is that it is possible to take a grammar specified in BNF and generate tables automatically for a parser. This means that changes to the syntax of a language can be accommodated quickly and it also ensures that the language being parsed matches the language specified in the written syntax. The problem with bottom-up parsing is that one must find the correct right side of a rule to perform a reverse derivation step. While this can be done efficiently when the program being parsed is syntactically correct, it is more difficult to perform error recovery when a syntactic error is discovered. There are two problems at this stage: to provide helpful information to the programmer so that the error can be found and corrected and to retain control so that parsing can continue without providing a spate of meaningless error messages.

The completion phase takes the derivation tree and constructs the abstract programs from it. This process involves abstracting those parts concerned with the meaning of the program from those that have only syntactic functions. In addition, the completion will add some things, making details explicit that were only implicit in the source program. For example, in a language like PL/I, those attributes that are not explicitly declared are manufactured through the application of some contextual rules and defaults. If there is no declaration for an identifier, then one is constructed, possibly with some attributes obtained from the context in which references to the identifier occur. An identifier, MASTER, that appears in the context

```
OPEN FILE(MASTER);
```

will be given the attribute file in its constructed declaration. At the end of the synthesis process, all the contextual implications of the source program will have been made plain and the abstract form of the program will be complete.

FURTHER READING

There are really not many works on the syntax of programming languages, aside from work on formal grammars and methods of implementation. The larger issues of readability and presentation of programs are seldom discussed.

One thoughtful work on the subject of syntax is Chapter 2 of the "Rationale for the Design of Ada" [see Ichbiah et al. 1979]. This discusses numerous issues concerning the presentation of the syntax of a programming language. An entirely different but relevant work is [Gannon and Horning 1976]. This paper describes an experiment intended to compare the utility of various forms for expressing programming language constructs.

On the subject of formal grammars, perhaps the most comprehensive treatment is given in [Cleaveland and Uzgalis 1976]. This work discusses the notion of context free grammars as well as development of BNF that allows context sensitive rules to be defined. This is done through the use of macro productions that will generate the infinite number of productions needed.

Other works of interest include [Ledgard 1977] and the survey of parsing techniques in [Aho and Johnson 1974], and a description, including a complete listing, of a simple compiler in [McKeeman et al. 1970].

EXERCISES

Exercise 2.1   Learning the P's and Q's of Syntax

There are many little and often annoying details that must be learned in a language. Some of these are covered in the following true-false quiz. Try it on Mini-language Core.

a. The first nonblank character in a program must be the p in `program`.

b. The last nonblank character in a program must be a semicolon.

c. The identifier `end` may be used as the name of an integer variable.

d. Only one statement may appear on a line.

e. The following sequence of characters is a well-formed comment:

    `-- The symbols -- may be used in comments.`

Exercise 2.2   Writing Context Free Grammars

See p.3
9/27/82

See pg. 45, 47, 51

A simple grammar for expressions is:

expression   ::=   term
              | expression + term

term   ::=   operand
              | term * operand

operand   ::=   X | Y | Z

Extend this grammar to include the subtraction and division operators, the use of parentheses to change precedence, and a prefix minus operator.

Exercise 2.3   Operator Precedence

Each of the two grammars G1 and G2 below defines the syntax of expressions involving identifier operands and the operations

+   infix plus
−   prefix and infix minus
*   multiplication
/   division
**   exponentiation

*Need to be able to handle A * − X*

These two grammars differ slightly in the order in which operations are evaluated.

Explain the effects of this difference, illustrating your answer by showing the differences in the two parse trees for at least three sentences expressions defined by the grammars. Describe the practical significance of this difference and give arguments in favor of choosing one of the grammars for describing the expressions.

Grammar G1

expression   ::=   expression-1
                 | expression + expression-1
                 | expression − expression-1

expression-1   ::=   expression-2
                 | expression-1 * expression-2
                 | expression-1 / expression-2

expression-2	: :=	identifier
	|	– expression-2
	|	expression-3

| expression-3 | : := | identifier ** expression-2 |

Grammar G2

expression	: :=	expression-1
	|	expression-1 + expression
	|	expression-1 – expression

expression-1	: :=	expression-2
	|	expression-2 * expression-1
	|	expression-2 / expression-1

| expression-2 | : := | expression-2 ** expression-3 |
| | \| | expression-3 |

| expression-3 | : := | identifier |
| | \| | – identifier |

Exercise 2.4   Writing a Grammar to Describe Trees

Consider the following trees:

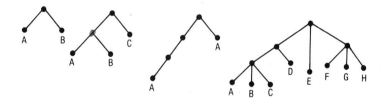

These trees can be represented by the lists:

```
(A B)
((A B) C)
(((A)) A)
(((A B C) D) E (F G H))
```

Write a grammar using the BNF variant of Table 2.2 to describe lists with one letter nodes.

Exercise 2.5   Extensions to Context Free Grammars

A context free grammar is sometimes either inadequate or clumsy for expressing some restrictions in the language it defines. As such, many forms of *extension* have been proposed.

One form of extension allows a grouping of n counters designated c1, c2, and so on, which may take on integer values. In the extended grammar, a rule is written

[p] left-side   ::= right-side [a]

where [p] is a *predicate*, a condition that must be satisfied before the rule is applied and [a] is an *action* to be performed after the rule is applied. The predicates and actions are expressions involving only counters and integer constants. For example, we may have:

[c2 < c1 + 3] left-side := right-side [c2 := c2 + 1]

A rule may be without a predicate or action. A rule with no predicate may be applied just as the rules of a contentional context free grammar are applied.

Suppose the following context free rules are used to define the syntax of identifiers and integers:

identifier	::=	letter
identifier	::=	identifier letter-or-digit
letter-or-digit	::=	letter
letter-or-digit	::=	digit
integer	::=	digit
integer	::=	integer digit

Assume the grammar has 26 rules for the nonterminal letter, each rule having a distinct letter as its right side. Similarly, there are 10 rules for the nonterminal digit to define the decimal digits.

Extend the rules to enforce the restriction that identifiers have no more than 10 characters and integers have no more than five digits.

Could a context free grammar *without* extensions be used to effect this sort of a length restriction? If not, explain why. If so, write a new set of rules for limiting integers to five digits.

Exercise 2.6   Describing BNF with BNF

See pg 10/4/82

Write a grammar to describe the BNF variant used in Table 2.2. Since the symbols you will be using in the meta-language will be the

a grammar defines a set, generally infinite, of the sentences that can be written in a language.

same as those of the language being described, you will have to use the technique of underlining such symbols in the language being described. This technique was introduced in Section 2.6. Your grammar will begin something like:

```
grammar     ::=     production...
production  ::=     variable ::= right-side
```

Exercise 2.7   The Shortest Possible Program

There are always a few tricky but interesting questions you can ask about a language. One of these concerns the shortest possible program you can write. Such a program would obviously do nothing when executed. Write one for Mini-language Core. How many non-blank characters are there?

3
Semantics

Through 95

Notes
9/22/82
9/22/82

You may have observed that, in the last chapter, no mention was made of what a program in Mini-language Core actually does; that is, what it means. Of course, symbols like + and if give clues to those experienced in programming languages. Nevertheless, we have deliberately separated the discussion of the written form of programs from their meaning. It is this question of meaning — the *semantics* — that we take up in this chapter.

We start by describing informally the semantics of Mini-language Core, whose syntax was given in Chapter 2 and is repeated here in Table 3.1, for reference. The way in which a programming language is defined raises a number of interesting but difficult questions. For example, how can precision be maintained without rendering the description inaccessible to the majority of readers? This and other questions concerning the semantics of languages are discussed following the presentation of Mini-language Core.

3.1 THE SEMANTICS OF MINI-LANGUAGE CORE

We now discuss the semantics of the mini-language corresponding to the syntactic categories given in Table 3.1.

Declarations

A declaration in Mini-language Core specifies one or more identifiers that can be used as variables in a program. Each declared variable can take on only integer values. An integer is a positive whole number, for example:

0   16   1776   12345

The maximum value of an integer is defined by a particular implementation and may vary from one implementation to another according to the characteristics of the host machine. However, the maximum value will not be less than 99999999.

The execution of a statement causes actions defined below to take place. The statements in a statement sequence are executed in the order in which they appear. However, some statements are compound in that they enclose other statement sequences. The execution of a compound statement and its enclosed statements is defined below. A program terminates *normally* after the execution of its last statement.

It is possible for the action specified by a statement to be meaningless. An attempt to execute such a statement causes the program to terminate *abnormally*. In addition, the execution of a loop statement, defined below, can result in its contained statements being executed endlessly. Hence, some programs may never terminate.

Thus there are only three possible outcomes to the execution of a program:

- Normal termination
- Abnormal termination
- Nontermination

The exact meaning of a program is defined only for programs that terminate normally.

Assignment Statements

An assignment statement causes the value of the expression at the time of execution to be associated with a variable. For example, we may have:

```
A := 0;       -- value of A is set to 0
B := B + 1;   -- value of B is incremented by 1
```

Execution of an assignment statement takes place as follows:

1. The expression given on the right of the assignment statement is evaluated according to the rules given below. If the expression contains any variables, their current value is used in the evaluation.

Table 3.1 Mini-language Core

```
program                ::=   program
                                 declaration...
                              begin
                                 statement...
                              end;

declaration            ::=   declare identifier [ , identifier ]... ;

statement              ::=   assignment-statement
                         |   if-statement
                         |   loop-statement
                         |   input-statement
                         |   output-statement

assignment-statement   ::=   identifier := expression ;

if-statement           ::=   if comparison then
                                 statement...
                           [ else
                                 statement... ]
                              end if;

loop-statement         ::=   while comparison loop
                                 statement...
                              end loop;

input-statement        ::=   input  identifier [ , identifier ]... ;

output-statement       ::=   output identifier [ , identifier ]... ;

comparison             ::=   ( operand comparison-operator operand )

expression             ::=   [ expression + ] factor
                         |   [ expression - ] factor

factor                 ::=   [ factor * ] operand

operand                ::=   integer
                         |   identifier
                         |   ( expression )

comparison-operator    ::=   <  |  =  |  ≠  |  >
```

2. The value obtained from the evaluation of the expression becomes the current value of the variable on the left of the assignment.

Provided that the evaluation of the expression does not terminate abnormally, the assignment statement will execute normally.

Input Statements

An input statement causes one or more integer values to be read from an external source, one value for each identifier given in the list of identifiers. Subsequent execution of the same or other input statements causes further values to be input. Each input value in the external source must be separated by one or more blank characters, and end-of-line boundaries are treated as single blank characters. For example, if the external data source contained

```
 0   5
16
```

then the input statement

```
input A, B, C;
```

would read these values into the variables A, B, and C respectively. For this set of data values, the input statement is thus equivalent to the assignments:

```
A := 0;
B := 5;
C := 16;
```

There are three kinds of error that can occur during the execution of an input statement:

1. The external data source contains fewer values than there are identifiers in the input statement. This is an *insufficient data error.*

2. The integer value read from the external data source is greater than the maximum allowed by the implementation. This is a *size error.*

3. One of the characters read from the external data source is an illegal character, other than a digit or blank. This is an *illegal character error.*

If any of these errors occur, the program is abnormally terminated.

Output Statements

Execution of an output statement causes the value of each of the variables in the list to be printed. Each value is preceded by the name of the variable and an = symbol. For example, the output statement

```
output A, B, C;
```

assuming that the values of **A, B,** and **C** are as given above, would result in the output:

```
A = 0    B = 5    C = 16
```

The output from an output statement starts on a new line and consists of the name of a variable, the = symbol, and the value, each separated by a single blank. The length of an output field is thus:

length(identifier) + length(integer-value) + 3

Fields are separated by three blanks. The length of an output line is defined to be 72 characters. If there is insufficient room left on a line to accommodate the next output field, a new line is started. An output field is not split between lines unless its length is greater than 72 characters.

There is one error that can occur during the execution of an output statement:

■ One of the variables in the list has not had a value assigned to it. This is the *undefined value error.*

If Statements

An if statement is a compound statement headed by a comparison. The comparison allows the programmer to make a choice of which statements are to be executed. The simplest form of an if statement contains only a comparison and one enclosed sequence of statements, for example:

```
if (A = 0) then
   INDEX    := INDEX - 1;
   PRODUCT  := PRODUCT * INDEX;
   output INDEX, PRODUCT;
end if;
```

Here, the two assignment statements and the output statement are executed only if the variable A has the value zero. If the value of A is not equal to zero, then none of the contained statements is executed.

If statements may have an else part, which contains an alternative sequence of statements to be executed if the comparison is false. For example, we may have:

```
if (A = 0) then
   INDEX    := INDEX - 1;
   PRODUCT := PRODUCT * INDEX;
   output INDEX, PRODUCT;
else
   INDEX := INDEX + 1;
   SUM    := SUM + INDEX;
   output INDEX, SUM;
end if;
```

Here, depending on the value of A, either the first three enclosed statements are executed or the second three enclosed statements are executed. An if statement terminates abnormally if the evaluation of the operands in the comparison leads to an error, as defined below.

Loop Statements

A loop statement is a compound statement that specifies that the statements within the loop are to be executed repeatedly for as long as the comparison at the head of the loop is true. For example, we may have:

```
while (CHANGE > 99) loop
   DOLLARS := DOLLARS + 1;
   CHANGE  := CHANGE - 100;
end loop;
```

Here the value of CHANGE is compared with 99. If it is greater than 99, the two enclosed assignments are executed and the process is repeated. If, for example, the value of CHANGE were initially 265, then the two assignments in the loop would be executed. The value of

CHANGE would then be 165 and the loop would be executed a second time. At this point, the value of CHANGE would be 65 and the execution of the loop statement would be complete. If the initial value of CHANGE were 65, the enclosed assignment statements would not be executed at all.

As in the if statement, the loop statement terminates abnormally if evaluation of the operands in the comparison leads to an error.

Expressions

An expression defines the computation of a value. An expression consists of one or more operands, separated by an operator +, - , or * meaning addition, subtraction, and multiplication. The operators are evaluated in order of decreasing precedence, defined by the rules:

- ■ The operator * has higher precedence than the + and - operators, which have equal precedence.

- ■ Operators of equal precedence are evaluated in textual order from left to right.

- ■ An expression enclosed in parentheses is evaluated to a single value before other operators.

Table 3.2 shows a number of example expressions and the order in which their components are evaluated.

There are two errors that can arise during the evaluation of an expression:

1. A variable in the expression has not previously had a value assigned to it. This is an *undefined value error*.

2. One of the operations leads to a value greater than the maximum permitted value defined by the implementation. This is an *overflow error*.

The occurrence of either of these errors causes abnormal termination of the program.

Comparisons

A comparison consists of two operands separated by one of the comparison operators, <, =, ≠, >, meaning less than, equal to, not equal to, and greater than respectively. If v1 is the value of the operand

Table 3.2   Evaluation of Expressions

Expressions	Sequence of Values Computed	Equivalent Expressions
A + B + C	x ← A + B y ← x + C	(A + B) + C
A − B − C	x ← A − B y ← x − C	(A − B) − C
A + B * C	x ← B * C y ← A + x	A + (B * C)
A * B + C	x ← A * B y ← x + C	(A * B) + C
A * B + C * D	x ← A * B y ← C * D z ← x + y	(A * B) + (C * D)
A * (B + C) * D	x ← B + C y ← A * x z ← D * y	(A * (B + C)) * D

x1 and v2 is the value of the operand x2, then the result of the comparison:

(x1 < x2)   will be true if v1 is less than v2
(x1 = x2)   will be true if v1 is equal to v2
(x1 ≠ x2)   will be true if v1 is not equal to v2
(x1 > x2)   will be true if v1 is greater than v2

Otherwise, the result of the comparison will be false.

Should the evaluation of one of the operands lead to an error, the program will be terminated abnormally.

Examples

The example shown at the end of Section 2.1 and reproduced here as Example 3.1, generates the Fibonacci series where, after the first

```
program
   declare COUNT, LIMIT;
   declare LAST_TERM, THIS_TERM, NEXT_TERM;
begin
   COUNT     := 0;
   LAST_TERM := 1;
   THIS_TERM := 1;
   input LIMIT;

   while (COUNT < LIMIT) loop
      output LAST_TERM;
      NEXT_TERM := LAST_TERM + THIS_TERM;
      LAST_TERM := THIS_TERM;
      THIS_TERM := NEXT_TERM;
      COUNT     := COUNT + 1;
   end loop;
end;
```

Example 3.1   Program to print the Fibonacci series

two terms, each term is the sum of the previous two. If the value read by the input statement were 10, the output would be:

```
LAST_TERM = 1
LAST_TERM = 1
LAST_TERM = 2
LAST_TERM = 3
LAST_TERM = 5
LAST_TERM = 8
LAST_TERM = 13
LAST_TERM = 21
LAST_TERM = 34
LAST_TERM = 55
```

Should the value read from the external data source be sufficiently large, the program will terminate with an overflow error during the execution of the statement:

```
NEXT_TERM := LAST_TERM + THIS_TERM;
```

The following is a very simple program with one assignment statement.

```
program
   declare A;
begin
   A := A + 1;    -- A has not been initialized
   output A;
end;
```

When the expression in this assignment statement is evaluated, the variable A has had no value assigned. Thus this program terminates abnormally and no output is generated.

3.2 DEFINING THE SEMANTICS OF A LANGUAGE

The semantics of a language give it an interpretation and provide a meaning to its expressions, statements, and programs. The symbols must be given an interpretation. We must be able to say, for example, that all the values in the language are integers and that all the operations performed on the values are operations in integer arithmetic.

In Section 3.1 we gave an informal but complete description of the meaning of all constructs in Mini-language Core. The problem of defining the semantics of a language is far from easy. The general goal, of course, is to specify the meaning of every well formed program in such a way that the programmer can understand its behavior unambiguously. There are two important concerns. First, the definition of the language must be *complete* — there must be no room for ambiguity as to the meaning of any construct. Second, the language should be defined in such a way that a programmer can *easily* refer to the language definition in order to answer questions about the language. These two goals, completeness and clarity, are not easy to satisfy separately and are very difficult to achieve together.

The semantics of most programming languages are, as we have done for Mini-language Core, defined informally. Only the context free syntax is defined formally. The definition of the semantics is usually through appeal to concepts presumably understood by the reader. Several techniques are commonly used.

Appeal to Mathematical Properties

Frequently, semantics are described by reference to commonly understood mathematical properties. When we defined the evaluation of expressions in Mini-language Core, for example, we appealed to the reader's background knowledge of integer arithmetic. Programming language conventions that limit the value that can be computed in any expression supplement the concepts of arithmetic.

The same principle applies to the definition of the semantics of comparisons. There, we assume knowledge about the ordering of integers and the way in which they can be compared.

Appeal to Mechanical Models of Computation

Another method of defining semantics is through the mechanical properties of the machine. This was used in explaining the sequence of statement execution. We assumed that the reader had in mind a model in which statements are processed one by one, based on the way in which computer instructions are executed. Concepts like if statements and loop statements are explained in terms of these properties. For example, the statements within the loop are executed repeatedly for as long as the comparison at the head of the loop is true. Futhermore, statements in a sequence of statements are executed one after another. Thus the reader of a definition can make use of the idea of the step by step execution of each statement in a program.

The concept of assignment is explained analogously. Here an appeal is made to the idea that each variable in a program has an associated location in which its value is stored. An assignment is viewed as a change of the value stored in a location.

Appeal to Abstraction

A very common, but more subtle, method of explaining the semantics of a language is by abstraction. Use is made of higher level concepts for the phenomena being explained.

For example, data that are sent for printing on an output device, such as a typewriter terminal, consist of a series of character codes. Some of these character codes are printable and represent the data, while others are not printed but control the output device, causing a new line, tabbing, or backspace. We can define the semantics of the output statement by the abstraction of fields in lines separated by blank characters. The abstraction of a group of characters representing the conceptual unit of an integer is used in describing the semantics of the input statement. Thus the execution of the input statement can be viewed as an abstracted operation that reads a succession of numbers from some external source of data.

Abstraction is also used in the description of the semantics of an array. It is viewed as a collection of items forming a table. Each item in the array has an index, and this index uniquely denotes a component of the array. Thus, rather than talking about computing the address of a component or saying that the components of arrays are stored in successive addresses in computer memory, which might not be true, we make the simple appeal to the concept of an indexed table.

3.3   SEMANTIC QUESTIONS

There are many questions related to the semantics of programming languages:

■   How can we present a precise definition of a language so that it is comprehensible to the average user?

■   How can we develop correct terminology, as well as avoid the profusion of computer jargon typically associated with the definition of a language?

■   How can we find abstractions for issues that are noted for their excessive detail, for example, input and output or arithmetic with real numbers?

■   How can we describe the conditions under which a program is erroneous?

■   How can we isolate those portions of a language that are dependent upon the implementation?

■   Last, is there a real need for formal definitions of semantics?

We treat these issues next.

Presentation of a Language

Programming languages are usually defined informally. Typically such descriptions employ normal prose, mixed with the use of tables, equations, and examples. Such is the case for the descriptions of our mini-languages in this and the following chapters.

One of the key decisions in describing a language is the order in which the concepts are presented. Typically, language descriptions take a bottom-up approach; that is, low level ideas, for example, numbers, identifiers, and character sets, are described first. The description slowly expands to include higher level parts of the language, for example, procedures, nesting of declarations, and, finally, programs.

This method presumes that the lower level concepts are easier to understand, and that a slow building of the user's knowledge will eventually lead to a comprehension of a complete program. Unfortunately, this method of description forces the reader to learn many features of a language whose utility may not be apparent until much more of the language is understood. As a result, there is some reason to believe that languages should be defined the other way around. This is the top-down order.

In a top-down presentation, the higher level concepts are given first, defined in terms of constructions that are to be specified later. All of the mini-language descriptions and all of the tables describing the syntax are arranged in this way. The category program is defined by the first production in terms of categories defined in subsequent productions.

We may argue that a top-down description of a language leads to a more rapid comprehension. Often this is because the lower level items, such as numbers and expressions, are common to most languages and the reader does not have to waste time rehearsing concepts that are already well known. More importantly, the general structure is outlined at the beginning and the details filled in subsequently according to the needs of the reader.

The major purpose of a language description has a considerable bearing on the choice of method. A definition intended for beginning programmers is likely to be organized differently from one for use by an experienced programmer as a reference. A description intended for beginners can appeal to little in the way of background knowledge. A programmer using a language as a reference uses it to answer certain questions about the language. Typical of such questions are: Is a semicolon needed here? Under what conditions will a particular construct lead to abnormal termination? What happens if I write this statement? Obviously, the choice of a good organization for a reference manual is a difficult issue and may be neither top-down nor bottom-up. Certainly a comprehensive index to any language description is essential.

People learn by examples, and with programming languages this is particularly true. Unfortunately, most language descriptions do not give realistic examples. The use of program fragments without a context or without a concern for style and clarity is all too frequent. For example, a construct like

```
while (I < J) loop
    J := J - 1;
end loop;
```

or even worse,

```
while (I < J) loop J := J - 1; end loop;
```

are hardly illuminating. From their identifiers, there is no inkling of the parts played by the variables I and J in the computation.

It may be argued that the development of good examples is difficult, and indeed it is. In this text, we too have occasionally used somewhat less than meaningful examples. On this point, we can only say, the better the examples, the better the language description.

Terminology

We now speak more about the words with which a language is described. A reference manual for a programming language is a compromise between a legal document describing the exact meaning of every feature in the language and a prose description suitable for the human reader. Typically, such descriptions introduce terminology and notations that have a special meaning with respect to the computer language.

One of the keys to the precision and clarity with which a language is described is the terminology used. Consider the simple and familiar term *value*. A value presumably denotes some object that can be constructed in a program. Thus it makes sense to speak of the value of an expression, the value existing on some input or output device, or the value returned by a function. This term is, however, used in other contexts.

For example, we often speak of the *value* associated with a parameter of a procedure, or the *value* of a variable given on the left side of an assignment statement. In these contexts, the term value is not quite so obvious. For example, the value associated with a parameter to a procedure may, in fact, mean the location of the corresponding argument. Similarly, the value of the variable on the left side of an assignment statement may also denote a location, rather than some object computed by the programmer. We consider this question in much greater detail in Chapter 4.

Similar problems arise with the two familiar terms *operator* and *operation*. We often speak of the addition operator and some times speak of the addition operation. Similarly, we speak of the assignment operator and sometimes of the assignment operation. Frequently, a clear definition of these two terms is not given.

In our description of the mini-languages we have made the following rather narrow distinction between these two terms. An operator can be applied to values to produce another value. Thus we speak of the addition operator or the equality operator. An operation is an action causing an effect on the internal state of the program. Thus we speak of an assignment operation and an input or output operation. This difference between an operation and an operator is one we also draw between a procedure and a function in Chapter 7.

There are many such related questions. What is "scope"? What is an "attribute"? What does it mean for an object to have a "location"? We discuss these particular points in later chapters.

These are typical of the kinds of issues that make the description of a programming language difficult. It is certainly true that the description of a programming language requires a great deal of care, and often a great deal of effort.

Specifying Details

Many features of a programming language involve numerous details. In Fortran, for example, the form and meaning of FORMAT statements is quite complicated because of the many options specifying the type and field width of items. A careful specification of all of the format options in Fortran typically takes pages and pages of text.

Another area of particular difficulty is the detailed behavior of arithmetic for floating point numbers. Specifying the resolution to which each arithmetic computation is evaluated, maximum and minimum values, the number of significant digits, and rounding or truncation conventions can be quite elaborate. Even with the simple Mini-language Core, the definition of these details is lengthy.

Errors

Programmers do not intend their programs to terminate abnormally. Nevertheless, errors occur, often to the great surprise of the programmer.

The specification of the conditions under which a program will terminate abnormally is an important part of any programming language description. All too often the specification of error conditions is not clearly defined.

In Mini-language Core there are several conditions that can lead to abnormal termination of a program. These are:

1. *Undefined value error.* This error occurs whenever an attempt is made to use the value of a variable that has not been assigned a value.

2. *Overflow error.* This error occurs whenever an attempt is made to compute a value greater than the maximum integer supported by the implementation.

3. *Insufficient data error.* This error occurs whenever an attempt is made to input a value from the external data source and no such value exists.

4. *Size error.* This error occurs whenever an integer value input from the external data source is greater than the maximum allowed by the implementation.

5. *Illegal character error.* This occurs whenever a character read from the external data source is other than a digit or a blank.

In addition, a program may be erroneous if it contains a loop that does not terminate.

Because Mini-language Core is such a small language, it has been possible to keep the number of semantic errors to a very small number. In real programming languages defining all the possible execution time errors is much more difficult, yet a complete definition must do so.

Implementation Dependencies

It is a fond wish for high level programming languages to be independent of the host machine and operating system on which they run. The program that runs on machine X should also run on machine Y without modification. To some degree, this is achieved. It is usually possible to move a program in one of the "standard" languages from one implementation to another without too much difficulty. This is because most programs make use of those parts of the language that are well understood and avoid the fringe areas.

Nevertheless, there are some areas that commonly give problems, for example:

■ *Maximum length of identifiers:* Different implementations of the same language, because of different machine characteristics, may find it convenient to set different bounds on the lengths of identifiers or discriminate between identifiers on different numbers of characters.

■ *Arithmetic precision:* The different word lengths of various machine architectures encourage arithmetic of different precision. This variance is compounded by a variety of number representations that bring computed results that may not be equal. For example, rounding on a two's complement machine may not give the same answer as rounding on a machine that uses a base ten representation.

■ *Character sets:* The character sets can be different from one implementation to another. While it is true that the sequence of letters in the alphabet is likely to be consistent, other important details are not. The two most popular character encodings are the ASCII set, which is a standard in the United States, and the EBCDIC scheme of IBM. In the ASCII code, the digits precede the letters; and in EBCDIC, the letters come first.

The choice of character set is generally made by the manufacturer of the hardware and is "built into" the hardware. It would therefore be difficult to implement a language that called for the ASCII character set on a machine that was designed for EBCDIC. Every time that two character strings were compared, special measures would have to be used, rather than making direct use of the hardware instructions.

Even beyond these kinds of issues, there is a tacit assumption that the implementation has adhered to the "standard" definition of the language. All too often this is not the case.

The definition of a language must therefore take care to separate those parts of the language that are to be consistent across all implementations from those that are left to the implementor's discretion. The parts beyond the core part of the language can be divided into three categories:

1. *Minimum requirement.* The definition may specify some minimum requirements, for example, the minimum number of characters used to distinguish between identifiers and a minimum for the largest number that can be represented. An implementation may make extensions beyond this minimum, however, a program that makes use of identifiers that are longer than the specified minimum might not be transportable from one implementation to another.

2. *Implementation defined.* This is closely connected to the first category in that the language specification would require that the documentation supplied by the implementor should augment the language definition by supplying certain details, such as the maximum number of characters used in discriminating identifiers.

3. *Deliberately undefined.* Certain details of a language can be left explicitly undefined, for example, the order in which subscript expressions in an array reference are evaluated. By

leaving them deliberately undefined, the programmer would know that programs that depend on these details are likely not to be movable from machine to machine; indeed, different versions of the same compiler may treat them differently.

In any case, a complete definition of a language must adopt a position on all details of the language.

Need For Formal Definitions

Computer science has already made considerable progress without having a generally accepted formal technique for defining programming languages, just as the English language was well developed before the advent of Johnson's *Dictionary of the English Language* in 1755. However, the lack of general use of formal definitions has not been without severe consequences. For example:

■   Language designers do not have good tools for careful analysis of their decisions.

■   Standardization efforts have been impeded by the lack of an adequate formal notation.

■   It is impossible to make a contract with a vendor for a compiler and be assured that the product will be an exact implementation of the language.

■   It is difficult to write reference manuals and tutorial texts without glossing over critical details.

■   The answers to detailed questions about a programming language frequently have to be obtained by trying an implementation or hoping for a consensus from several implementations.

Most of these problems would be avoided if there were good formal definitions for the languages. There would then be a single place for the precise details of each language, and no question would be left unanswered. Importantly, there would be a tendency to improve the design of a language by bringing its complexities out into the open. It is easy to say, "Language X is block structured and jumps out of blocks are permitted." But without a formal description of language X, the consequences are not so obvious.

Among the characteristics that are important to the successful use of any method are:

1. *Completeness:* There must be no gaps in the definition. In particular, there must be no questions about the syntax or semantics of the language that cannot be answered by means of the definition.

2. *Clarity:* The user of the definition must be able to understand the definition and to find answers to his questions easily. While it is obvious that some facility with the language is essential before being able to understand the definition fully, the amount of effort required should be small.

3. *Naturalness:* The naturalness of a notation has a very large effect on the ability of a user to understand a definition. The naturalness of a notation is more important than its conciseness, although there is a relation between the two.

4. *Realism:* Although the designer of a language may wish to be free from such mundane restrictions as finite numeric ranges and bounded storage, these restrictions are realities of an implementation. The definition provided by the designer, which is the implementor's manufacturing specifications, must specify exactly where restrictions or choices can be made and where the designer's unobstructed landscape must be modeled exactly.

3.4 FORMAL DESCRIPTIONS OF PROGRAMMING LANGUAGES

As explained, there is a need for the precise and understandable specification of programming languages. Many different techniques have been attempted. The methods that have been used range from simple context free grammars with informally described semantics to complete mathematical definitions. In this section we will discuss some of the techniques used in completely formal definitions.

A full discussion of formal definition techniques is far beyond the scope of this text. The reader who wishes a more detailed introduction to this area is referred to the paper [Marcotty et al. 1976]. In this section, we simply highlight three dominant definition techniques.

Operational Definitions

One of the earliest proposals for the rigorous definition of a programming language was Garwick's suggestion [1963] that an actual implemention be used. The major objections to this technique are the inevitable encroachment of the host hardware into the language being defined and the restricted availability of the definition. To escape these objections the IBM Vienna Laboratories developed the idea of a hypothetical machine as proposed in [McCarthy 1962], [Elgot and Robinson 1964], and [Landin 1965] on which to make an implementation. This work led to the Vienna Definition Language (VDL) and was used originally for a formal definition of PL/I [Lucas and Walk 1969].

In VDL a formal definition is based on a hypothetical computer that is not based on any real hardware. This is the *abstract machine*, as shown in Figure 3.1. It has a state with general components and some primitive instructions. The meaning of a program is defined by the sequence of changes in the state of the abstract machine as the program is executed. The rules of execution are defined by an algorithm, the Interpreter.

To make a distinction between those properties of a program that can be determined statically and those that are intrinsically connected to the dynamics of the program's execution, the original program is transformed into an abstract form before execution. This transformation is performed by another algorithm, the translator, which corresponds to the early phases of a compiler in a real implementation. During the transformation, the context sensitive requirements on syntax can be checked.

The state of the abstract machine used as the base of a VDL definition of Mini-language Core would have five components:

1. *The program:* the abstract program constructed by the translator.

2. *The control:* defining the part of the abstracted program currently being interpreted

3. *The store:* the storage part of the abstract machine

4. *The input file*

5. *The output file*

The idea underlying this type of formal definition is that, although the abstract machine is divorced from reality, it is simple enough that it is impossible to misunderstand its operation. Once the abstracted

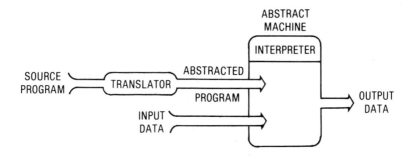

Figure 3.1 The VDL definition scheme

program has been understood, one merely has to trace through it, step by step, to determine its precise meaning.

Axiomatic Definitions

The axiomatic definition differs significantly from the operational approach just described. Instead of relying on a model of execution, the definition of the constructs of the language is designed so that it is possible to prove properties about programs built from the constructs. The meaning of a construct is given in terms of *assertions* about the computation state before and after execution of the construct. The definition associates an axiom with each kind of construct in the language. The axiom states what can be asserted after execution of the construct based on what was true before. Thus the definition of a statement can be expressed as:

$$P' \ \{statement\} \ P$$

Here, P' is the set of assertions that are true before execution of the statement, and P the set of assertions that can be derived from P' after execution of the statement.

For the assignment statement, we have the axiom

$$P[expression \rightarrow identifier] \ \{identifier := expression\} \ P$$

The notation $P[expression \rightarrow identifier]$ denotes the set of assertions obtained from P by replacing all occurrences of the identifier by the value of the expression. In a sense, the axiom for assignment appears to be the wrong way around, since we are deriving the assertion that must be true before assignment from the assertion that is true afterward. This initially counter-intuitive definition reflects the fact that any assertion derived after execution of the statement must be true when the identifier is replaced by the expression before execution of the statement. Thus, for example, we have

$(A + B + C) > 0$ $\{D := A + B;\}$ $(D + C) > 0$

As another example, consider the loop statement of Mini-language Core

```
while comparison loop
    statement...
end loop;
```

We know that when the loop terminates, provided that it does, the comparison will be false. In addition to asserting that the comparison is false, it will be possible to make other assertions after execution of the loop. These will depend on what was true before the loop was executed and on the effect of executing the sequence of statements contained in the loop. Since it is impossible to assert how many times the loop will be traversed, it is only possible to state that those assertions P_{inv} that were true before execution of the loop and that are not made false by execution of the loop will still be true after the loop has terminated. These assertions are known as the *loop invariant.* Thus, the axiom for the loop statement is

P_{inv} { loop-statement } P_{inv} & not(comparison)

Axiomatic definitions of the statements show nothing about *how* the statements are executed. They describe only assertions about values before and after execution. Our attention is turned away from the mechanics of execution toward more static and easier to observe objects, assertions. The assertions that are true *after* executing one statement are those that are true *before* executing the next statement. By using the first-order predicate calculus to link assertions, it is possible to derive assertions about results at termination of the entire program.

The technique of axiomatic definition grew out of work described in [Floyd 1967], where assertions were attached to links of flowcharts. The application to the definition of programming languages has been mainly developed in [Hoare 1969]. It was used to define some of the semantics of Pascal in [Hoare and Wirth 1973].

used by Tennent pg. 5

Denotational Definition

This approach to the definition of semantics is based on the idea that every construct in the programming language can be defined in terms of mathematical entities that model their meaning. These entities are the *denotations*. As a very simple example of this, we can say that the expressions (4 + 2), (12 − 6), and (2 * 3) all denote the same number, the number denoted by 6.

The denotational approach to defining semantics was developed by Strachey and Scott, e.g. see [Scott and Strachey 1972]. Over the years this method of defining semantics has gained considerable popularity. It can be argued that this method is the only one that addresses fundamental semantic issues. Unfortunately, it has been often associated with a great deal of specialized and often complex notation. This has hampered the understanding of its underlying ideas.

Two of the most important of these are the concepts of an "environment" and a "store." An environment is viewed as a function that maps identifiers into locations. The identifiers are those existing in a program. The locations are abstract entities somewhat similar to those needed in an underlying implementation. For example, in a program with two declared identifiers, say A and B, the environment for this program would be denoted as:

A → location-1
B → location-2

This function intuitively reflects the idea that the declaration of a variable also implicitly introduces a declaration of a location in which its values can be stored.

The idea of a store is also modeled as a function. In the above case, we would have a store mapping each location into some value that can be stored in the location, for example:

location-1 → value-1
location-2 → value-2

With this greatly oversimplified view of the method, we can take a view of semantics as follows.

The semantics of a *declaration* is a function mapping an environment and a store into a new environment and store. The new environment is derived from the old by the addition of an identifier mapped into some newly created location. The new store is derived from the original store by mapping this location into an initially undefined value. The semantics of a *statement* is a mapping from a store into a new store where the new store is derived from the original store by updating the value associated with a location. One must also introduce abstract definitions of both input and output files in order to define the semantics of a program involving input-output.

More generally, we may view the semantics of a "program" as a mapping from an input and an output file into a new input and output file. In order to define this mapping we need to define the concept of a *state*. A state is defined as a 4-tuple consisting of the following:

<Environment, Store, Input-file, Output-file>

The state is used to model the internal behavior of the program.

One of the important ideas associated with this method of semantic definition is the "undefined" value. An undefined value is treated just as any other value; for example, evaluation of an expression may produce an undefined value if an error is detected during its evaluation. In particular, the domain of integers introduced by Mini-language Core may be viewed as a set of objects containing the whole numbers through the maximum integer of the implementation, plus the undefined value. The undefined value is used to model error conditions.

A full discussion of this method of semantics takes us into the very deep foundations of programming languages. Rather than attempt any more than a brief introduction, further readings on this topic are suggested at the end of this chapter.

Interrelation of the Three Approaches

The aim of the definition of a programming language is to specify the meaning of all programs in that language. A compiler provides one such definition. To get the semantics of a particular program, it is necessary to determine its behavior under the standard implementation. This is expressed as a machine state transformation of the computer. This involves all the details of the compiler and the supporting operating system. The problem of proving the correctness of any other implementation under these circumstances is horrendous.

In order to simplify this definition we can use a simpler abstract machine and supporting system. This is the operational approach. Although it is simpler than an actual compiler, the problem of proving implementation correctness is still very difficult.

The denotational method specifies a mathematical "value" for each construct in the language. It also allows us to talk about equality;

two constructs are equal if they both denote the same value. Thus the task of proving two implementations equivalent now becomes one of demonstrating that they are both realizations of the same mathematical objects. To express it in this way is by no means to dismiss the problem as now simple; it is still extremely difficult, particularly for a large language; however, it is now conceptually much easier.

The axioms of a language are really theorems on the mathematical entities of the corresponding denotational definition.

It is not helpful to regard these three approaches as *competing* or that one method is *better* than the other. They are really different aspects of the same problem. The operational approach is likely to be of most value to the implementor, since it describes the language in a familiar algorithmic metaphor. The axiomatic definition should give the programmer the tools needed to prove the correctness, formally or informally, of a program. Finally, denotational definitions are likely to help the language designer, since they bring out the underlying mathematical structure of the language.

3.5 THE CORRECTNESS OF A PROGRAM

It is a common view that a program is either correct or incorrect. Correctness is thus viewed as some kind of absolute property of a program. Strictly speaking, this view may be valid, but in practice it is not always helpful.

The language definition, the programmer, and the user of a program all provide different views of correctness. The following is a list of various interpretations of correctness in order of increasing difficulty of attainment.

1. The program contains no context free syntax errors.

2. The program contains no context free or context sensitive syntax errors.

3. The program contains no syntax errors and executes to a normal termination.

4. The program contains no syntax errors and there exists some set of input data for which the program executes to normal termination to yield the correct result.

5. The program contains no syntax errors and, for a typical set of input data, executes to normal termination to yield the correct results.

6. The program contains no syntax errors and, for deliberately difficult sets of test data, executes to normal termination to yield the correct results.

7. The program contains no syntax errors and, for all possible sets of input data that are valid according to the problem specification, executes to normal termination to yield the correct results.

8. The program contains no syntax errors and, for all possible sets of input data, executes to normal termination to yield the correct or reasonable results.

The beginning programmer will, for a short while, be happy with levels 1 or 2. Eventually the programmer will generally be satisfied with level 6. The user, of course, would like to see all programs at level 8 but must come to realize that this may be prohibitively expensive.

From the point of view of the definition of most programming languages, any program that has no syntax errors and executes to normal termination is a correct program and has a meaning. That the program does not produce correct results from the programmer's point of view does not destroy its validity. It is still a correct program written to a specification other than the one that the programmer intended.

Some languages allow the programmer to include assertions as part of the program. These can then be checked against the statements in the program either during compilation with the help of a theorem prover, or during execution with extra machine instructions. For such languages, the programmer's view of correctness of results has some meaning. However, it should be remembered that the statements and the assertions are really two different ways of saying the same thing. All that can be checked is that these two versions match. There can be no guarantee that what was written down matched what the programmer or user had in mind.

3.6   A FURTHER VIEW OF TRANSLATION

In Section 2.5 we described how, during compilation, the source program is converted to the abstract program. In this section we review the conversion of the abstract program to the object program. This phase of the compiler often involves two parts, *optimization* and *code generation.*

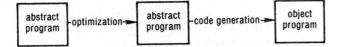

The goal of optimization is to make the object program as small and as fast as possible. To do this, transformations are applied to the abstract program that make it more efficient but do not change its meaning. The term *optimization* is a misnomer, since to produce a truly *optimal* version of a program would generally involve discarding the original program and substituting the best possible algorithm for performing the desired task. All that can generally be achieved is a *better* program than can be produced without optimization.

Typical transformations that can be done during optimization are:

■ *Folding:* performing operations whose operands have values that are known during compilation.

For example,

    I := 4 + J - 5;

can be transformed to

    I := J - 1;

A less obvious example is that the pair of assignments

    I := 3;
    J := I + 2;

can be transformed to

    I := 3;
    J := 5;

■ *Elimination of redundant operations:* This generally involves factoring out common subexpressions.

For example, the three assignments

```
A := 6 * (B + C);
D := 3 + 7 * (B + C);
E := A * (B + C);
```

can be transformed to

```
TEMP := B + C;
A    := 6 * TEMP;
D    := 3 + 7 * TEMP;
E    := A * TEMP;
```

where **TEMP** is a new variable created by the compiler to hold the value B + C.

■   *Loop optimization:* Usually this means moving expressions whose values do not change within a loop out of the loop.

Consider, for example, the Mini-language Core loop statement:

```
while (COUNT < LIMIT) loop
   input SALES;
   VALUE := SALES * (MARK_UP + TAX);
   output VALUE;
   COUNT := COUNT +1;
end loop;
```

The computation of the value **MARK_UP + TAX** is performed each time the loop is executed, yet its value does not change. The loop is transformed to

```
TEMP := MARK_UP + TAX;
while (COUNT < LIMIT) loop
   input SALES;
   VALUE := SALES * TEMP;
   output VALUE;
   COUNT := COUNT +1;
end loop;
```

Although the examples of optimization transformations just given are shown as transformations of the source program, in most compilers it is the abstract program that is transformed. In all cases, the transformation must preserve the meaning of the program. Depending on the skill with which the source program was written, factors of about two in improvement may be obtained by using optimization techniques.

The transformations during optimization are generally independent of the target machine for the compilation. The characteristics of this machine become of great importance during the final stage of the compilation. At that point, the abstract program is translated into the machine instructions of the target machine and the object program is output in a form suitable for the target machine's operating system. Some functions called for in the program may require the use of library subroutines. The code generation stage must construct the necessary calls for these subroutines so that they can be incorporated in the final object program.

Even during the code generation phase some transformations akin to those that are done during optimization can take place. The difference between these and the previous ones is that the characteristics of the target machine are taken into account. Typical of these transformations is the movement of constant address calculations to the outside of loops.

With all the optimization transformations, it is essential that the meaning of the program not be changed. The compiler must make a very careful analysis of the program to make sure of this and, if there is the slightest doubt, the form of the program must be left unchanged. We shall see in later chapters that the design of a language can have a profound effect on what transformations can be performed.

FURTHER READING

On a subject as broad as semantics the possible readings are numerous. We list but a few.

The general subject of language design and semantic issues, in particular, are treated in [Hoare 1973] and [Richard and Ledgard 1977]. Both of these papers are quite readable and tend to emphasize directions in design, rather than specific proposals for improvement. A much more rigorous but somewhat less readable exposition of the language design area is given in [Ichbiah et al. 1979]. This document, "Rationale for the Design of the Ada Programming Language," examines almost every area of language design.

Another view of the programming languages is given in [Strachey 1972]. This short report presents a thoughtful analysis of programming languages by simply discussing the kinds of objects denoted by programming constructs.

In the area of formal definition, a rather elaborate survey is given in [Marcotty et al. 1976]. This paper not only surveys the area of formal definition techniques but presents a small language similar to Mini-language

Core whose syntax and semantics are defined using four different formal techniques.

Another comparative view of formal definition techniques is given in [Donahue 1976]. Papers on the origins of definition techniques include the work in [Strachey 1966] and [Landin 1964].

The Vienna Definition Approach to defining semantics has received considerable attention in the literature. A fundamental paper on this topic is [Lucas and Walk 1971]. A further description of this technique can be found in [Lee 1972].

The functional or denotational approach to defining semantics has evolved over the years. Surveys of this approach are given in [Stoy 1977] and [Gordon 1979]. Of these, the text by Stoy is more comprehensive, and the paper by Gordon is more readable to the uninitiated. The origins of this approach are discussed in [Scott and Strachey 1972] and [Scott 1970]. A fairly comprehensive bibliography on this approach is given in [Donahue 1976]. A survey of this approach is also given in [Tennent 1976].

There are a large number of works on axiomatic definition of languages and proofs of program correctness. The early work by Floyd [1967] gives one of the first attempts at work in this area. Also of importance are the work [Hoare 1969] and the classic axiomatic definition of Pascal given in [Hoare and Wirth 1973]. Again, a good bibliography in this area as well as a comparison of axiomatic approaches with the denotation approach is given in [Donahue 1976].

EXERCISES

Exercise 3.1   Defining a Language

In Output, how are negative numbers handled.

The description of Mini-language Core was quite carefully written. Nevertheless, a thorough reading of the description reveals a number of points in which the exact meaning of a program is not explicitly stated. Enumerate four such points.

Note: Problems like those found above are commonplace in language descriptions. In commonly used (and thus much larger) languages, the possibilities for imprecision are much greater.

Exercise 3.2   Programming in Mini-language Core

The numbers on the pages of a book go in ascending order; the first page is 1, the second 2, and so forth.

If you are a typesetter in a printing shop, you need to have sufficient digits to print the page number for each page. For example, in a book with only 51 pages, you need:

5	Zeros	7	Fives
16	Ones	5	Sixes
15	Twos	5	Sevens
15	Threes	5	Eights
15	Fours	5	Nines

Assuming you never have to print a book with more than 1,000 pages, write a program in Mini-language Core to input the number of pages in a book and to output the number of each digit required.

Exercise 3.3   Proofs of Correctness

The following program computes the greatest common divisor of X and Y.

```
program
    declare X, Y, GCD

begin
    input X, Y;
    while (X ≠ Y) loop
        if (X > Y) then
            X := X - Y;
        else
            Y := Y - X;
        end if;
    end loop;
    GCD := X;
    output GCD;
end;
```

Using the mathematical properties of greatest common divisors, for example,

$$gcd(X, Y) = gcd(Y, X)$$
$$gcd(X, Y) = gcd(X+Y, Y)$$

give a formal proof of correctness for this program.

see my 1
10/6/82

my 1
10/18/82

Exercise 3.4   Writing a Reference Manual

Consider the following strange looking language.

A program is a sequence of string replacement rules of the form

L → R

where L and R are strings of characters. Some of the rules may have a period after the arrow, as in

L →. R

In both cases, the replacement R may be an empty string. The input to each program is itself a character string.

A program is executed as follows. The sequence of rules is scanned for the first rule, such that the string L given on the left side occurs within the input string S. Then the leftmost occurrence of L within S is replaced by R, giving a new input string S'. This process is reiterated until a rule with a period is executed, or until no substitution is possible, at which point the program terminates.

The final value of the input string is the output of the program.

This language is known as a Markov Normal Algorithm [1954] and can, in fact, express any computable operation. For example, the program

B → D
C → F
0 → I

transforms the string COBBLER into the string FIDDLER, and the program

B → D
C →. T
0 → I

transforms the string COBBLER into the string TODDLER.

Consider also the following program for taking a parenthesized string of letters from the alphabet {I, O, N, X} and producing a string where the initial letters are reversed:

Rules

II*	→	I*I	*1*
IO*	→	O*I	*2*
IN*	→	N*I	*3*
IX*	→	X*I	*4*
OI*	→	I*O	*5*
OO*	→	O*O	*6*
ON*	→	N*O	*7*
OX*	→	X*O	*8*
NI*	→	I*N	*9*
NO*	→	O*N	*10*
NN*	→	N*N	*11*
NX*	→	X*N	*12*
XI*	→	I*X	*13*
XO*	→	O*X	*14*
XN*	→	N*X	*15*
XX*	→	X*X	*16*
(I*	→	I(	*17*
(O*	→	O(	*18*
(N*	→	N(	*19*
(X*	→	X(	*20*
()	→ .		*21*
)	→	*)	*22*

I nput String
Output String

For example, the input

(INNOX)

gives the output

XONNI

Now for the exercise. Write a reference manual for this "programming language." In the course of writing your reference manual, you will discover that you will have to specify some details not covered in our informal description. You should draw on your experience and inventiveness to supply these details.

Exercise 3.5   Proper Terminology

Imagine for the moment that you are writing a glossary of terms for Mini-language Core. Give precise definitions for each of the following terms, using at most two sentences for each definition:

program	integer
declaration	value
statement	operator
identifier	operand
expression	location
comparison	

Exercise 3.6   Optimization

The following program in Core does not do anything sensible. However, apply the optimization techniques of folding, elimination of redundant operations, and loop optimization to transform it into a more efficient program.

```
program
    declare A, B, C, D, E;
begin
    input A;
    B := 1;
    C := 2;
    if (A < 5) then
        D := B*C + 3;
        while (C ≠ 10) loop
            E := B + C;
            C := C + 1;
            if (A > 3) then
                D := A * B + D;
            else
                while (E < 10) loop
                    D := A*B*C + E;
                    E := E + 1;
                end loop;
            end if;
            E := A*B + D;
            A := A + 1;
        end loop;
    else
        D := B*C + A;
    end if;
    B := C * D;
    C := B - D;
    output A, B, C, D;
end;
```

Explain and justify each transformation that you make.

Dominant Features

4
Names, Locations, and Values

Notes 10/4/82
10/6/82

A programming language is designed for the manipulation of objects, for example, numbers, strings, people's names, colors, and so forth. An object that is to be operated on by a program has two attributes:

1. The place where it is stored; this is its "location."

2. Its value; this value may change during the course of the program's execution.

We use the term *location* rather than *address*, since address is a hardware concept that may have no meaning in a programming language. An object can occupy only one location, yet it may occupy several hardware addresses. For example, on a byte-addressed machine, a number may occupy more than one byte. The value of a pointer variable in PL/I may often be thought of as an address, and the built-in function ADDR encourages this thought; in fact, the pointer value might not be a physical address but an index into a vector of actual addresses. In general, for a given location, we can always obtain the value that is stored there.

The objects manipulated by a program are identified by names. However, sometimes names are used to mean the location of an object; and, at other points in the same program, the name can be used to mean the value stored at that location. Thus, in the Fortran statement

    J = J + 1

the J on the left is used to refer to a location, while the one on the right means the value stored at that location.

In the following excerpt from Lewis Carroll's *Through the Looking Glass*, the White Knight demonstrates the problem:

> "...The name of the song is called '*Haddocks' Eyes*'!"
>
> "Oh, that's the name of the song, is it?" Alice said, trying to feel interested.
>
> "No, you don't understand," the Knight said, looking a little vexed. "That's what the name is *called*. The name really is '*The Aged Aged Man*.'"
>
> "Then I ought to have said 'That's what the *song* is called'?" Alice corrected herself.
>
> "No, you oughtn't: that's quite another thing! The song is called '*Ways and Means*': but that's only what it is *called* you know!"
>
> "Well, what *is* the song then?" said Alice, who was by this time completely bewildered.
>
> "I was coming to that," the Knight said. "The song really is '*A-Sitting on a Gate*': and the tune's my own invention."

The White Knight is showing the difference between:

1. the song — "*A-Sitting on a Gate*"
2. What the song is called — "*Ways and Means*"
3. The name of the song — "*The Aged Aged Man*"
4. What the name is called — "*Haddocks' Eyes*"

Consider the statement about a program:

The value of the variable X is pi.

This really means:

X is the name of the place where the number called pi is stored at this moment.

Thus, to draw a parallel with the White Knight's distinctions:

1. The number — 3.1415926535
2. What the number is called — pi
3. The name of the number — some location in storage
4. What the name is called — X.

If we return to our example of the Fortran assignment

J = J + 1

we can clarify the problem by saying that the J on the left gives a *reference* and the J on the right gives a *value*. Thus a reference identifies a location at which a value is stored. Some writers use the terms *l-value* (left value) for location and *r-value* (right value) for the value stored in the location.

Mini-language Ref, defined next, will help clarify some of the issues involved in names.

4.1 MINI-LANGUAGE REF

Mini-language Ref derives its reference mechanism from Algol 68. Its context free syntax is defined in Table 4.1.

A program consists of a sequence of declarations followed by a sequence of statements. Each identifier used in these statements must appear exactly once in the declarations.

A declaration associates a type with one or more identifiers. The type of an identifier defines the type of value to which it may refer or represent. The value can be a constant, in which case the type *integer constant*, followed by an = symbol and the value. The value can also be a variable, in that case, the type specification is *integer* preceded by zero or more ref symbols.

If we declare the value associated with an identifier to be constant, for example

    declare PAGE_LENGTH: integer constant = 63;

Identifier becomes a notation for the constant value.

then the identifier essentially becomes a notation for the constant value. The two assignments

    X := PAGE_LENGTH;

and

    X := 63;

are exactly equivalent. The symbol = in the declaration indicates that the identifier is identically equal to the given value throughout the program; it cannot be changed. This has two advantages: the meaning of the constant value in the program is more easily understood from the name than its value and, should the value have to be altered, only one statement in the program would need to be changed.

Advantages of declaration Name & Integer = 63

Table 4.1   Mini-language Ref

```
program            ::=   program
                             declaration...
                         begin
                             statement...
                         end;

declaration        ::=   declare identifier [ , identifier ]... : type ;

type               ::=   integer constant = integer
                   |     [ ref ... ] integer

statement          ::=   assignment-statement
                   |     input-statement
                   |     output-statement

assignment-statement ::= identifier := expression ;

input-statement    ::=   input   identifier [ , identifier ]... ;

output-statement   ::=   output identifier [ , identifier ]... ;

expression         ::=   [ operand + ] operand

operand            ::=   integer
                   |     identifier
```

S1B program font

If the value associated with the identifier is to be variable, then there are many different kinds of values that can be associated with the identifiers, depending on the type specifications.

If the type specification does not contain any occurrences of the symbol ref then the associated identifiers refer to integer values. If the type specification contains a single ref symbol, then the values to which the associated identifiers refer are themselves references to integer values; that is, the values identify locations in which integer objects are stored. If the type specification contains two ref symbols, then the values to which the associated identifiers refer are references to locations that contain references to integer values, and so on.

use of
ref

In each case, starting with an identifier and following the chain of references, one eventually finishes at a location that contains an integer value. The number of links is defined by the number of ref symbols in the specification of the type. Since the language does not impose an upper bound on the number of ref symbols in a declaration, there are arbitrarily many different types in any program.

The executable statements are assignment statements, input statements, and output statements, all of which have familiar syntax.

Consider the very simple program:

```
program
    declare X  : integer;
    declare ONE: integer constant = 1;
begin
    input X;
    X := X + ONE;
    output X;
end;
```

This program reads in a positive integer value, adds one to the value, and prints the result.

This simple program uses an identifier that refers directly to an integer value similar to the variable X in the declaration:

```
declare X: integer;
```

This variable, like all variables, must be given a value, either by assignment or input, before it can be used in an expression.

When we declare a variable as having the type *integer constant*, we are saying that the identifier is identically equal to an integer value, that is, the *mode* of the identifer is integer. The identifier X declared to be of type integer has associated with it an integer value that can change during program execution.

Since X refers to integer values, its mode is reference-to-integer. Compare this with the variable Y declared as:

```
declare Y: ref integer;
```

Here Y is a variable that refers to reference-to-integer values. Thus the mode of Y is a reference-to-reference-to-integer.

Executing the assignment

```
Y := X;
```

sets the value of Y to be a reference to the integer value to which X refers. Executing the assignment

```
X := 7;
```

does not change the value of Y, still a reference to the integer value to which X refers, but it does change that integer value. Thus the integer value that is at the end of the chain of references that starts with the identifier Y is changed.

To obtain the integer value at the end of this chain of references, the value of Y must be *dereferenced* twice, corresponding to the two occurrences of *references-to* in the mode of Y. This mechanism is extended for variables declared with more than one ref symbol.

The operator + represents addition. To evaluate an expression that consists of the + operator and operands that are identifiers, the value of each identifier must be dereferenced as many times as needed to obtain an integer value.

For an assignment statement to be legal, the identifier on the left must not be declared with *integer constant* and one of the following must be true, either:

1. The expression consists of more than one operand, a single identifier that has been declared to be an *integer constant* or an integer, and the identifier on the left is declared without any ref symbols.

2. There is an identifier on the right side, and the number of ref symbols in the declaration of the identifier on the left side is at most one greater than the number of ref symbols in the declaration of the identifier on the right side.

For example, given the declarations

```
declare A: integer constant = 5;
declare B: integer;
declare C: ref integer;
declare D: ref ref integer;
```

both the assignments

integer := integer constant

```
B := A;
C := D;
```

ref integer := ref ref integer

O K

satisfy the requirements above. On the other hand, the assignments

ref integer := integer constant

```
C := A;
D := B;
```

Wrong

ref ref integer := integer Rule!

both violate the conditions and are thus illegal.

<u>Execution of a legal assignment is as follows:</u>

1. The expression consists of more than one operand, a single identifier declared with the type *integer constant* or an integer.

   The value of the expression (which by definition is an integer value) is copied into the location associated with the identifier on the left.

2. The expression is an identifier.

Case 2.1: The number of ref symbols in the declaration of the identifier on the right is one less than the number of ref symbols in the declaration of the identifier on the left.

   In this case, a reference to the location associated with the identifier on the right is copied into the location associated with the ~~location~~ *identifier* on the left.

Case 2.2: The number of ref symbols in the declaration of the identifier on the right is greater than or equal to the number of ref symbols in the declaration of the identifier on the left.

   In this case, the value contained in the location associated with the identifier on the right is obtained. This value refers to a location. This value is dereferenced, that is, it is replaced by the value contained in the location to which it refers. The dereferencing operation is performed a number of times equal to the excess number of ref symbols in the declaration of the identifier on the left. The resulting value is

right

copied into the location associated with the identifier on the left.

For the assignment to be executed without error, it must be possible to perform the required number of dereference operations. Notice that in case 2.2, each time a value is obtained from a location, that location must contain a defined value; that is, the location must have had a value assigned to it either by an assignment statement or by an input statement.

Input and output statements specify the reading and writing of integer values. On input it must be possible to dereference each identifier by the number of ref symbols given in its declaration. On output it must be possible to dereference each identifier in the output statement fully to obtain an integer value. Otherwise, the input or output action is in error.

As an illustration of the dereferencing mechanism, consider the program of Example 4.1. After the fifth assignment has been executed, two chains of references will have been set up and the state will be as shown schematically in Figure 4.1. Note that REF_REF_INT_F has not been assigned a value.

```
program
    declare INT_A, INT_B: integer;
    declare REF_INT_C, REF_INT_D: ref integer;
    declare REF_REF_INT_E, REF_REF_INT_F: ref ref integer;
begin
  1  INT_A := 1;
  2  INT_B := 2;
  3  REF_INT_C := INT_A;
  4  REF_INT_D := INT_B;
  5  REF_REF_INT_E := REF_INT_C;   -- state shown in Figure 4.1
  6  REF_INT_C := INT_B;           -- state shown in Figure 4.2
  7  INT_A := REF_REF_INT_E;
     input    REF_REF_INT_E;       -- state shown in Figure 4.3  — Day 3
     output   REF_INT_D;
end;
```

Example 4.1   Dereferencing in Mini-language Ref

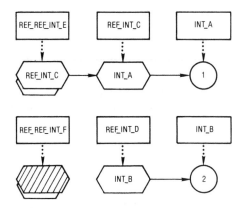

Figure 4.1 State after execution of the fifth assignment of Example 4.2

The next assignment

```
REF_INT_C := INT_B;
```

causes the value of **REF_INT_C** to refer to the location associated with **INT_B**. No other value is changed. The situation after executing this statement is as shown in Figure 4.2.

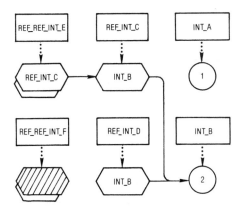

Figure 4.2 State after executing REF_INT_C := INT_B;

$INT\_A := REF\_REF\_INT\_E;$

The final assignment causes the value of REF_REF_INT_E to be dereferenced twice to obtain the integer 2, which is copied into the location associated with INT_A. The input statement causes a value, say 3, to be read from the input file and assigned to the variable found by following the chain starting at REF_REF_INT_E. The semantics of Mini-language Ref require that this chain be set up by a sequence of assignment statements before an input statement is executed. The result is depicted in Figure 4.3. The final statment thus prints the value 3.

Notice that an attempt to execute

```
output REF_REF_INT_F;
```

in place of the given output statement is in error, since the value of REF_REF_INT_F is undefined and cannot be dereferenced to produce an integer.

4.2 DECLARATION AND ASSIGNMENT

Consider a declaration of a variable, such as:

```
declare A: integer;
```

This states that A is the name of a variable. A variable has two things:

a. A location
b. A value

Thus associated with the name A is a reference to a location, one that can contain a particular kind of object; in this case, an integer object. This association may be represented pictorially as:

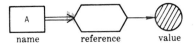

name   reference   value

A declaration of a variable creates this structure with an undefined value in the location. Once the location associated with the identifier A has been created, it cannot be changed although the value stored in the location can be. The identifier A is said to be bound by the declaration. Since A always refers to a location that can only contain an integer object, it always refers to an integer.

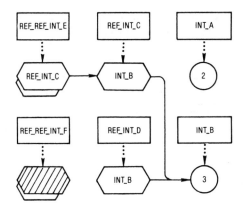

Figure 4.3   Final state of Example 4.1

Next consider the assignment:

```
A := 5;
```

Execution of this statement puts a copy of the integer object 5 into the location associated with the identifier A, giving:

A new variable does not have a value until it has been explicitly assigned. A program that attempts to obtain the value of a variable before it has been assigned is in error.

The digit 5 is the name of a constant whose value is the integer 5. The role of locations is made clear in Algol 68, where the declaration

```
real X
```

is an abbreviation for the declaration:

```
ref real X = loc real
```

Here X is a constant whose value is a reference to a real value; *loc real* is a generator that acquires the location that is to be defined as the value of X; that is, X is identically equal to a reference-to-real value that is given by *loc real.* In this case we have

S1B program font

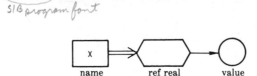

Thus

    real X

really declares X to be the name of a constant value, the location where a real value may be stored. Thus the location associated with X cannot change, but the real value that is stored in the location can.

Returning to our mini-language, consider the declaration

    declare A, B: integer;

and the statements:

    A := 5;
    B := A;

By the second assignment we mean: obtain the value associated with A and copy it into the location associated with B. Thus, the execution of this second assignment may be represented as:

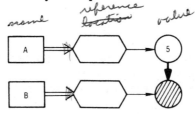

It is possible to have more than one name referring to a single value. For example, in Mini-language Ref, consider the declaration

    declare REF_A: ref integer;

Here REF_A is a variable that refers to a location that can contain reference-to-integer objects. Such a variable is somewhat like a PL/I pointer variable, but is constrained to take only values that are references-to-integers.

Next consider:

```
declare A, B: integer;
declare REF_A: ref integer;
A     := 5;
REF_A := A;
B     := REF_A;
```

The declarations set up the following:

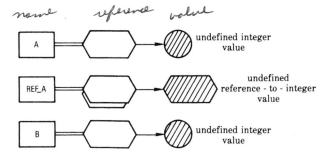

Note that a location can only contain objects of a particular type. For this reason, we use different shapes in the diagrams.

The assignment

```
REF_A := A;
```

causes the location associated with A to be assigned to the location associated with REF_A.

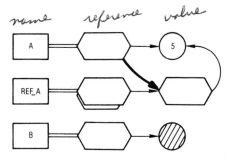

Thus A and REF_A both refer to the same integer value, though REF_A refers through an extra level of indirection. The assignment

```
B := REF_A;
```

causes a simple dereferencing operation to be applied to the value in the location associated with the variable REF_A. This value is the location associated with A. Dereferencing this gives the value 5, which is copied into the location associated with B.

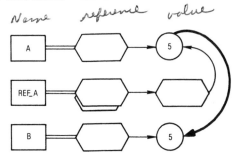

Notice, if we now execute the assignment statement

```
A := 10;
```

this will change both the value that A refers to directly, as well as the value that REF_A refers to indirectly.

In a language like PL/I, for example, it is possible to have two names that refer directly to the same value. The PL/I declaration

```
DECLARE X FIXED,
        Y FIXED DEFINED X;
```

gives rise to the naming structure:

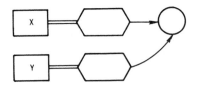

As we have seen, when a name is used in a program sometimes its location and sometimes the object contained in that location is meant. Consider, for example, the Pascal program

```
program EXAMPLE (INPUT, OUTPUT);
   var
      A: INTEGER;

   procedure P (var B: INTEGER);
   begin
      B := B + 2
   end;

begin
   A := 1;
   A := A + 1;
   P(A)
end
```

Here A is used with two distinct meanings. In the expression:

```
A + 1
```

A really means some *value*. Once we are given the value of A, we can perform the required addition without concern about the name of A or the location of the value of A.

On the left side of the assignment, A really denotes some *location*. Once we are given this location, we can proceed with the assignment without concern about the name A or its value.

In the procedure invocation P(A), A really means its location; for on invocation, the parameter B of procedure P is associated with the *location* of A. Hence the occurrence of B on the left side of

```
B := B + 2
```

refers to the location of A (whose value is to be changed), whereas the occurrence of B on the right side denotes the value stored in the location of A.

4.3 A MODEL OF STORAGE

In general, a store is a carrier of information that may be realized in computer hardware as immediate access main storage or by some other technique that has longer access time. From the point of view of the programming language, it is the holder of the objects that are manipulated by the language. It thus stands between the abstract world of the language and the real world of hardware realization.

As we described earlier, associated with a variable is a location, and an object may be stored in that location, both of which must be represented in our model. A store provides a mapping, S, between locations and values; that is, given a location loc, we can obtain a value v. Thus we can write:

    v = S(loc)

The store S may only be a partial mapping since there can be locations that have no defined value if none has been assigned.

As the contents of the store are changed, so too, are the mapping changes. After the value of a location has been changed, applying the mapping to the same location gives a different value. An assignment thus changes the mapping S into a new mapping S'.

A particular assignment changes the value in a location loc from S(loc) to v' such that

    v' = S'(loc)

where

    S'(x) = if (x = loc) then v' else S(x)

that is, an assignment changes the value of one location only.

So far we have considered assignment only; there are also the operations of allocation and freeing that can be performed on storage. The mapping S allows a certain set of values for loc; there are only certain locations that are valid. This corresponds to the amount of storage that can be accessed at any particular time. The set L is the set of *active locations.*

Allocation is the inclusion of new locations in the set L of active locations. Allocation may be implied by a declaration of a variable or by an explicit command, like the ALLOCATE statement of PL/I or the *heap* statement of Algol 68. Allocation is an operation on the mapping S to produce a new mapping, S'. Suppose loc is not a member of the set of active locations L, then

    (ALLOCATE loc)(S) = S'

where

    S'(loc)

is undefined, and

    S'(loc') = S(loc')

for all loc' in L. Thus the set of active locations L' consists of the set L with the additional element loc.

We may define the operation of freeing similarly. Examples of this are the implicit freeing of storage at the end of a block in a language like Algol or an explicit command, such as FREE in PL/I

    FREE(loc)(S) = S'

where loc is a member of the set L, and

    S'(loc') = S(loc')

Here loc' is a member of the new set of active locations L' derived from L by deleting loc; that is, for all loc' $\neq$ loc, the freeing operation leaves them unchanged.

So far we have only considered elementary values made up of the single primitive objects manipulated by the language. We discuss objects that are collections of other objects in Chapter 6.

4.4 SYMBOL TABLES

A *symbol table* is an implementation concept used to translate a program into a form suitable for execution. Conceptually a symbol table is a dictionary providing a correspondence between identifiers and their properties. These properties include names, their attributes, and machine addresses. It is referenced constantly during compilation: during syntax analysis for its construction and during code generation for its information.

Consider the program declarations

    declare A, B: integer;
    declare C, D: ref integer;
    declare E, F: ref ref integer;

A simple symbol table might be

Identifier	Attribute	Address
A	int	100
B	int	101
C	ref int	102
D	ref int	103
E	ref ref int	104
F	ref ref int	105

The identifiers and attributes are inserted during analysis of the declarations. The addresses are inserted before code generation. The table is later used during code generation to construct appropriate machine instructions for execution of the program.

FURTHER READING

More than any other, the concept of assignment separates programming languages from conventional mathematical systems. Without assignment, the world of programming languages would be quite different.

Perhaps the most thoughtful work of assignment is a very early one, [Strachey 1967]. This paper may be difficult to obtain, but it presents a number of early fundamental ideas about programming languages.

EXERCISES

Exercise 4.1   Names, Locations, and Values

The occurrence of an identifier can imply the use of either the location associated with the identifier, or the value associated with the identifier. Which of these uses of the identifier A is made in the following PL/I or Pascal statements? Not all are from the same program.

	PL/I	*Pascal*
a.	A = 3;	A := 3
b.	B = A;	B := A
c.	CALL A;	A
d.	A(1) = 2;	A[1] := 2
e.	ALLOCATE A;	NEW(A)
f.	X = A -> Y;	X := A↑
g.	GOTO A;	goto A
h.	OPEN FILE(A);	RESET(A)

Exercise 4.2   Explicit Dereferencing   *H 2   -see pg. 4 10/6/82*

We have already remarked that in many languages the two instances of the identifier I in the assignment statement

pg. 3 of 10/20/82
DEC

```
I = I + 1;
```

denote either the location associated with I or the value contained in that location. In the systems programming language Bliss [Wulf et al. 1971] <u>an identifier always denotes a location</u> and not the object stored at that location. <u>In order to access the object stored in the location, the programmer must explicitly dereference the identifier with the . prefix operator.</u> Thus the assignment would have to be written:

Location   dereference to obtain the object

```
I := .I + 1;
```
I := .I+ 1

Consider a variant of Mini-language Core in which the same rule obtains. Using this variant, write a program that builds an equivalent structure and produces the same output as the program shown in Example 4.1. *2 pg. 112*   *use double dots ?*

Exercise 4.3   Mini-language Ref

Consider the fragment of Ref program:

```
program
    declare ONE        :  integer constant = 1;
    declare TWO        :  integer constant = 2;
    declare A, B       :  integer;
    declare RC, RD     :  ref integer;
    declare RRE, RRF   :  ref ref integer;
    declare RRRG, RRRH:  ref ref ref integer;

begin
    A     :=  ONE;
    B     :=  A + ONE;
    RC    :=  A;
    RD    :=  B;
    RRE   :=  RC;
    RRF   :=  RD;
    RRRG  :=  RRE;
    RRRH  :=  RRF;
end;
```

Given the state after executing this fragment, for each of the following statements state whether it is legal (and describe its effect) or illegal (and give reasons).

```
a.  A     := RRRG + B;
b.  RRRH := RC;
c.  RC    := RRRH;
d.  RC    := RRRH + RD;
e.  RRRH := RRE;
f.  RRF   := RRRG;
g.  RRF   := RRRG + TWO;
h.  input RC;
i.  RD    := RC;
j.  B     := RRRG;
```

Exercise 4.4 Reference Variables

There are two different views of reference variables. In Mini-language Ref, like Algol 68, Pascal, and Ada, a reference (or pointer) variable may only designate an object of a specific type which is specified before the program is compiled. The other view, exemplified by PL/I, is that a pointer variable can designate any kind of object, for example, the fragment:

```
DECLARE
    I   FIXED,
    F   FLOAT,
    IB  FIXED BASED,
    FB  FLOAT BASED,
    P   POINTER;

I = 1;
F = 1.0E0;
P = ADDR(I);       /*  P now designates I   */
P -> IB = 2;       /*  The value of I changed to 2  */
P = ADDR(F);       /*  P now designates F   */
P -> FB = 2.0E0;   /*  The value of F changed to 2.0  */
```

Thus P can be used to designate both a fixed and a floating point object. The location is obtained from the value of P and the type is obtained from the associated based identifier, IB or FB. There is, however, the restriction that the type obtained from the associated based identifier must match the type of the object in the designated location. For example, given the state at the end of the above fragment, the statement

```
P -> IB = 3;
```

would be illegal since P, at this stage, designates a floating point object and the type obtained from the associated based identifier is fixed point.

Discuss the relative advantages and disadvantages of these two views of reference variables. *See pg 10/26/62 pg.6 § 5.6*

Exercise 4.5 Multiple Assignment *—H 2 — See pg 4/10/61rz pg 1 - 10/18/8z*

PL/I has the multiple assignment statement of the form

$$ref_1, ref_2, \ldots, ref_n = exp;$$

107,109 variable 109,110,124,359

where ref_1, ref_2, through ref_n are references and exp is an expression. There are a number of possible rules for executing this kind of statement, for example:

1. Evaluate exp to obtain a value val
   For i = 1 to n step 1 *Operational definition*
       evaluate ref_i to obtain a location loc_i
       assign val to location loc_i

2. Evaluate exp to obtain a value val
   For i = n to 1 step -1 *— opposite of #1*
       evaluate ref_i to obtain location loc_i
       assign val to location loc_i

3. Evaluate ref_1 to obtain a location loc_1 *Adds, don't see benefit*
   Evaluate exp to obtain a value val
   Double assignment Assign val to loc_1
   For i = 2 to n step 1
       evaluate ref_i to obtain location loc_i
       assign val to location loc_i

4. Evaluate ref_n to obtain a location loc_n *Opposite of #3*
   Evaluate exp to obtain a value val
   Assign val to loc_n
   For i = n-1 to 1 step -1
       evaluate ref_i to obtain location loc_i
       assign val to location loc_i

5. For i = 1 to n step 1 *2 For's*
       evaluate ref_i to obtain a location loc_i *Need to have some intermediate table for $ref_i \to loc_i$*
   Evaluate exp to obtain a value val
   For i = 1 to n step 1
       assign val to location loc_i

Not a random word
number order
✓ compiler could
✓ at in any order
it wants to

6. Evaluate exp to obtain a value val
   For each value of i, 1 < i < n, taken in <u>undefined order</u>
       evaluate ref$_i$ to obt$\overline{a}$in location loc$_i$
       assign val to location loc$_i$

There are, of course, other possible sets of rules. <u>Discuss the possible
advantages and disadvantages of each of the six given rules. Choose one
of these methods or another that you feel would be the best and explain
why</u>.

Note: You may start by considering the assignment

    A(J-1), A(J), A(J+1) = J;

where A is an array. Also, the possible semantics of the statements have
been described in an algorithmic manner. <u>These algorithms are for
definitional purposes only and are not intended as implementation
models</u>.

Exercise 4.6   Declarations

All the mini-languages and many real languages, such as Pascal
and Ada require that the declaration of a variable occur before it is
used. For example, in Pascal you can say

```
const
    NUMITEMS = 10;
var
    A:  array [1 .. NUMITEMS] of INTEGER;
```

but not

```
var
    A:  array [1 .. NUMITEMS] of INTEGER;
const
    NUMITEMS = 10;
```

Discuss the advantages and disadvantages of this requirement, both
from the point of view of the user and of the implementor.

5
Control Structures

thru 149

The power of computers comes in large part through the programmer's ability to specify the sequence in which the statements of the program are to be executed. The execution sequence is defined by such techniques as loop and if statements. Statements of this sort are called *control structures.*

The choice of control structures in a language has long been a subject of controversy, and for good reason. One of the keys to clarity is the set of control structures used.

Although a great deal has been written on the subject of control structures, the debates and polarized opinions remain. On one side, we have the view that only conditional and simple loop structures should be used. On the other side, there is the view that high-order structures, like exits, are essential to good programming. In this chapter we treat simple conditional and looping structures. The goto statement and high-order structures are treated in Chapter 9.

5.1 MINI-LANGUAGE D

In order to provide a focus for our discussion, we define a mini-language whose essential ingredient is, of course, a set of control structures. The syntax of this language, Mini-language D, is specified in Table 5.1.

Control Structures

In Mini-language D, there are three ways in which the sequence of statement execution may be specified:

1. Sequential execution
2. Conditional or selective execution
3. Iterative execution

In sequential execution the statements are executed precisely in the order in which they are written, for example:

Sequential

```
input X, Y;
X := X + 1;
Y := Y + 1;
output Y, X;
```

Conditional execution in Mini-language D is expressed by the if statement. In its full form this statement is:

Conditional

```
if condition-expression then
    statement...
else
    statement...
end if;
```

Execution of an if statement begins by the evaluation of the condition-expression. If its value is true, then the sequence of statements between the then and else symbols is executed. If its value is false, the sequence of statements between the else and end if symbols is executed. In both cases, after execution of the appropriate statement sequence, control passes to the statement following the if statement; the first statement after the end if; symbols.

In an alternative form of the if statement, the else part is omitted:

```
if condition-expression then
    statement...
end if;
```

In this case, if the condition-expression evaluates to true, the statement sequence between the then and end if symbols is executed. Otherwise, control passes immediately to the statement following the if statement.

Table 5.1   Mini-language D

program   ::= program
                                               declaration...
                                           begin
                                               statement...
                                           end;

declaration   ::= declare identifier [, identifier]... ;

statement   ::= assignment-statement | if-statement
                        | loop-statement | input-statement
                        | output-statement

assignment-statement   ::= identifier := integer-expression ;

if-statement   ::= if condition-expression then
                                statement...
                          [else
                                statement...]
                            end if;

loop-statement   ::= while condition-expression loop
                                statement...
                            end loop;

input-statement   ::= input identifier [, identifier]... ;

output-statement   ::= output identifier [, identifier]... ;

condition-expression   ::= [condition and] condition
                        | [condition or] condition

condition   ::= comparison
                        | (condition-expression)

comparison   ::= (operand comparison-operator operand)

integer-expression   ::= [operand +] operand
                        | [operand -] operand

operand   ::= integer | identifier
                        | (integer-expression)

comparison-operator   ::=   < | = | ≠ | >

The iterative control structure in Mini-language D is the loop statement, which specifies that a sequence of statements, the *body of the loop*, is to be executed repeatedly. There is only one form of loop statement, the while loop, in which the loop body is prefixed by a condition-expression. This structure has the form:

Loop statement

```
while condition-expression loop
    statement...
end loop;
```

Each time control arrives at the top of the loop, the condition-expression is evaluated. If its evaluation gives the value true, the body of the loop between the loop and end loop symbols is executed. When execution of the loop body is complete, control is returned to the top of the loop and the condition-expression is re-evaluated.

Thus, *before* any execution of the body of the loop, the condition-expression at the head of the loop is evaluated; it is the result of this evaluation that determines whether the body is to be executed or the loop is to be terminated. Note that the value of the condition-expression, were it to be evaluated *during* the execution of the loop body, has no effect on the termination of the loop. If the condition-expression has the value false initially, the body of the loop is never executed; and the loop statement has no net effect.

A condition-expression is either a single condition or a pair of conditions separated by one of the logical operators and and or. A condition is either a comparison of two integer operands or a parenthesized condition-expression. A condition-expression consisting of two conditions separated by the and operator evaluates to true only if both conditions evaluate to true. A condition-expression consisting of two conditions separated by the or operator evaluates to true if either or both conditions evaluate to true. The order in which the components of a condition-expression are evaluated is defined by the parentheses, just as in the arithmetic expressions.

Other Features

Programs in Mini-language D, of course, have variables; and all variables in a program must be declared. A variable can only have integer values.

The remaining statements in the language are the common:

- Assignment statements
- Input statements
- Output statements

Examples

We next turn to some example programs. Example 5.1 shows a simple program for converting nautical or 24-hour clock time into the more common 12-hour notation. A flag AM_OR_PM specifies morning (0) or afternoon (1). For example, if 1830 is given as input, the program outputs:

```
HOURS = 6     MINUTES = 30    AM_OR_PM = 1
```

The basic structure of this program is quite simple. The integer value of the nautical TIME is input, and the number of HOURS and the number of MINUTES are calculated. If the number of HOURS or MINUTES is out of range for a valid time, the value input for TIME is printed. Otherwise, the appropriate time is printed.

5.2 BASIC CONTROL STRUCTURES AND FLOWGRAPHS

In the study of flow of control, it is useful to represent a program as a *flowgraph*. This is a set of nodes, representing actions in the program, connected by directed lines that represent the sequence in which the actions occur during program execution, the flow of control. There are three kinds of nodes:

■ *Basic actions:* These are represented by rectangles and denote actions that can change the values of variables but cannot alter the flow of control. Thus a basic action node has only one flow line leaving it.

■ *Conditions:* These are represented by diamonds and denote actions that can change the flow of control but cannot alter the values of variables. A condition node has two flow lines leaving it, implying that a binary choice of flow sequence is being made.

■ *Joins:* These are represented by a simple junction of flow lines. Joins do not denote any action and thus cannot change the values of variables and have only a single flow line leaving them.

We now discuss a class of simple control structures called D-structures, D for Dijkstra [as in Bruno and Steiglitz 1972]. A D-structure is either a

```
program
    -- This program reads in an integer value representing the time
    -- on a 24-hour clock and prints out the corresponding 12-hour
    -- clock time. If the input value does not represent a correct
    -- time, the input value is printed.

    declare TIME, HOURS_AND_MINUTES, HOURS, MINUTES, AM_OR_PM;
begin
    input TIME;
    HOURS_AND_MINUTES := TIME;
    HOURS            := 0;
    while (HOURS_AND_MINUTES > 100) loop
        HOURS_AND_MINUTES := HOURS_AND_MINUTES - 100;
        HOURS             := HOURS + 1;
    end loop;
    MINUTES := HOURS_AND_MINUTES;

    if (HOURS > 23) then
        if (HOURS = 24) and (MINUTES = 0) then
            AM_OR_PM := 0;
            HOURS    := 12;
            output HOURS, MINUTES, AM_OR_PM;
        else
            output TIME;
        end if;
    else
        if (MINUTES > 59) then
            output TIME;
        else
            AM_OR_PM := 0;
            if (HOURS = 0) then
                HOURS := 12;
            else
                if (HOURS > 11) then
                    AM_OR_PM := 1;
                    if (HOURS > 12) then
                        HOURS := HOURS - 12;
                    end if;
                end if;
            end if;
            output HOURS, MINUTES, AM_OR_PM;
        end if;
    end if;
end;
```

Example 5.1   A Mini-language D program

■ *Basic action:* For example, an assignment statement, procedure call, or input-output statement;

or it is constructed from simpler D-structures, each using one of the following forms:

■ *Sequence*

$$s_1 \; s_2 \; ... \; s_n$$

of two or more D-structures s_1 through s_n.

■ *Conditional structure*

```
if c then
    s₁
else
    s₂
end if;
```

where c is a condition and s_1 and s_2 are D-structures.

■ *Iterative structure*

```
while c loop
    s
end loop;
```

where c is a condition and s is a D-structure.

D-structures may be represented in the form of flowgraphs as shown in Figure 5.1. We use the convention in all flowgraphs that the true branch is always shown on the left of the node.

Since the basic actions are such that no transfers of control can occur during their execution, then we can say that they are *one-in, one-out* structures; that is, control enters by only one path and leaves by only one path. The assumption we have made is that there is no mechanism by which control can return from a procedure to a statement other than the one immediately following the call statement. D-structures built from one-in, one-out actions are themselves one-in, one-out structures.

A program that is constructed entirely from D-structures is itself a D-structure. Consequently, it will have only one entry and one exit. The control schemes of Mini-language D correspond exactly to the construction rules for D-structures. As a result, all programs written in Mini-language D are D-structures.

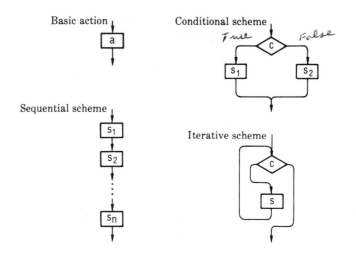

Figure 5.1   Flowgraph representation of D-structures

```
program
    -- This program reads a number of integer
    -- values and prints their maximum value

    declare NUM_VALUES, CURRENT_MAX,
            NEW_VALUE,  VALUE_COUNT;

begin
    input NUM_VALUES;
        VALUE_COUNT := 0;
        CURRENT_MAX := 0;

        while (VALUE_COUNT < NUM_VALUES) loop
            input NEW_VALUE;
            if (NEW_VALUE > CURRENT_MAX) then
                CURRENT_MAX := NEW_VALUE;
            end if;
            VALUE_COUNT := VALUE_COUNT + 1;
        end loop;
        output CURRENT_MAX;
end;
```

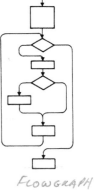

FLOWGRAPH

Figure 5.2   A Mini-language D program and its flowgraph

A program that is a D-structure can be readily diagrammed as a planar flowgraph. Figure 5.2 shows a Mini-language D program and the corresponding flowgraph. Notice that an if-then statement can be considered as an if-then-else structure in which s_2 is null, that is, in which s_2 performs no action.

More generally, the flow of control of any program, whether D-structure or not, can be depicted as a flowgraph. Figure 5.3 shows the flowgraph of a program that is not a D-structure. Since the program is not a D-structure, it cannot be written in Mini-language D. The program

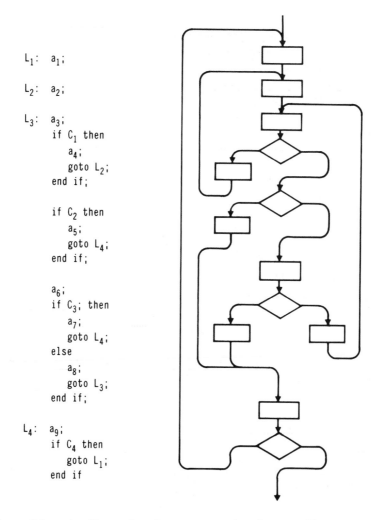

```
L1:  a1;

L2:  a2;

L3:  a3;
     if C1 then
        a4;
        goto L2;
     end if;

     if C2 then
        a5;
        goto L4;
     end if;

     a6;
     if C3; then
        a7;
        goto L4;
     else
        a8;
        goto L3;
     end if;

L4:  a9;
     if C4 then
        goto L1;
     end if
```

Figure 5.3   An Example of a program that is not a D-structure

corresponding to the flowgraph, also shown in Figure 5.3, is written with explicit transfers of control. Here, execution of a statement

    goto label;

results in program execution continuing at the statement prefixed by the label.

5.3   THE FUNDAMENTAL CONTROL STRUCTURE THEOREM

We now turn to the classic theorem of Boehm and Jacopini [1966], which shows that D-structures are sufficient for the construction of any program. This result, virtually unnoticed at first, has had a far-reaching effect on programming and has spawned much controversy about the proper use of control structures.

In this section we give an informal proof of the theorem. A more formal version of the proof given here is contained in [Mills 1972]. The implications of this result are discussed in the following section.

The basic conclusion can be stated simply as:

For any proper program there exists an equivalent program that is a D-structure.

By "any proper program" we mean any computer program, no matter what control structures are used, provided:

1. There is precisely one entry and one exit to the program.

2. For every node in the flowgraph representation of the program, there is at least one path from the entry point, through that node, to the exit point.

This latter restriction rules out programs containing infinite loops and statements that are not reached by the flow of control from the programs at entry point.

By *equivalent program* we mean a program that will always give the same result as the original one for the same input data. Two equivalent programs may have very different flowgraphs. For example, we can compare two programs that calculate the square root of their input. One obtains the result by successive approximation, while the other uses a table look-up method. These two programs will be equivalent if their results are exactly equal for all possible input values.

The proof of the existence of an equivalent D-structure program consists of a step-by-step method of deriving a D-structured flowgraph that is equivalent to the flowgraph for the original program. This derived flowgraph corresponds to a D-structure program equivalent to the original one.

Proof of the Fundamental Control Structure Theorem

To convert a program to an equivalent one that is a D-structure, we first construct a flowgraph G corresponding to the original program. We then make a sequence of changes to G, working from the input point in a step-by-step manner until the whole flowgraph is a D-structure. At each stage, the change to be made is determined by the first component of the unexamined part of the flowgraph.

There are three cases to consider:

Case 1: The first component of G is an basic action, a.

Hence G is of the form

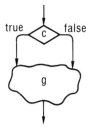

~ unexamined part of G

where g is an as yet unexamined part of G. This case is simple: we already have a sequence of two structures and we apply our step-by-step process to g.

Case 2: The first component of G is a conditional, c.

In this case, G is of the form:

We perform the conversion by constructing two flowgraphs g_1 and g_2 from g. The flowgraph g_1 is derived from g by making a copy of those parts of g that can be reached from the true branch of c. Similarly the flowgraph g_2 is constructed by copying those components of g that are reached by the false branch of c.

Although both g_1 and g_2 may contain copies of identical parts of g, neither g_1 nor g_2 can contain more components than g. We now replace g by g_1 and g_2 to form the flowgraph

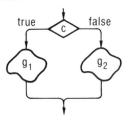

and apply our process to g_1 and g_2 separately.

As an example of this case, consider the flowgraph G of Figure 5.4. The equivalent flowgraph that is derived from it is shown in Figure 5.5. Notice that both g_1 and g_2 contain a copy of the action a_4. Although g_1 and g_2 are, in this case, already D-structures, in general this will not be the case.

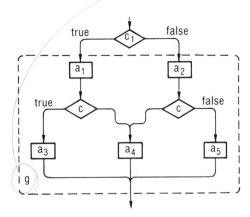

Figure 5.4   An example of flowgraph case 2

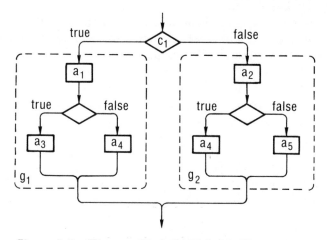

Figure 5.5   Flowgraph derived from Figure 5.4

<u>Case 3:</u> The first component of G is a junction.

The flowgraph G is thus of the form:

<u>In this case, our action depends upon the next component in G, that is, the first component of g. Again, there are three cases to consider.</u>

<u>Case 3.1:</u> The first component of g is an action.

In this case, the flowgraph G has the form:

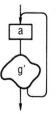

Here we transform G by moving the junction to the other side of the action a and inserting a copy of the action into the flowpath from g' to the junction. This gives the flowgraph:

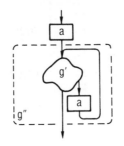

We then apply our transformation process to the flowgraph g".
As an example of this case, consider the flowgraph:

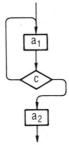

As a result of the transformation just described we obtain the structure:

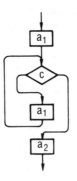

which, again, turns out to be a D-structure.

Case 3.2: The first component of g is a conditional.

Here the flowgraph G has the form:

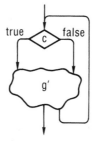

This case is not so easy. As we did in Case 2, we construct two flowgraphs, g_1' and g_2', that consist of all the components of g' that can be reached from the true and false branches of c, respectively. Both g_1' and g_2' may have two exits, one for the return to c and one that is linked directly to the exit from g'.

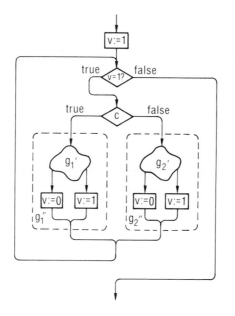

Figure 5.6 Derived Flowgraph in case 3.2

In order to make the transformation in this case, we must choose a new variable, say V, that can take the values 0 and 1. We insert a new action node before the junction that assigns the value 1 to V. In each of the flowgraphs g_1' and g_2' we insert actions on each of their exit lines. On the exit line that leads back to c, the new action assigns the value 1 to V and on the exit line that goes directly to the exit of G, the action assigns the value 0 to V. Finally, we join the exit lines from both g_1' and g_2' back to c and insert a new conditional that tests the value of V between the junction and c.

Do not despair! Our derived flowgraph is now as shown in Figure 5.6. Effectively, what we have done is to put g inside an iterative schema that will continue to loop until the value of V has been set to 0. This will happen when control passes along the exit line of g_1' or g_2' that was directly connected to the exit of G. The transformation process is then applied separately to the new flowgraphs g_1'' and g_2'' shown in Figure 5.6.

Case 3.3: The first component of g is also a junction.

Here we have a flowgraph of the form:

The conversion here is simple.   We transform G into:

The trick here is to see that our revised flowgraph is closer to a D-structure. This is illustrated in Exercise 5.4.

This completes our informal proof. We suggest that you convert one of your own programs to an equivalent D-structure using this method. The exercises at the end of this chapter also pose a few transformation problems.

5.4   COMMENTS ON THE THEOREM AND ITS PROOF

The impact of the theorem is that it is possible to write *any* program as a D-structure. The theorem *guarantees* that any problem can be programmed using only D-structures. If you stick to using only D-structures from the very start, you are sure to have enough ammunition to write your program. In particular, if your programming language includes only the following control statements

1. Sequences of one or more statements

2. Conditional statements of the form

   ```
   if condition then
       statement...
   else
       statement...
   end if;
   ```

3. Loops of the form

   ```
   while condition loop
       statement...
   end loop;
   ```

or their equivalent, then this is all you need, at least theoretically.

Of lesser importance is the method by which the theorem is proved. It is a proof by construction. We take an arbitrary flowgraph and keep on transforming it according to the rules until we reach an equivalent D-structure. It should be clear that converting a program using the method shown in the proof does not always result in a clearer or more efficient program. In many instances the converted program will even be less efficient and far less clear. There are methods of mechanical restructuring that are more effective, [for example, Arsac 1979], but this topic is far beyond the scope of this text. The important point is that restructuring a poorly designed algorithm in a mechanical way will probably not improve it. A clear structure should be there from the outset.

5.5   OTHER ONE-IN, ONE-OUT CONTROL STRUCTURES

There are other one-in, one-out control structures that allow the clear expression of some algorithms. These structures are available in some programming languages, particularly those designed more recently. In this section we will discuss several of these structures. All have the important property that they are one-in, one-out.

By a one-in, one-out control structure we mean a control structure that always has one entry and one exit, and for which any substructure also has precisely one entry and one exit. For example, in a structure of the form

```
if condition then
    statement-1
    statement-2
    statement-3
end if;
```

pg 134

our definition excludes the use of any statement, say statement-2, to cause an explicit branch out of the if-then statement.

As you may have noticed in Example 5.1, the simple form of the if statement in Mini-language D is not very satisfactory when there are many possible conditions. The statement becomes deeply indented and difficult to understand. A simple language design approach to this problem would be to extend the definition of the if statement to:

```
if-statement   ::=    if condition-expression then
                          statement...
                      [ elsif condition-expression then
                          statement... ]...
                      [ else
                          statement... ]
                      end if;
```

This is similar to that found in the programming language Ada. Execution of this form of the statement consists of evaluating each of the condition-expressions in the order in which they appear until the first one with the value true is encountered. At this point, the corresponding sequence of statements is executed. After execution of the statement sequence, control passes to the statement following the if statement. If none of the condition-expressions evaluates to true, the statement sequence that follows the else symbol is executed if it exists; otherwise control passes directly to the statement following the if statement.

This form of the if statement is useful in problems where a choice of actions is determined by the first of several conditions that is true. For example, it allows statements like:

```
if (DISCRIMINANT > 0) then
   PRINT ('TWO REAL ROOTS');
elsif (DISCRIMINANT = 0) then
   PRINT ('ONE ROOT');
else
   PRINT ('TWO IMAGINARY ROOTS');
end if;
```

This is clearer than using the nested if-then-else statement:

```
if (DISCRIMINANT > 0) then
   PRINT ('TWO REAL ROOTS');
else
   if (DISCRIMINANT = 0) then
      PRINT ('ONE ROOT');
   else
      PRINT ('TWO IMAGINARY ROOTS');
   end if;
end if;
```

With many conditions, the point becomes even more evident.

An important one-in, one-out structure found in many languages is the case statement. It is a form of conditional statement where the actions to be carried out depend upon the value of an expression given at the head of the case statement. In a simple form, it has a structure like that found in Ada:

```
case expression of
   when value-1  => statement...
   when value-2  => statement...
   . . .
   when value-n  => statement...
end case;
```

Here the expression following the case symbol is evaluated and its value is compared in turn with each of the values that follow the when symbols. As soon as a match is found, the corresponding sequence of statements is executed.

There are many variants of this kind of statement. One of the most useful contains an *otherwise* option to cover any values not explicitly given. For example, we may have:

```
case I of
   when 0     =>  -- what to do if the value of I is 0
   when 1     =>  -- what to do if the value of I is 1
   otherwise  =>  -- what to do for all other values of I
end case;
```

case

There are a number of questions that must be resolved by the language designer when specifying such a statement. For example:

Considerations in designing a language using CASE

■ Must all the conditions be mutually exclusive?

■ Are the conditions evaluated strictly in the order in which they appear?

■ Suppose that none of the conditions evaluate to true. Is it an error if there is no otherwise option?

The situations where the conditions need not be mutually exclusive and where more than one may be true are discussed in Chapter 15.

Loop Variations

For iteration structures, there are numerous useful forms. One of them is a variant of the while loop where, instead of testing the termination condition before each iteration, it is tested after the body of the loop has been executed. Thus at least one iteration of the loop is guaranteed. This can be expressed in the form:

```
loop
   statement...
end loop when condition;
```

at least one iteration of loop is performed

In most existing languages this structure is written with a syntax using the keywords *repeat* and *until* for example, as:

```
repeat
   statement...
until condition;
```

This form of loop is especially useful when the condition depends on a value that is initialized within the loop, for example:

```
repeat
   -- some statements
   input X;
   -- other statements
until (X = 0);
```

Another useful form is the *for loop*, where the number of iterations of a loop is specified beforehand; and at each iteration a variable, called the *control variable*, is assigned one of a sequence of values. A simple example can be shown by a loop that computes the sum of 100 input values:

```
SUM := 0;
for I := 1 to 100 loop
   input X;
   SUM := SUM + X;
end loop;
```

This structure also has many alternative forms. For example, we may have a loop that terminates when either the control variable completes its assigned values or when a condition is satisfied:

```
SUM := 0;
for I := 1 to 100 while (not END_OF_INPUT_FILE) loop
   input X;
   SUM := SUM + X;
end loop;
```

Here too, there are a number of points that must be resolved by the language designer, for example:

■ Can the value of the control variable be changed inside the body of the loop?

■ What is the value of the control variable immediately after terminating the loop?

All of these structures illustrate a general point. Even within the basic framework of one-in, one-out structures, of which D-structures are a part, it is possible to provide considerable expressive power.

Another set of one-in, one-out control structures based on nondeterminism is discussed in Section 15.5.

FURTHER READING

The practice of using only one-in, one-out control structures is generally attributed to Dijkstra. His famous Letter to the Editor [1968a] hurled the challenge to the goto statement. A later work [1972] presents a thoughtful treatise on programming, in which only one-in, one-out control structures were used. These two works are classics in the area.

The proof of the Boehm and Jacopini theorem given in this chapter is taken from the work [Mills 1972]. Another form of this theorem that gives the stronger result that for every proper program there exists an equivalent program that is a D-structure with one occurrence of the iterative structure is in [Cooper 1967]. An interesting account of the history of these two forms of the theorem is in [Harel 1980].

EXERCISES

Exercise 5.1   Programming Mini-language D

Write a program in Mini-language D to check the relationship between the height and weight of men. The input consists of pairs of integers representing a man's height and weight respectively. The input is terminated by a height of zero.

If the height is less than 62, then the man is in category 1. If the height is greater than 75, then the man is in category 2. Otherwise if, the man's weight is less than 124 plus 4 times the amount by which the man's height exceeds 62, the man is in category 3. If the man's weight is greater than 143 plus 4 times the amount by which the man's height exceeds 62, the man is in category 4. Otherwise the man is in category 5.

For each pair of numbers input, output the corresponding category number.

Make a second version of your program using a variant of Mini-language D that also contains the alternative forms described in Section 5.5.

Exercise 5.2   Elimination of Goto's

Restructure the following program to eliminate as many goto's as possible by using the control structures of Mini-language D.

```
program
    declare X, MAX_VALUE;
```

```
begin
      input MAX_VALUE;
      goto 3;
   1: if (X = 0) then
         goto 9;
      else
         goto 5;
      end if;
   5: if (X > MAX_VALUE) then
         goto 6;
      else
         goto 4;
      end if;
   9: output X;
      goto 7;
   3: input X;
      goto 1;
   6: X := X + 1;
   8: X := X + X;
      goto 9;
   4: X := X + 2;
      goto 8;
   7: output MAX_VALUE;
end;
```

use mini Lang D?
15 pts   meanwhile?

Exercise 5.3   Conversion of a Flowgraph

Convert the flowgraph shown below into a functionally equivalent one built from a sequence, if-then-else and do-while structures only. You can introduce boolean variables if needed. The aim is to produce the clearest possible flowgraph for the algorithm. Compare the clarity of the structured flowgraph with the original unstructured one.

pg 131
mini Language D

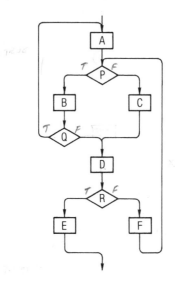

Exercise 5.4 Using the Boehm and Jacopini Theorem

Consider the following two flowgraphs. These are both examples of Case 3, in which the first component is a rejoin point. Using the method of the Boehm and Jacopini Theorem, convert these two flowgraphs to a D-structure.

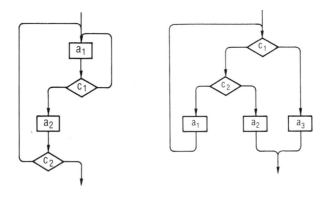

Exercise 5.5   Designing an If Statement

In the design of any language feature, a choice must be made among alternative designs. Consider the following alternative syntax equations for if statements:

1. *Mini-language D:*

```
if-statement   ::=   if comparison then
                         statement...
                  [ elsif comparison then
                         statement... ]...
                  [ else
                         statement... ]
                  end if;
```

2. *Pascal-like:*

```
if-statement       ::=   if comparison then
                             unit-statement
                      [ else
                             unit-statement ]

unit-statement     ::=   statement   SIB TEXT FONT
                   |     begin
                             statement...
                         end;
```

3. *Choice-like:*

```
if-statement   ::=   select
                     when comparison => statement...
                 [ when comparison => statement... ]...
                 end select;
```

In alternative 3, the first true comparison determines which statements are executed. Faced with the above choices, choose one alternative and justify your choice.

154 Chapter 5

Exercise 5.6 Loop Invariants

In Section 3.4 we alluded briefly to invariant relations of loops. Suppose Mini-language D included arrays. Then in the loop

```
    I := 1;
    X := A[1];
    while (I ≠ N) loop
S1      I := I + 1;
S2      if (A[I] > X) then
S3          X := A[I];
        end if
    end loop;
```

the invariant relation is that X contains the maximum value of the first I elements of the array A. Verify that executing the body of the loop does not change the invariant relation.

Consider next the following program fragment to reverse the order of the first N values in the array A:

```
    LOWER := 1;
    UPPER := N;
    while (LOWER < UPPER) loop
        TEMP     := A[LOWER];
        A[LOWER] := A[UPPER];
        A[UPPER] := TEMP;
        LOWER    := LOWER + 1;
        UPPER    := UPPER - 1;
    end loop;
```

Determine the invariant relation of the loop and then show that this relation, together with the condition for loop termination (LOWER > UPPER), demonstrates that the program has executed correctly.

Exercise 5.7 Conversion of a Program

Consider the following program:

```
program
   declare X;
begin
      input X;
  1. if (X > 1) then
         goto 2;
     X := X + 1;
     if (X >5) then
         goto 2;
     X := X + 1;
     goto 1;
  2. output X;
end;
```

Convert the program to a D-structure *without* introducing new variables, or show that it cannot be done.

Exercise 5.8 **Prettyprinting of Control Structures** - See pg 146 - middle of page

One design requirement for features in a programming language is that they be able to be displayed in a readable fashion. Consider the following alternatives for Mini-language D:

```
a.  if (X > Y) then X := Y;
                  else Y := X;
        end if;
```

```
b.  if (X > Y) then
           X := Y;
        else
           Y := X;
        end if;
```

```
c.  if (X > Y)
           then
               X := Y;
           else
               Y := X;
        end if;
```

Each of these versions is debatable. In the general use where there may be several contained statements, nested structures leading to wide lines of text, or no else part, the issue is even more debatable.

Your problem is to choose one of the following positions, and support it with a three or four page position paper. Even if you disagree with them all, you must choose one.

1. Any prettyprinting conventions should be chosen by the programmer. In particular cases, options (a), (b), or (c) may be individually desirable, and each should be allowed.

2. All conditional statements should be displayed as in option (b) above. No exceptions should be allowed.

3. All conditional statements should be displayed as in option (c) above. No exceptions should be allowed.

4. Prettyprinting is an over-rated issue. It tends to emphasize small concerns at the expense of more important issues.

Don't be bashful.

6
Data Types

Thru pg. 185

A program manipulates abstract objects that represent real world objects. The closer the properties of an abstract object mirrors those of the corresponding real world object, the easier it will be to understand the program. Early programming languages permitted only numbers as abstract objects, all real world objects had to be represented by numbers. Since early programming was largely computational, the mapping between real and abstract was generally simple, though by no means perfect. As the need to represent other kinds of objects, for instance characters, increased, the limitation to numerical objects became more inadequate. With improvements in the design of programming languages, more varied and useful kinds of objects have been allowed.

In this chapter we discuss the kinds of objects that can be an intrinsic part of languages. We begin by describing Mini-language Type, which can operate on different kinds of objects, that is, data of various types. This mini-language serves as a basis for a discussion of the concept of *type* in programming languages. This discussion is limited to the *primitive types* of a language, that is, the types that are part of the language. In Chapter 10, we take up the issue again, with a discussion of techniques that allow the programmer to specify new data types that closely match the real objects of a given problem.

6.1   MINI-LANGUAGE TYPE

The context-free syntax of Mini-language Type is given in Table 6.1. Note here that the symbol ƀ represents the single blank space character.

As usual, a program in Mini-language Type consists of a sequence of declarations followed by a sequence of statements. The declarations specify the type of value that can be associated with each identifier. The statements define the operations to be performed on values associated with declared variables.

A declaration specifies that a given list of identifiers can refer only to objects of the given type. The types in Mini-language Type are either simple or composite. The simple types include the integers (for example, 10 and 1776), strings of characters (for example, 'ABC' and '123'), and the boolean values true and false. Note that the integer 123, denoting the numeric value one hundred and twenty three, is different from the string '123', denoting the three characters for the digits representing one, two, and three.

Simple

The composite types in Mini-language Type are arrays of a given simple type and record structures. For example, an array TABLE with ten integers is declared as

Composite

```
declare TABLE: array [1..10] of integer;
```

and a record structure COMPLEX_NUM representing a complex number is declared as:

```
declare COMPLEX_NUM:
    record
        REAL_PART: integer;
        IMAG_PART: integer;
    end record;
```

All identifiers referenced in the program must be declared exactly once. A variable is either:

■   An identifier, in which case, its type must be simple and given in the declaration for the identifier.

■   An identifier declared to be an array followed by a bracketed expression; in which case, it denotes some array component whose type is specified in the declaration for the identifier.

Table 6.1 Mini-language Type

program	::=	program
		    declaration...
		begin
		    statement...
		end;

declaration	::=	declare identifier [, identifier]... : type ;
type	::=	simple-type | array-type | record-type
simple-type	::=	integer | string | boolean | CHAR
array-type	::=	array [bounds [, bounds]...] of type

record-type	::=	record
		    identifier : type ;
		    [identifier : type ;]...
		end record;

bounds	::=	integer .. integer
statement	::=	assignment-statement | if-statement | input-statement | output-statement
assignment-statement	::=	variable := expression ;

if-statement	::=	if expression then
		    statement...
		[else
		    statement...]
		end if;

input-statement	::=	input variable [, variable]... ;
output-statement	::=	output variable [, variable]... ;
expression	::=	[operand operator] operand
operand	::=	variable | integer | string | boolean | (expression)
variable	::=	identifier | variable.identifier | variable [expression]
string	::=	' character... '
boolean	::=	true | false
operator	::=	< | = | ≠ | > | + | – | * | / | cat | and | or
character	::=	letter | digit | special-character
special-character	::=	ƀ | + | – | * | / | : | ; | – | . | , | \$ | % | = | ≠ | > | <

■   An identifier declared to be a record followed by a dot and an identifier; in which case, it denotes some component of a record whose type is specified in a record declaration.

Thus a variable always references a simple integer, string, or boolean value.

For example, using the declaration of TABLE above, the variable TABLE[3] is of type integer and denotes the third element of the array TABLE. Similarly, using the declaration of COMPLEX _NUM above, COMPLEX _NUM.REAL _PART is a type of integer component of the record structure named COMPLEX_NUM.

There are four varieties of statement in Mini-language Type, each of the usual form:

1. An assignment statement: Both the variable and the expression must be of the same simple type.

2. An if statement: The conditional expression must be of boolean type.

3. An input statement.

4. An output statement.

Notice that if TABLE were declared to be an array of strings, then TABLE[3] would be of type string and the statement

```
TABLE[3] := 'XXXX';
```

would assign the string **XXXX** to the third element of **A**.

Variables may be combined by operators in an expression to form new values. The operators +, -, and *, are defined over integers to yield their conventional result.

The relational operators < and > are defined over integers and give a result of type boolean. The equality operators = and ≠ are defined over any two objects of the same simple type and also yield a result of type boolean.

The operators and and or are defined over two boolean values and perform the boolean "and" and "or" operations on the two values. The operator cat is defined over two string values and yields the string consisting of the concatenation of the two values.

For example, consider the declarations:

```
declare X, Y, I, J: integer;

declare ITEM_FOUND, NO_MORE_ITEMS: boolean;
declare TEXT: string;

declare TABLE: array[1..10] of integer;
declare ITEM:  array[1..10] of string;

declare COMPLEX_NUM:
   record
      REAL_PART: integer;
      IMAG_PART: integer;
   end record;
```

The following expressions are legal:

Expressions of type integer:

```
223
(X+2)
(X / 10)
(2 * (X - Y))
TABLE[I]
COMPLEX_NUM.REAL_PART
```

Expressions of type string:

```
'UUW'
TEXT cat 'ABC'
ITEM[I] cat ('A' cat ITEM[J])
```

Expressions of type boolean:

```
true
(ITEM[I] = 'A')
TABLE[I] = COMPLEX_NUM.REAL_PART
ITEM_FOUND
ITEM_FOUND or NO_MORE_ITEMS
```

Here we see a number of expressions whose values are integer, string, or boolean. Note that, for simplicity, no precedence rules specifying the order of operations are needed for Mini-language Type, as all expressions with more than one operator must be parenthesized.

Examples

The following program is illegal:

```
program
    declare A: integer;
begin
    A := 'XYZ';    -- A is not of type string
end;
```

This example shows a fundamental property of most languages with several types. Once a variable is declared to have a certain type, in this case integer, the type cannot be changed during execution. It is thus illegal to assign values of another type (for example, string) to it.

The next program is also illegal:

```
program
    declare A, B: integer;
begin
    A := 0;
    B := (3 or A);   -- or is an illegal operation for integers
end;
```

The error here is the attempt to use an operation that is only applicable to boolean values and applying it to two integer values.

The next example can give an error during execution:

```
program
    declare A: integer;
begin
    input A;    -- input value might not be an integer
    A := A + 1;
    output A;
end;
```

If a variable is declared to be of a certain type and thus can take on only values within that type, an attempt to input a value of a different type will result in an error during execution. In particular, if the input statement attempts to read a string or a boolean value, an execution error occurs.

Finally, the following shows a program that adds two complex numbers:

```
program
    declare I, J, RESULT:
        record
            REAL_PART: integer;
            IMAG_PART: integer;
        end record;
begin
    input I.REAL_PART, I.IMAG_PART;
    input J.REAL_PART, J.IMAG_PART;

    RESULT.REAL_PART := I.REAL_PART + J.REAL_PART;
    RESULT.IMAG_PART := I.IMAG_PART + J.IMAG_PART;

    output RESULT.REAL_PART, RESULT.IMAG_PART;
end;
```

Demo. of Record Variables

This illustrates the use of record variables.

6.2 THE MEANING OF TYPE

A view of programming is shown in Figure 6.1. The problem to be solved by the computer is presented as a real world algorithm that manipulates real world objects. For example, the algorithm takes objects such as names, hours worked, and salaries, and produces a payroll.

Programming consists of describing a computer model of the real world algorithm through a programming language. To model the algorithm, the programmer must choose a representation of the objects in the problem from the possibilities afforded by the programming language.

The choice of representation can have a great effect on the clarity and correctness of the computer algorithm. Thus, for example, a floating point number would not be a suitable representation of a social security number, since there are likely to be inaccuracies introduced in converting it to and from the real world form. A character string representation would be better in this case.

With each set of objects of a particular type that can be manipulated in a programming language, there is a corresponding set of operations that can be performed on objects. In Mini-language Type, addition, subtraction, multiplication, division, and the four comparison operations can be performed on integer objects. However, concatenation and tests of equality and inequality are the only valid operations for string objects.

A consequence of a particular choice of representation of a real world object is the set of operations that can be performed on the object in the model. Each operation permitted by the language should have a corresponding meaning in the real world; for example, dates might be represented by integers. This would mean that all the operations that are available for integers could be performed on the modeled dates. While two dates may be subtracted to give a time interval, there is no analogue of the addition, multiplication, or division of dates in the real world.

This view of programming leads to a definition of types:

A type is a collection of objects and operations that can be validly performed on the objects.

For example, the type "dollars" may be viewed as a collection of quantities, $1, $2, etc., along with certain operations. For example, it is meaningful to "add" or "subtract" two dollar amounts to yield another dollar amount. It is also meaningful to "multiply" a dollar amount by an integer or a percentage to yield another dollar amount.

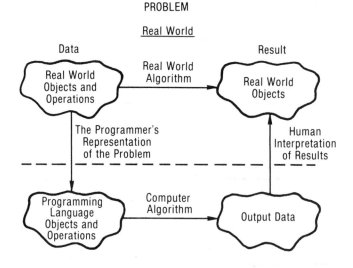

PROBLEM

Figure 6.1   Model for a typical programming task

Generally sophisticated types such as dollars and percentages are not included directly within a programming language. Rather, most programming languages, like Mini-language Type, provide a few basic types that the programmer must use in order to define meaningful computations on a class of real world objects. Languages that allow the programmer to define data types that are a close match to the problem objects will be discussed in Chapter 10.

6.3 PRIMITIVE TYPES

In this section we discuss several kinds of primitive types: boolean types, integer types, and other numeric types.

Boolean Types

Perhaps the simplest of all types found in programming is the boolean type. This type contains only two values, true and false. Operations on values of this type vary from language to language, as do the operations for almost every type. Typical operators include:

not: a unary operator for negating a boolean value.

or: a binary operator for computing the logical "or" of two boolean values.

and: a binary operator for computing the logical "and" of two boolean values.

Other operators are usually provided for mapping non-boolean values into true or false. The most common, of course, is the equality operator. This operator maps two values, for example, two integers or two arrays, into true if the values are equal, and into false otherwise.

Some languages do not have boolean values in the pure sense. For example, in PL/I the bit string '0'B is treated as false and '1'B is treated as true. Cobol allows only indirect use of boolean values. Instead, it permits conditional expressions, for example

```
IF (X = Y) THEN ...
```

but does not permit boolean valued variables or functions that return boolean values.

Character and String Types

The manipulation of characters is fundamental to many programming problems, since communication with users is generally via sequences of characters. The real requirement is not to handle characters by themselves but to manipulate sequences of several characters in juxtaposition. These sequences are usually known as *strings*.

There are two kinds of operations that can be performed on strings.

1. Those that treat strings in their entirety; comparison, assignment, and building longer strings through concatenation.

2. Those that require the decomposition of strings into substrings.

This differentiation is reflected by the two, essentially opposing, approaches used to provide string manipulation in languages.

String as the Primitive Type

Access to constituent substrings is provided by means of special operations and functions. Typical of these operations is the substring function of PL/I. This function has the form

```
SUBSTR(s, n, m)
```

where s is a string value (variable or constant), and n and m are integer values denoting respectively the starting position of the substring and its length. Thus the value of

```
SUBSTR('ABCDEFG', 3, 2)
```

is the substring CD. In addition, an operation, generally concatenation, is provided for building a string out of substrings. This is the approach that we have taken in the Mini-language Type; though, for simplicity, no substring operation has been supplied.

A Single Character as the Primitive Type

A string is treated as an array of characters. This approach has been taken in Pascal and Ada. We will return to this method in Section 6.4 when arrays are discussed.

The approach taken by Mini-language Type has been to say that all variables declared to be of type string can take string values of any length. To implement this kind of string satisfactorily requires a complex dynamic storage management capability, which may explain why such facilities are comparatively rare in languages. We discuss the storage management problems in Section 13.3. The simple alternative to the variable length method is to require that all string variables be declared with a length. When a string value is assigned to a string *Pad or* variable, the value will be padded on the right with blanks if it is too *Truncate* short or truncated if it is too long.

In addition to the fixed length string approach, PL/I also offers a half-way position between that and the implementation problems of completely variable length. The declaration

```
DECLARE STR CHARACTER(20) VARYING;
```

specifies that STR can be assigned string values up to a maximum length of 20 characters. Above that length, the values are truncated as is done for fixed length strings. A similar approach is taken in Basic.

Numeric Types

Numerical calculations have always had an important role in the use of computers. All programming languages manipulate numeric data. Even in languages designed for non-numeric work, Snobol for example, there is a need for numbers to act as counters, field widths, and control values in computation.

An important difference between the numeric values in programming languages and those in mathematics is that the computer values all have finite representations. Thus they are frequently approximations to their real world equivalents. There is no way that a completely accurate value of pi can be represented in a computer. The need to represent objects with a wide range of number values, even if the representations were approximate, resulted in the floating point form.

Numeric types generally fall into one of three classes:

1. *Integer:* used for exact arithmetic on whole numbers within a fixed range.

2. *Fixed point:* used for non-integer values with a fixed number of digits before and after the radix point.

3. *Floating point:* used for non-integer values with a fixed number of significant digits and a widely varying magnitude.

Lexical Issues

The written form of numeric values is largely determined by conventional usage. To aid readability, some languages allow a break character to divide lengthy sequences of digits. For example, the denoting

```
1000000      -- PL/I, Mini-language Type
1 000 000    -- Algol 60, Fortran
1_000_000    -- Ada
```

are different ways of writing the same integer.

The written representation of fixed point numbers is generally of the form:

```
digit-sequence.digit-sequence
```

For clarity, neither digit sequence should be null, and the radix point should always be required.

The written form of floating point forms values has an essential difference from integer and fixed point values due to the need for an exponent. Frequently, the beginning of the exponent part is marked with the letter E, for example:

```
3.14259E0
10E+2
```

With the above syntax rules, it is possible to determine the type of all written numeric values. In languages where there are no implicit type conversions, it is possible to enforce the rule that only constants of the appropriate type can be used in assignments and expressions. This discipline has the important advantage that different types of arithmetic are distinguished; the exact computations are separated from the approximate.

Integer Types

In programming languages, the integer type has a finite set of values, the largest of which is determined either by an implementation or by the language definition. Integers are by far the most common of the numeric types. Since integers can be represented exactly on all digital computers, the usual operations of addition, subtraction, and multiplication can be provided without surprising results, even if the actual machine representation is in a base other than the conventional decimal. Should the result of these operations be outside the finite range of permitted values, an execution error will result.

In many languages, the integer type also includes the operators:

div   for integer division,
mod   for the remainder after integer division.

For example,

```
5 div 3  =   1
5 mod 3  =   2

-5 div 3  =  -1
-5 mod 3  =  -2
```

In addition, relational operators like < and = are usually defined over integers and yield a boolean result.

Fixed Point Types

Values of a fixed point type are similar to integers in that they are uniformly spaced over a range. Two quantities are required to specify this range:

Precision: the total number of digits used for representing the value.

Scale: the number of digits in the fractional part of the value.

Thus the number 123.4567 has a precision of 7 and a scale of 4. This definition is equally applicable to numbers represented in bases other than the conventional decimal; for example, the fixed point binary number 11011.11101101 has a precision of 13 and a scale of 8.

Languages that provide a fixed point type generally allow the user to declare variables with different precisions and scales. Because these two quantities must be taken into account, the operations on fixed point values are more complex than the corresponding operations on integer values.

The concept of fixed point assignment is reasonably simple to define. The value must be copied into the target location so that its radix point is in the correct place. We align decimal quantities in this way when we write them down on paper. Fixed point variables, however, have the added problem that their precision and scale are fixed. The language must define what is to happen when the precision and scale of the assigned value do not match those of the target variable.

If the value has more fraction digits than the target, then the value must be truncated to fit, either with or without rounding. If the value has more digits before the point than the target, the situation is more serious. A radical decision is to disallow any assignments that might lead to this situation. While this restriction can be detected during compilation, it is probably too severe for most users. The alternative is to define such assignments to be execution errors. This requires special checking during execution, which may be thought to be too expensive. However, to ignore such cases is likely to lead to unreliable programs.

The operations of addition, subtraction, and multiplication present further complications. In each of these there is the possibility that the precision of the result will exceed that of either operand. For example, if X is a fixed point variable with precision 5, scale 3, and value 12.345, then the value of the expression X*X is 152.399025. This has a precision of 9 and a scale of 6.

In an actual implementation, there will be an upper bound to the precision of a fixed point number. There is a problem similar to the one with assignment just described. Again, the radical solution of forbidding any expressions whose result might exceed this bound on the precision is too restrictive. We must expect that the result of some expressions will exceed the bound and that possible truncation may occur. It is the task of the language designer to find the most useful method for controlling this loss of information.

The amount of truncation must be calculated during compilation, otherwise we would be duplicating the effect of floating point arithmetic. There are two main approaches, truncation at the right end and truncation at the left end. Truncation at the right, while avoiding the loss of significant digits, involves a loss of accuracy in all results. This abandons the accuracy of fixed point computation without gaining the flexibility of floating point. Truncation at the left end preserves accuracy, but brings the same problem that exists in assignment of detecting loss of significant digits during execution.

The operation of division is still more complicated due to the potential requirement for infinite precision to represent the quotient. A discussion of this is beyond the scope of this book. A more complete discussion of fixed point arithmetic is to be found in [Nicholls 1975].

Floating Point Types

A floating point value has two parts, a *fraction* and an *exponent.* The fractional part is sometimes called the *mantissa.* It represents the significant digits of the value. The exponent is a scaling factor to be applied to the fraction to obtain the proper value.

From the programmer's point of view, the major characteristics of floating point values are:

- There is only a finite set of values.
- They do not contain the set of integers as a subset.
- They are not uniformly distributed.

In some languages, for example, Fortran, Algol, and Ada, the floating point type is referred to as a *real* type. As can be seen from these properties, the behavior of the floating point type is considerably different from the real numbers of mathematics.

The fact that the set of floating point values does not contain the integers as a subset leads to many anomalies in floating point arithmetic. These contribute to the complexity and inaccuracy of floating point computations. A full discussion of floating point arithmetic is beyond the scope of this book; for further information, see [Knuth 1969].

Operations

One feature that is common to the three numeric types is the set of arithmetic operators. Although these operators are written with the same symbol for each type, they connote somewhat different actions. For example, fixed point addition maintains the position of the radix point, whereas floating point addition adjusts its position to accommodate a range of values. The use of a single symbol to denote an operation whose meaning is determined by the operand types is called *overloading* or polymorphism. Probably the two most common overloaded operations are the relations = and ≠ which generally apply to all types.

Conversions

In our everyday pencil and paper calculations, we treat all numeric data as being of a single type, numbers. We do not think whether they are integers, rationals, or irrationals. In programming, things are not so simple; there are different numeric types with separate representations.

In Mini-language Type, there is only one numeric type, integer, so the problem of assigning one type of numeric value to a variable of another does not arise. In most languages, this problem exists and these assignments are usually allowed. The same numeric value may have different representations in separate numeric types. The mappings between these representations are generally called *conversions*. Algol 68 and Pascal use the term *coercion*. Conversions from integer to fixed point, from fixed point to floating point, and from floating point to complex can generally be done without loss of information. A coercion of this sort is called a *widening*.

As the number of numeric data types in a language increases, so does the number of possible conversions. Some languages, for example, Pascal and Algol 68, insist that almost all conversions be done through the explicit use of a function. For example, to convert a real value to an integer in Algol 68, the function *entier* is used. At the other end of the scale, PL/I has the deliberate policy of defining all mappings between data types whenever they have a "reasonable" meaning. These implicit conversions can lead to programming errors that are accepted by the compiler as a reasonable conversion. The advantage of the Pascal and Algol 68 kind of approach is that the programmer is made aware of almost all conversions, and we support this view.

6.4 ARRAY TYPES

A fundamental property of the values belonging to the simple types is that they are indivisible without special action, like the use of a *substring* function. The modeling of objects, like a deck of cards, a birth certificate, or a bank account, brings up the general issue of *composite* types. Objects of a composite type are not indivisible, but have components bearing some relation to each other.

Every programming language offers one or more built-in composite types. Among others, Fortran has arrays, Cobol has record structures, Pascal has sets, Lisp has lists, and APL has vectors.

The composite types in a language are critical to the ease with which real world objects can be represented. For example, representing a bank account is quite easy in Cobol and representing a network is quite easy in Lisp, but not necessarily vice versa. In this section we discuss an elementary composite type, the array, where all the components are of the same type. In the next section, we discuss a different composite type, the record. The components of records can be of differing types.

The array is perhaps the most familiar composite type in programming. An array is basically a mapping from a range of contiguous integers to a set of elements. These integer values are called the *index* or *subscript* values.

In its simplest form, an array is a representation of a table. For example, consider a table that represents the number of people waiting in line at each of five counters. In Mini-language Type this array might be declared by:

```
declare QUEUE_LENGTH: array [1..5] of integer;
```

An intrinsic property of an array is that the value of any one of its elements can be changed without affecting the value of any of the other elements.

The range of index values of an array defines the number of elements of the array; this is the size of the array. In most programming languages the range of index values must be specified by the programmer.

The point at which the size of an array must be known is a subject of considerable difference in programming languages. For example, consider the following cases:

```
declare A: array [1..5] of integer;
```

Here the size of the array is defined at the time the declaration is written:

```
declare N: integer constant = 5;
declare A: array [1..N] of integer;
```

Here the size of the array is defined at the time the declaration of the constant N is written:

```
procedure F (N: integer):
    declare A: array [1..N] of integer;
```

In this fragment of a procedure, N is a parameter whose value is established when the procedure is invoked. Thus the size of the array is only determined at execution time and can vary from one invocation to another.

Finally, consider:

```
type VECTOR is array (INTEGER range <>) of FLOAT;
type VECTOR_REF is access VECTOR;
A: VECTOR_REF;

A := new VECTOR(1..100);
```

In this fragment of Ada, the array A has an access type, which means that its value is allocated at run time. This value does not exist until the *new* operation is executed. In the declaration of A, the number of elements is specified as being determined by an initially unspecified integer range. This range is given at the time the storage for the array is obtained by executing the new operation. In this example, the array will have 100 elements.

Generally, once the size of an array has been established, it does not change during its existence. Algol 68, however, allows the size of arrays that are declared with flexible bounds to be changed by assignment.

Usually languages permit arrays to have more than one index. For example, in an extension to Mini-language Type, one might write the declaration:

```
declare B: array [1..5, 1..10] of integer;
```

Such an array can be thought of as a rectangular arrangement of elements with five rows and ten columns. Usually, each of the sets of bounds is referred to as a *dimension*. The array B has two dimensions. An array of one dimension is often called a *vector*.

Conceptually the elements of an array may be of any type, including simple types and other composite types, including arrays. In practice, most languages place restrictions on the types of elements, often restricting the elements to simple types.

The basic operation on an array is element selection, that is, a reference to the value of an element in the array. This operation is usually denoted by giving a bracketed expression following the array name. For example, for the array A, a reference to an element is denoted by

```
A(3)
A(I)
A(I + 1)
```

in Ada, Fortran, and PL/I, but

```
A[3]
A[I]
A[I + 1]
```

in Mini-language Type, Pascal, and Algol.

Sometimes it is convenient to be able to reference a subpart of an array as a single entity. In Algol 68 it is possible to treat the three elements of A with subscripts 2, 3, and 4 as an array by the reference A[2:4]. This is called a *trimmed* reference. A similar concept is found in the Ada *slice*. If B is a one-dimensional array then the reference B(2 .. 8) references elements 2 through 8.

Assignment to array elements is allowed in every language with array types. In some languages the assignment operation is also allowed on complete arrays. For example, if A and B are 10-element arrays of integers, then

```
A := B;
```

copies the values in B to A. This raises the issue of arrays of constant values, a feature that is present in few languages. For example, one might allow the initialization of A to be specified as

```
A := (1..10 => 0);
```

as is done in Ada. Most languages, however, allow assignment only on an element-by-element basis, as in Mini-language Type.

A Note on Strings

As mentioned in Section 6.3, an alternative to the primitive type string is the use of arrays of elements of the primitive type character. The rationale behind this view is that the basic unit is really the character, and the composite type array properly reflects the construction of the string. However, in order to provide the proper access to substrings and variable length strings, we need a mechanism like trimmed references and flexible bounds as in Algol 68. This poses considerable implementation problems. Conceptually, we believe that representing strings as arrays is unwieldy, and that strings deserve to be a type in their own right.

6.5 RECORD TYPES

A programmer must often deal with objects having a number of different components. For example, a driving license may be viewed as an object having a:

```
Driver: a name consisting of a
          First name:      a string of letters
          Middle initial: a single letter
          Last name:      a string of letters

License number:  an eight digit number
```

```
Expiration date: a calendar date consisting of a
              Month: a number from 1 to 12
              Day:   a number from 1 to 31
              Year:  a four digit number

Driving code: a character
```

The type used for collections of related objects is often called a *record*. Basically a record type contains a collection of components, each of which may be of a different type. Each component has a name and a value.

For example, a record of type LICENSE can be declared in Mini-language Type by:

```
declare LICENSE:
   record
      DRIVER: record
                    FIRST_NAME    : string;
                    MIDDLE_INITIAL: string;
                    LAST_NAME     : string;
             end record;
      LICENSE_NUM: string;
      EXPIRATION_DATE: record
                          MONTH: integer;
                          DAY  : integer;
                          YEAR : integer;
                       end record;
      DRIVING_CODE: string;
   end record;
```

Notice, for example, that though the original description of the license specifies the license number as a number, it is really a sequence of digits. It does not make sense to multiply a license number by five. Similarly, the month, day, and year of expiration are not really integers, although it is convenient to perform limited numerical calculations, for example, computing when to send out the renewal notice, two months before expiration.

The basic operation on record types is component selection. For example, to refer to the driving code component, we write:

```
LICENSE.DRIVING_CODE
```

This is the method used in Ada, PL/I, Pascal, and Euclid. Algol 68 and Cobol take a different point of view, by writing:

```
DRIVING CODE of LICENSE      -- Algol 68
DRIVING-CODE in LICENSE      -- Cobol
```

This approach seems to focus most attention on the component, while the Ada, PL/I, Pascal, and Euclid view attaches more importance to the record as a whole.

The value of the reference LICENSE.DRIVER is also a record, so that it is possible to write:

```
LICENSE.DRIVER.LAST_NAME
```

A reference to the component of a record behaves just as a reference to the component of an array. For example, we may have:

```
LICENSE.LICENSE_NUM          := '022325795';
LICENSE.EXPIRATION_DATE.YEAR :=
        LICENSE.EXPIRATION_DATE.YEAR + 4;
```

In practice, record types may have several components that are themselves records, and references to these components are common. As a result, references to records may become long and tedious. Consider the simple problem of assigning the following values to the components of the name of a DRIVER:

```
LICENSE.DRIVER.FIRST_NAME     := 'HENRY';
LICENSE.DRIVER.MIDDLE_INITIAL := 'F';
LICENSE.DRIVER.LAST_NAME      := 'LEDGARD';
```

There are several solutions to this problem. One solution, similar to PL/I and Cobol, allows omission of component names as long as the shortened reference can be uniquely identified. For example, if there were no other records in the program with the component names FIRST_NAME, MIDDLE_INITIAL, or LAST_NAME, the above sequence could be written as:

```
FIRST_NAME     := 'HENRY';
MIDDLE_INITIAL := 'F';
LAST_NAME      := 'LEDGARD';
```

This solution has one severe disadvantage in that to understand which record variable is being referenced requires knowledge of the declarations for all record variables. It also tends to produce awkward naming conventions in the attempt to keep component names distinct from each other.

Another solution, offered by Pascal, is the inclusion of a statement specifying a local context for a statement sequence. For example, the above sequence may be written as:

```
with LICENSE.DRIVER do
   begin
      FIRST_NAME     := 'HENRY';
      MIDDLE_INITIAL := 'F';
      LAST_NAME      := 'LEDGARD';
   end;
```

Here, the with clause provides the top level qualifier over the part of the program contained between the begin and end. The Pascal solution has a disadvantage when other variables are included in the body of the with statement, in that it is not always clear to the reader which references need qualification.

Still another solution offered by Cobal, Euclid and Ada allows the programmers to declare a name as a shorthand reference to record components. For example, we may declare something like

```
ME: renames LICENSE.DRIVER;
```

and then have:

```
ME.FIRST_NAME     := 'HENRY';
ME.MIDDLE_INITIAL := 'F';
ME.LAST_NAME      := 'LEDGARD';
```

This convention avoids the disadvantages of the other two solutions but still requires all record variables to be qualified by a prefix. However, if the prefix is chosen carefully, this will add to the clarity of the program.

Variant Records

As mentioned earlier, there are cases where the information within a record may be missing or where additional information may be required when another record component has certain values. In our license example, a driver may not have a middle initial, and the driving code may indicate a special or a restricted permit requiring other information. This kind of structure is generally handled with a record variant.

A record type with a variant part must have a special component called a tag and a selection mechanism giving the various substructures for possible values of the tag. For the selection mechanism denoting the variant we shall use a case-like notation, similar to that for case statements. This method is borrowed from the preliminary version of Ada.

To represent our license example in full, we can write the declaration of Example 6.1. Here, the component DRIVING_CODE is used as a tag, and the following case structure defines the record variant. When the tag value is S, the information for a special vehicle type is included; when its value is R, the information for a restricted permit is included; when the tag HAS_MIDDLE_INITIAL has a false value, the variant is explicitly stated as being null or empty.

Each variant of a record type can take a separate set of values. Thus the complete record type with all its variants can take the union of these sets of values. It is common to refer to such record types as *unions* and to refer to those that contain a tag field to distinguish between the variants as *discriminated unions*. Those unions where the language does not insist on the tag field are known as *free unions*.

Algol 68 provides an example of unions. To take a simple case, a variable could be declared to be a union of integer and boolean values. The value of such a variable is either of type integer or type boolean, depending on which type of value was last assigned to the variable. The language requires that, each time the value of the union variable is used, the programmer must provide explicit checks to determine if the current value is of the correct type. Union variables do not contain an explicit tag as in variant records, but do have internal coding to record the type of the current value.

Variant records, while useful, raise some difficulties with reliability and implementation. First, there is the question of assignment to the tag field. The value of the tag is set when the record object is created. While the program must be able to assign values with an ordinary statement to components of the record, assignment of a new value to the tag is a very different question. To change the tag really implies a change in the structure of the record. From the implementation view, this could imply a change in the amount of storage required for the record. Ada specifically forbids the assignment to tags, while Pascal allows them.

A second question is that of reference to a record component that is not prescribed by the value of the tag. For example, in the record LICENSE, if the value of DRIVING_CODE is 'S', then a reference to the element VEHICLE_TYPE is valid, whereas a reference to the element CORRECTIVE_LENSES is not. Checking the validity of such references results in an overhead during execution. For the programmer, guarding against such errors can be difficult.

Another serious problem is the design of a readable syntax. It is not obvious from the above syntax that DRIVER has potentially four components, and nested record types with variants make the problem even more acute.

```
declare LICENSE:
   record
      DRIVER: record
                  FIRST_NAME: string;
                  LAST_NAME : string;
                  HAS_MIDDLE_INITIAL: boolean;    -- tag
                  case HAS_MIDDLE_INITIAL of
                  when true  => MIDDLE_INITIAL: string;
                  when false => null;
                  end case;
              end record;

         LICENSE_NUM: string;

         DRIVING_CODE: string;      -- tag
         case DRIVING_CODE of
            when 'S' => record
                           VEHICLE_TYPE    : integer;
                           PASSENGER_PERMIT: boolean;
                           ZONE_CODE       : boolean;
                        end record;
            when 'R' => record
                           CORECTIVE_LENSES : boolean;
                           DAYLIGHT_ONLY    : boolean;
                           AUTO_TRANSMISSION: boolean;
                        end record;
            else     => null;
         end case;

         EXPIRATION_DATE: record
                           MONTH: integer;
                           DAY  : integer;
                           YEAR : integer;
                          end record;
      end record;
```

Example 6.1   A record variant

Record Mapping

Once the programmer has defined a record, the layout of the fields in the computer storage must be determined. This is generally done by the compiler. It must be done according to a well-defined set of rules to ensure compatibility between separately compiled parts of a complete program.

Generally the precise way in which the fields are laid out is of little consequence to the programmer. The actual addresses usually have no meaning in the language. On the other hand, where interlanguage communication is required, as for instance, when data generated by a Cobol program being processed by a PL/I program, that the mapping from declaration to addresses becomes important. Two languages may map their records differently and appropriate programming will be required for the records produced in one language to be read in the other.

The simplest mapping would be to put each component of a record immediately adjacent to its declared neighbors. This is practical only in a computer where each bit of storage can be addressed individually. On most computers only groups of bits, words or bytes, for example, are accessed directly. Information that does not fall on these particular boundaries requires extra machine instructions, generally masking and shifting, for access. In order to avoid this, *padding* must be inserted between the end of one field and the beginning of the next. Thus there is a choice between inefficient programs and inefficient use of storage. PL/I takes account of this by allowing the programmer to specify for each field whether it is to be ALIGNED on a storage boundary to permit efficient access at the cost of extra storage.

In addition to the question of storage use versus execution time, the language itself places two requirements on the storage mapping. First, the mapping of a record component must be independent of its position in the record that contains it. Second, in order to access a component of a record, the attributes of only those subitems that occur between the beginning of the record and the component being referenced need be known. These are both needed to allow access to parts of a record without having knowledge of the whole record, for example when a component of a record is passed as an argument to a separately compiled procedure.

A more complete description of the problem of storage mapping, including a discussion of particular algorithms, is in [MacLaren 1970].

although the checking may not be done rigorously in all implementations. Such languages are said

184 **Chapter 6** *to be strongly typed.*

6.6 TYPE CHECKING

The partitioning of objects into types allows each assignment to be checked for a match between source value and target variable. The validity of each operation for its operands can also be verified. If these tests can be made during compilation, *before* execution, then we say that the type checking is *static*. Ada, Fortran and Algol 68, for example, have static type checking. These three languages allow the type checking to be complete with no chance of a mismatch slipping through; they are said to be *strongly typed*. Pascal, on the other hand, because it allows the tag field of variant records to be changed is not strongly typed.

If the type checking can only be done *during* execution then the type checking is *dynamic*. APL and Pal are examples of dynamically typed languages.

The essential difference between statically and dynamically typed languages is that in a statically typed language, the type is associated by declaration with an identifier. In a dynamically typed language, the type is associated with the value. This is implemented by storing type information with each value. Any type of value can be assigned to a variable. Before any operation is applied to a value, the type of the value is examined to see if it is compatible with the operation.

Dynamic type checking is usually simple to implement. However, since the checkup is performed during execution, there is a considerable machine time penalty. Furthermore, since type errors can only be found by execution, it is generally impossible to verify that a program contains no type errors. It is often claimed that dynamic typing allows the programmer greater flexibility; however, it is not clear that this gain is sufficient to offset the loss of reliability.

Some languages avoid the idea of type altogether. These are generally the high-level *systems programming* languages. Examples of such languages are Bliss and BCPL. In Bliss, any contiguous set of bits in storage can be named and from the language's point of view, merely contains a pattern of bits. Various operations, such as integer arithmetic, comparison, or boolean operations, may be applied to these bit patterns. The interpretation placed on a particular bit pattern and the consequent transformation performed by the operator is an intrinsic property of the operator and not of its operands.

The argument for type checking is one of security. A language that regards the store as a homogeneous array of words is very error prone. It is only possible to make trivial checks on the use of data. The rationale behind strong type checking, as opposed to dynamic type checking, is that a large number of errors can be detected before the program is run when it is feasible to make extensive checks.

The counter argument is that strong typing removes a lot of the flexibility that programmers find useful, particularly in systems programming. Two examples illustrate this kind of flexibility.

■ The need for arrays of heterogeneous elements. For example, in an interpreter, a stack for expression evaluation may have to consist of integer, floating point, and boolean components. Although each element in the stack assumes only one fixed type during its lifetime, the underlying static array element appears to have a varying type. This could be achieved by Algol 68 unions.

■ The realization of implicit type conversions. For instance, a floating point variable might need to be treated as a bit string for printing its internal representation during error analysis of numerical computation. PL/I provides a conversion function, UNSPEC, for precisely this purpose.

The arguments between the two views continue with no resolution in sight.

FURTHER READING

In the literature, works solely on the concept of type have been overshadowed by the rather large effort in the area of type definition discussed in Chapter 10. Nevertheless, we mention here a few relevant references.

An early work [Morris 1973] discusses the now prevalent view of a type, which is characterized by a set of objects as well as operations over the objects. A later paper [Brosgol 1977] discusses a number of issues relevant to types.

A paper by Haberman [1973] presents a critique of the view of types in the programming language Pascal. As is often the case in this text, type issues are also extensively discussed in the rationale for the preliminary version of Ada [Ichbiah et al. 1979].

EXERCISES

Exercise 6.1 Programming in Mini-language Type

On many computer systems, a calendar date is expressed in six-digit form. For example,

02 22 43

means the month 02, day 22, year 1943, or in more familiar terms we use day to day:

```
FEBRUARY 22, 1943
```

Write a program in Mini-language Type to read in three integer numbers and output the corresponding date in day-to-day notation. If the integers do not represent a valid date, an appropriate message should be printed.

For example, with

```
13 22 43
```

the output should be:

```
NOT A VALID DATE
```

Don't forget about leap year.

You must take note that in the mini-languages, each printed value is prefixed by the variable name and an equal sign. Thus your output may be something like:

```
MONTH = FEBRUARY
DAY = 22
YEAR = 1943
```

Exercise 6.2   Strong typing

In Section 6.5 we mentioned that the strong typing in Pascal is not complete because the tag field of a variant record can be changed during execution. Explain how some type checking in Pascal can be defeated in this way. It is said that such loopholes are necessary in certain applications such as system programming. Discuss this argument.

Exercise 6.3   Mixed Mode

Some languages with multiple data types (modes) allow *mixed mode* expressions. In PL/I, for example, an expression may involve operands of many different types that are converted at run time if necessary to compatible modes before the operators are applied. In other languages, operands that are not of the correct mode for an operation must be explicitly converted by using a set of functions provided in the language for that purpose.

For example, if J were an integer, in PL/I one could write the expression

```
(J + '3')
```

while in the other class of languages, one would have to write this as

```
(J + CHAR_TO_INT('3'))
```

where CHAR_TO_INT is a function which performs character string to integer conversion. What are the advantages and disadvantages of each scheme?

Exercise 6.4   Literals for Arrays

In some languages it is possible to write values for both composite objects and for simple objects. For example, in Ada, a ten-element array A may be set to zero with the assignment:

```
A := (1..10 => 0);
```

For a five-element array where elements are

11, 14, 10, 16, and 11

we may write

```
(11, 14, 10, 16, 11)
```

where the array elements are listed in positioned order, or alternatively,

```
(1 => 11;  2 => 14;  3 => 10;  4 => 16;  5 => 11)
```

where the index values are identified. Discuss the pro's and con's of these two notations.

Exercise 6.5   Array Access

Consider a language in which arrays may have many dimensions. The number of dimensions and the bounds on the dimensions are fixed by the declaration and may not be changed dynamically. Suppose a particular array has n dimensions with lower bounds l_1, l_2 through l_n and upper bounds u_1, u_2 through u_n and that the array is stored as a contiguous set of elements. Describe how the location of a particular element of the array can be calculated from it subscripts.

Exercise 6.6   **String Handling**

In Section 6.3, we described how character strings can either be viewed as a primitive type of the language, as in Mini-language Type, or treated as vectors of the primitive type character. By designing additional syntax and semantics, compare two variants of Mini-language Type demonstrating the two methods of character string representation. The comparison should be based on the operations:

   A. Concatenate two strings to form a new string.
   b. Extract a portion of a string.
   c. Search within a string for a given substring.
   D. Obtain the length of a string.
   E. Delete a substring or replace it by another substring, not necessarily of the same length.
   F. Insert a string within another string at a specified point.

Note: To do this exercise well, you will need to think carefully.

7
Procedures and Parameters

The use of subprograms is a familiar programming concept. Charles Babbage's Analytical Engine in 1840 already had provision for the use of a group of punched cards for performing a frequently used part of a larger calculation. Now, it is hard to imagine a programming language that does not offer a subprogram facility in some form.

Subprograms allow the programmer to package computations and parameterize their behavior. There are two forms of subprograms, procedures and functions. A procedure subprogram is a sequence of actions that is invoked by a call statement. A function subprogram is a sequence of computations that results in a single value and is invoked from within an expression. Usually, control returns to the point of invocation after execution of the subprogram, thus forming another one-in, one-out control structure. Both forms of subprogram invocation represent operational abstractions that simplify the programs that contain them.

There must be some means of passing data between the subprogram and the program that calls it. The usual method of passing data is through parameters in the subprogram and through global variables. In this chapter, we use a mini-language to provide a basis for discussing procedures and the various mechanisms used for passing data. Global variables are discussed in Chapter 8. The special properties of functions are described in Chapter 11.

Before describing the Mini-language, there is a question of terminology that must be clarified. In different languages, various terms are used to describe the data passed between procedures. For example:

argument
Passed

■ The information that is *passed to* a subprogram by a caller is termed the argument in Fortran and PL/I. In Ada, Pascal, and Algol, it is called the actual parameter. We will use the term *argument*.

Parameter
Received

■ The information that is *received from* a caller by a subprogram is termed the dummy argument in Fortran; the formal parameter in Ada, Pascal, and Algol; and parameter in PL/I. We will use the term *parameter*.

7.1   MINI-LANGUAGE PROCEDURES

We begin with our mini-language, as described in Table 7.1.

A program in Mini-language Procedures consists, as usual, of a sequence of declarations followed by a sequence of statements. There are two types of declarations, for variables and for procedures.

Variable declarations introduce simple variables and arrays that take integer values. Array variables contain an unspecified number of components. For example, we may have:

```
declare X, Y, TOTAL;    -- three integer-valued variables
declare A, B: array;    -- two arrays with integer components
```

All variables used in the statement part of a program must be declared exactly once.

A procedure declaration defines a procedure subprogram and contains the following parts:

■ an identifier that is the name of the procedure,

■ the names of any parameters and their mode,

■ the declaration of any variables local to the procedure,

■ a sequence of statements comprising the *body* of the procedure.

Table 7.1   Mini-language Procedures

```
program                ::=   program
                                 variable-declaration...
                                 procedure...
                             begin
                                 statement...
                             end;

variable-declaration   ::=   declare identifier [ , identifier ]... [: array];

procedure              ::=   procedure identifier ( parameter-list ) :
                                 variable-declaration...
                             begin
                                 statement...
                             end;

parameter-list         ::=   parameter [ , parameter ]...

parameter              ::=   identifier : parameter-mode

parameter-mode         ::=   value | result
                         |   value_result | location
                         |   name

statement              ::=   assignment-statement | call-statement
                         |   input-statement | output-statement

assignment-statement   ::=   variable := expression ;

call-statement         ::=   identifier ( expression [ , expression ]... ) ;

input-statement        ::=   input variable [ , variable ]... ;

output-statement       ::=   output variable [ , variable ]... ;

expression             ::=   [ expression + ] operand

operand                ::=   integer | variable | ( expression )

variable               ::=   identifier | identifier [ expression ]
```

For example, consider the procedure declaration:

```
procedure SUM_FIVE_TIMES (I: value, J: value, SUM: result):
   declare TEMP;
begin
   TEMP := I + J;
   SUM  := TEMP + TEMP + TEMP + TEMP + TEMP;
end;
```

This procedure has the following characteristics:

1. Its name is SUM_FIVE_TIMES.

2. It has two parameters I and J of mode value, and another parameter SUM of mode result.

3. There is one local variable named TEMP.

4. The body contains two assignment statements.

In Mini-language Procedures, all variables used within the body of a procedure must either be declared in the procedure or be parameters. The meaning of the different parameter modes will be discussed below. There are four kinds of statements in Mini-language Procedures. An assignment statement causes the value of an expression to be assigned to an integer variable or to a component of an array. Input statements allow integer values to be read into a variable. Output statements allow the values of variables to be printed. Finally, a call statement consists of the name of a declared procedure and arguments corresponding to each parameter associated with the procedure. The number of arguments must equal the number of parameters declared in the procedure. For example, we may have:

```
X := 7;
Y := 9;
SUM_FIVE_TIMES(X, Y, TOTAL);
output TOTAL;
```

The third statement invokes the procedure SUM_FIVE_TIMES. When control returns from executing the procedure, the value of the variable TOTAL is five times the sum of the values of X and Y, that is 80. The next statement to be executed is the output statement.

Note that, since TEMP is a local variable belonging to the procedure SUM_FIVE_TIMES, this variable cannot be referred to by any statement outside the body of the procedure. Also, the rules of *the* mini-language preclude any reference from the body of a procedure to variables declared outside the procedure except through the argument parameter correspondence, which we shall next describe.

We now turn to the exact mechanism by which procedures are invoked. A call statement consists of the name of the procedure to be invoked followed by a parenthesized list of expressions, the argument list. During the execution of a call statement, two things take place:

(1) A correspondence between the arguments in the argument list and the parameters in the procedure is established in left-to-right order. The *i*-th argument corresponds to the *i*-th parameter. The rules for passing the argument to the procedure being called are then applied to each separately.

(2) Control is transferred to the first executable statement of the body in the invoked procedure.

When the last statement in the called procedure has been executed, control is returned to the statement following the call statement.

The way in which the argument is passed to its corresponding parameter depends on the mode of the parameter. Since the rules are applied to each parameter separately, we will describe the rules by assuming that each procedure has only one parameter. Where there is the possibility of interaction among several parameters, this will be discussed.

We use the terms *pass by value, pass by result,* and so on to indicate the way in which information passes between argument and parameter. Sometimes the terms *call by value, call by result*, and so on are used for the same concept. We prefer to reserve *call* for the actual invocation of a procedure.

Pass by Value   *Inputs to a procedure*

Here the parameter acts as a local variable belonging to the procedure. This local variable is initialized with the value of the corresponding argument. Since the parameter is purely a local variable, any change of its value during execution of the procedure can have no effect on the corresponding argument. An argument passed by value can be an integer-valued expression.

Pass by Result   *Outputs from a procedure*

In this case the parameter again acts as a local variable, but its value must be initialized locally within the procedure body. After the statements of the body have been executed, the value of the parameter is assigned to the corresponding argument. In this case, of course, the argument must be a variable.

We see here the dual roles of pass by value and pass by result. Arguments passed by value are expressions that provide *inputs* to a procedure; arguments passed by result are variables that receive *outputs* from a procedure.

Summary
Pass by value &
result

Pass by Value-Result

Pass by value-result combines the effects of pass by value and pass by result. The parameter is considered as a variable local to the procedure: its initial value is given by the value of the corresponding argument, and the final value of the parameter is assigned to the argument on completion of execution of the procedure. In this case as well, the corresponding argument must be a variable.

Pass by Location

Here again, the argument must be a variable. The parameter is considered as a local variable of the procedure, but its location is the location of the argument. Thus any reference to the value of the parameter is considered to be a reference to the value of the argument, and any assignment to the parameter is an assignment to the location of the corresponding argument, thus changing the argument's value.

Pass by Name

→ *if an assignment to the parameter is made inside the procedure; otherwise it can be any expression.*

This case is the most difficult. ~~Again,~~ the argument must be a variable. A reference to a parameter that is passed by name is a direct use of the corresponding argument.

The pass by name mechanism can be modeled as a textual modification to the procedure at the time of invocation. Each reference in a statement to the parameter is replaced by the text of the argument. This is accompanied by a relaxation of the rule against referring to variables that are neither parameters nor local variables. For example, in the procedure:

```
procedure ADD_ONE(X: name):
begin
    X := X + 1;
end;
```

Execution of the call

    ADD_ONE (V);

results in executing the procedure body with X replaced by V. Thus the call to the procedure is equivalent to executing the assignment:

    V := V + 1;

Similarly, execution of the call

    ADD_ONE (COUNT);

is equivalent to executing the assignment:

    COUNT := COUNT + 1;

If arguments are scalar, same as pass by location.

For arguments that are scalars, as V and COUNT, pass by name has the same effect as pass by location. However, if the argument is a reference to an array component, the effect is somewhat different. Execution of the call

    ADD_ONE (A[COUNT]);

is equivalent to executing the assignment

    A[COUNT] := A[COUNT] + 1;

and the component of the array A that is incremented depends on the value of COUNT *at the time the statement is executed*. This point will be illustrated in the following examples.

Some Examples

To clarify the issues of parameter passing in Mini-language Procedures, we now present a series of small examples.
Consider the following very simple procedure:

```
program
    declare A, B, SUM;

    procedure ADD(X: value, Y: value, R: result):
    begin
        R := X + Y;
    end;

begin
    A := 2;
    B := 3;
    ADD (A, B, SUM);
    output A, B, SUM;
end;
```

This is the very model of what a procedure is conceptually. Here the procedure ADD takes two input values, named X and Y, and has a single output named R. The net effect of the procedure is simply to add X and Y and return the value through R.

The statement part of the main program calls the procedure ADD with two input arguments A and B, and another variable SUM intended to store the result of calling the procedure ADD. The final values of A, B, and SUM are then printed. These are 2, 3, and 5.

To illustrate the effects of parameter passing modes we use a rather well known example, that of swapping the values of two variables passed as arguments. Examples 7.1 through 7.4 are identical except for the modes in which the arguments are passed. In each example, a variable I is set to 3, a variable A[I] is set to 6, and a procedure to swap the values of the two variables is invoked. Finally, the values of I and A[I] are printed.

In Example 7.1 the parameters of the swapping procedure are called by value. For value parameters, the corresponding arguments are used solely as initial values. As a result, the assignments to the parameters X and Y in the procedure have no effect on the arguments. Thus the procedure does not perform the desired action. Execution of the procedure has left the values of I and A[I] unchanged.

In Example 7.2 the parameters are passed by location. Thus any assignment to X and Y results in assigning the values to the corresponding location of the variables given as arguments, in this case the locations in which I and A[I] are stored. Thus, this procedure has the desired effect, as shown by the output of the program. Note that it is the value of I at the time the call statement is executed that determines the component of A referenced by Y. That is, the location that is passed is evaluated at the time the procedure is invoked and before the first statement in the body is executed.

```
program
   declare I;
   declare A: array;
   procedure SWAP_BY_VALUE(X: value, Y: value):
      declare TEMP;
   begin
      TEMP := X;
      X    := Y;
      Y    := TEMP;
   end;
begin
   I    := 3;
   A[I] := 6;
   output I, A[3];
   SWAP_BY_VALUE (I, A[I]);
   output I, A[3];
end;
```

Output
```
   I = 3    A[3] = 6
   I = 3    A[3] = 6
```

Example 7.1   Pass by value

```
program
   declare I;
   declare A: array;
   procedure SWAP_BY_LOCATION(X: location, Y: location):
      declare TEMP;
   begin
      TEMP := X;
      X    := Y;
      Y    := TEMP;
   end;
begin
   I    := 3;
   A[I] := 6;
   output I, A[3];
   SWAP_BY_LOCATION(I, A[I]);
   output I, A[3];
end;
```

Output
```
   I = 3    A[3] = 6
   I = 6    A[3] = 3
```

Example 7.2   Pass by location

*because 6
array*

*7.3
Pass by
Name*

In Example 7.3 where the parameters are passed by name, we have a rather surprising result. The values of I and A[3] are set to 3 and 6, respectively, as before. Then the procedure call SWAP_BY_NAME (I, A[I]) is executed. This is equivalent to executing the statements:

```
TEMP := I;
I    := A[I];
A[I] := TEMP;
```

This execution results in 3 being assigned to TEMP, 6 to I, and then 3 to A[6]! The value of A[3] is left unchanged.

*7.4
Pass by
Result*

In Example 7.4, the arguments are passed by result. Since result parameters can only provide return values to their corresponding arguments, and must be given initial values by statements in the procedure, execution of this program will result in a run-time error. The error will occur when the assignment of the value of X to the local variable TEMP is attempted, since X is given no value within the body of the procedure. Notice that this error occurs despite the fact that the argument corresponding to X has a value.

These examples show some of the consequences of the various methods of passing arguments. We return to this discussion in Section 7.4.

7.2   PROCEDURES AS ABSTRACTIONS

The procedure facilities in a programming language can be a powerful tool for coding clear, modular programs. Not only do these facilities allow the programmer to "factor out" frequently executed sections of code but, more importantly, they provide a basic unit for abstraction of program modules. This abstraction can have a great effect on program readability by exposing the program's logical structure.

When procedures are used effectively, they allow the program to be presented in levels of abstractions. The top-most level, the main program, defines the outer structure of the program. The successive lower levels give increasing details about the computations needed to obtain the desired result.

Perhaps the most primitive facility for procedures is evident in Basic and Cobol. In these languages procedures have no parameters and must rely on global variables but, still, units of computation can be grouped into modules and invoked through some form of procedure call.

```
program                                         I | 6
   declare I;
   declare A: array;                            [ . | 3| . | 3| | ]  A
   procedure SWAP_BY_NAME(X: name, Y: name):
      declare TEMP;
   begin
      TEMP := X;     TEMP := I        3       Replaces @ each step
      X    := Y;     I = A[I]         6
      Y    := TEMP;  A[I] := TEMP    A[6] = 3
   end;
begin
   I    := 3;
   A[I] := 6;
   output I, A[3];
   SWAP_BY_NAME(I, A[I]);
   output I, A[3];
end;
```

Output
```
   I = 3    A[3] = 6
   I = 6    A[3] = 6
```

Example 7.3   Pass by name   pg. 196

```
program
   declare I;
   declare A: array;
   procedure SWAP_BY_RESULT(X: result, Y: result):
      declare TEMP;
   begin                    I initialized      FINAL
      TEMP := X;              X [ ? ]          [ ]  Stores X is undefined
      X    := Y;             Y [ ? ]          [ ]
      Y    := TEMP;        TEMP [ ? ]         [ ]
   end;
begin
   I    := 3;
   A[I] := 6;
   output I, A[3];
   SWAP_BY_RESULT(I, A[I]);
   output I, A[3];
end;
```

Output
```
   I = 3    A[3] = 6
   *** ERROR: ATTEMPT TO EVALUATE AN UNDEFINED VARIABLE X
```

Example 7.4   Pass by result   pg. 195

Example 7.5 shows the use of procedures in Cobol. The names of procedures are given as paragraph headers and procedures are invoked using a *perform* statement, ~~and~~ as:

```
PERFORM PRODUCE-PAGE-EJECT.
```

This perform statement invokes the paragraph named PRODUCE-PAGE-EJECT, and after execution of this paragraph control returns to the calling sequence.

Even with this simple scheme, we see a basic value in providing procedures in a programming language. In particular, they allow named units of computation to be extracted from the program text and to be invoked when needed. The simple procedure facility of Cobol brings up an important issue not present in Mini-language Procedures. Notice that in the Cobol program of Example 7.5, execution of the procedure takes place as if the procedure were inserted in place at the point of call. As a result, the effect of the procedure takes place directly upon the variables that can be referenced at the point where the procedure is invoked. This is in sharp contrast to Mini-language Procedures, where all variables in a procedure are local and the effect of the procedure takes place only by assignment to arguments of the call.

In most programming languages, procedures may achieve an effect by both methods. That is, a procedure may affect its arguments or may affect variables that can be referenced at the point where the procedure is called. This brings up the whole idea of global variables, as well as the concepts of block structure and the nesting of procedures. These topics are saved for treatment in Chapter 8. Our intent here is to present procedures in their simplest form, without these additional linguistic complexities.

Procedures have one clear and strong advantage from our point of view. In our discussion of control structures, we noted the simplicity gained if the flow of control in a program followed a one-in, one-out strategy. Procedures fit perfectly within this scheme. Even with the somewhat simple procedure structure in Cobol, we see the value of using these one-in, one-out abstractions.

In order to follow a strict one-in, one-out structure, procedures can have only a single entry point and a single exit. In Mini-language Procedures, the programmer is not allowed any choice in this matter. In other languages it can be different. PL/I, for example, permits a procedure to have several entry points, each with its own name that can be called separately. Ada, Fortran, and PL/I also allow the programmer

```
PREPARE-ACTION-RPT.
    PERFORM   PRODUCE-PAGE-EJECT.
    PERFORM   PRODUCE-ACTION-RPT-HEADER.

INCORPORATE-NEXT-TRANSACTION.
    PERFORM   GET-NEXT-TRANSACTION-REC.
    IF (NOT   EOF-SALE-TRANSACTION-FILE)
        PERFORM GET-MATCHING-MASTER-REC
        IF (MATCHING-MASTER-REC-OBTAINED)
            PERFORM UPDATE-MASTER-REC
            ADD 1 TO NUM-OF-UPDATES
        ELSE
            PERFORM HANDLE-UNMATCHED-TRANSACTION.

    . . .


PRODUCE-PAGE-EJECT.
    MOVE SPACES TO RPT-LINE.
    WRITE RPT-LINE BEFORE ADVANCING PAGE.

PRODUCE-ACTION-RPT-HEADER.
    ACCEPT TODAYS-DATE IN ACTION-RPT-HEADER FROM DATE.
    MOVE ACTION-RPT-HEADER TO RPT-LINE.
    PERFORM FREE-RPT-LINE.

GET-NEXT-TRANSACTION-REC.
    READ SALE-TRANSACTION-FILE
        AT END MOVE 1 TO SALE-TRANSACTION-FILE-STATUS.

GET-MATCHING-MASTER-REC.
    MOVE SALESPERSON-ID-NUM IN TRANSACTION-REC
        TO ID IN MASTER-REC.
    MOVE 0 TO MATCHING-MASTER-REC-STATUS.
    READ SALESPERSON-MASTER-FILE
        INVALID KEY MOVE 2 TO MATCHING-MASTER-REC-STATUS.

HANDLE-UNMATCHED-TRANSACTION.
    IF (NUM-OF-UNMATCHED-TRANSACTIONS = 0)
        PERFORM PRODUCE-LINE-SKIP
        PERFORM PRODUCE-UNMATCH-IST-HEADER.
    PERFORM LIST-UNMATCHED-TRANSACTION.

    . . .
```

Example 7.5   Use of procedures in Cobol

to use a return statement to specify that control is to return to the calling procedure. Thus it is possible to construct a procedure that is no longer a one-in, one-out structure. It is clear that these extra facilities add complexity to programs. What is not so clear is whether this added complexity brings with it an equivalent simplification to the reader.

7.3 ARGUMENTS AND PARAMETERS

Of course, procedures cannot exist in isolation. They must have some form of data communication with the point at which they are called. Parameters are an important part of almost every facility for procedures, for it is through parameters that we generalize the action of a procedure.

The identifiers used for the parameters of a procedure have no effect on its meaning. Thus the effect of

```
procedure ADD (X: value, Y: value, R: result):
begin
    R := X + Y;
end;
```

is precisely the same as the effect of

```
procedure ADD (ITEM1: value, ITEM2: value, SUM: result):
begin
    SUM := ITEM1 + ITEM2;
end;
```

where the identifiers have been changed. Parameter identifiers are purely local to the procedure and have no connection with any identifiers used outside the procedure. Because Mini-language Procedures has a rule against declaring an identifier more than once, there is no chance of a parameter identifier being the same as a locally declared variable. If this rule were relaxed then it would be possible for a parameter identifier to be the same as an identifier used for a variable elsewhere in the procedure. Nevertheless, the two uses of the identifier are quite separate, and a call statement like

```
ADD(SUM, ITEM1, ITEM2);
```

would invoke the procedure ADD, using the values of the variables SUM and ITEM1 and assign the result to the variable ITEM2. This independence between the two sets of identifiers is essential to the procedure's role as an abstraction. The user does not need to be aware of the internal details of the procedure in order to be able to use it.

Conceptually we may view a procedure in rather simple terms. In particular, parameters may be classed as:

■ *Inputs:* The inputs provide values from the caller that are to be used within a procedure. If we view a procedure like a function, inputs are arguments in the traditional sense.

■ *Outputs:* The outputs of a procedure convey the values returned to the calling environment. Again, if we view a procedure as a function, outputs correspond to the value computed by a function. While normally a function may return only a single value, with procedures, several outputs may be computed.

■ *Updates:* The updates characterize those objects in a calling environment that are used both as inputs and as outputs by a procedure. Because of the use of assignment in programming languages, it is frequently the case that an object, for example an array or variable, will need to be modified by a call to a procedure.

This rather simple view of procedures is illustrated as follows:

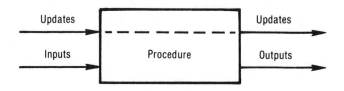

Generally speaking, each parameter-mode of Mini-language Procedures models one of these three types of parameters. Unfortunately, it is the nature of programming languages that such a simple view of parameter passing is often not sufficient to characterize their behavior. We now turn to the various methods by which arguments are passed.

Passing by Value

Argument passing by value is used in many computer languages, for example, Algol 60, Pascal, Algol 68 and Snobol. The reason for the popularity of this method is its analogy to the arguments of a function, where values are provided in order to compute the result.

The simple description of passing by value is that the parameters are treated as local variables. Initial values are provided by copying the values of the corresponding arguments. However, all is not quite so easy.

One of the debits of call by value is that the operation of copying the value of an argument into the location used for the corresponding parameter may be an expensive operation. This is especially true when *large* objects are passed. Imagine for the moment a procedure with two parameters, the first being a thousand element array and the second being an integer valued variable. Assume that the first parameter is called by value, and the second by result. The body of the procedure simply sums all of the elements in the array and passes the result back to the calling environment via the second variable.

Although copying such a large array is expensive, the operation is necessary, since in general a value parameter may be modified in the body of the procedure, and thus a local copy of the array is needed.

This problem is nicely solved in Ada by *in* parameters. Such parameters are similar to *value* mode parameters but may not be targets of assignments. Thus, the value of such a parameter acts as a local constant whose value is initialized by the procedure call. There is no need to copy the values supplied as an argument when the procedure is invoked. Since no updates to the parameter are allowed within the procedure body, the compiler can check this and generate code that refers directly to the actual argument.

Passing by Result

Passing by result is a relatively rare method of argument passing, but exists in Algol W and Ada. In a sense, passing by result is the converse of passing by value, in that the values of the corresponding arguments are set on completion of the execution of the procedure body. Passing by result thus directly models the principle of outputs mentioned above. Of course, the arguments corresponding to a parameter passed by result must be variables.

There are two potential problems with result parameters that can only be resolved by careful language design and definition. If a procedure has more than one result parameter, there is the possibility that it will be invoked by a call statement that associates two of them with the same variable, for example a call statement like P(I, I);. If, after execution of the procedure, the two parameters have different values, the question of the order in which these two values are assigned to I arises.

Mini-language Procedures does not specify this ordering and it is left to the decision of the implementor. For this reason, a call statement like this is generally regarded as a programming error or at least as poor programming practice. Indeed, some languages specifically forbid such calls because the results are indeterminate.

2. The second problem arises where an argument passed by result is a subscripted variable whose subscript depends on other arguments in the same call. For example, if the procedure Q has two result parameters and it is invoked by the call statement:

```
Q (A[I], I);
```

Here, the language definition must specify carefully whether the location of the first argument is evaluated before or after the procedure Q is executed. The effect of the procedure can be quite different in these two cases. In this particular example, the effect of the procedure will also depend on the solution taken in the first problem. In languages where global variables exist, the situation is more complex.

Perhaps the reason for the general lack of passing by result in programming languages is that the same effect can usually be achieved with passing by location. However, in general we feel that the notion of outputs of a procedure is so important that a parameter passing convention strictly for this case is well justified.

Passing by Location   *Passing by reference*

Passing by location, sometimes known as *passing by reference*, is a popular method of argument passing. This method exists in Fortran, Cobol, Pascal, PL/I, and Algol 68. The popularity of this method must be due to its simplicity and its direct analogy with the idea that variables have a location from which their values can be obtained or updated. Passing by location models update parameters for a procedure.

Pass by location can be implemented efficiently, for its implementation only requires the computation of the address of each argument, which is then associated with the corresponding parameter.

Like passing by result, there are two areas where careful attention to the details of the design must be given. Again, the first one concerns the same variable being used as two arguments and thus associated with two different parameters. That is, both parameters are associated with the same location. The two parameters are said to be *aliases*. Generally, the term is used to cover the situation where two different identifiers in a segment of a program refer to the same location. There are other ways in which this can occur as we shall see in Chapter 8.

Procedures in which there are aliases are difficult to understand. In addition, when there is a potential for aliasing there are certain optimizations that cannot be performed for fear of changing the meaning of the program. In PL/I, where arguments are passed by location, procedures are often compiled separately from the call statements that invoke them. In these circumstances, it is impossible for the compiler to determine whether any aliasing exists; the conservative approach must be taken, by omitting the optimization.

 2. The second area of design concerns the restriction that arguments that are passed by location must be variables. Certainly, if an argument were an expression, its value could be stored in a temporary location and this passed to the corresponding parameter. This would then mean that an assignment in the procedure to the parameter would be an assignment to the temporary value. This would allow the parameter to continue in its role as one of the procedure's local variables. Such an assignment would have no effect in the calling environment. It is an open question of language design whether passing arguments that are expressions by location should be allowed.

Passing by Value-Result

In spirit, this method of passing arguments is similar to passing by location. The value of the argument, which must be a variable, is assigned as the initial value of the corresponding parameter. When the procedure completes execution, the final value of the parameter is assigned to the argument variable. Like passing by result, passing by value-result is rare but it does exist in Algol W.

Because of the copying of values that is required, this method of passing arguments is less efficient than passing by location. However, since the parameter is a variable in its own right, there can be no danger of aliasing. Thus there is a greater potential for optimization than there is with location mode parameters.

A sharp difference between passing by location and passing by value-result occurs in cases where an *exception* condition arises during execution of the procedure. Exception conditions are discussed in Chapter 14, but a brief point will be made here.

Consider a procedure with one value-result parameter. Let us assume that arithmetic is performed on the parameter and that during the arithmetic computation, a value is computed that lies beyond the maximum numeric value handled by the implementation. This is an *overflow* condition. In this case, a program will usually terminate abnormally, and then the values of variables can often be inspected.

With passing by value-result, inspection of the corresponding argument will reveal that the value is the same as that obtained when the procedure was invoked, as no change to the value of this variable is performed during execution of the procedure body. With passing by location, however, the value stored in the location may be altered.

Inspection of the value of the variable given as an argument will show such a change. Thus the two methods of parameter passing may differ under abnormal termination conditions.

Passing by Name

Historically, passing by name has received much attention in the literature. Yet its use is very rare, and to our knowledge, exists only in Algol 60.

The relative unpopularity of this method is due to the surprises it can give the programmer and to its inefficiencies. This method of passing arguments stems directly from the Lambda Calculus [Church 1941].

The characteristic of passing by name is the *deferred evaluation* of the argument. In the other modes of argument passing, the argument is evaluated *before* the body of the called procedure is executed. Instead of passing a value or location to a name parameter, a rule for evaluating the argument is passed. This rule is used whenever the argument is referenced. In Section 7.1, we described this process through the metaphor of textual substitution. This metaphor works well for a small language like Mini-language Procedures, however, in a more complex language, it soon loses its simplicity if it is to remain accurate. The problem is that the application of the rule for evaluating the argument is only valid in the context of the call statement. Thus, if the argument is A[I] and there is a variable I declared in the called procedure, simple textual substitution does not tie the I in A[I] back to the calling context.

7.4 VALUE-RETURNING PROCEDURES

A value-returning procedure is one that is invoked as a function reference in an expression. It thus computes a value that is used in the next stage in evaluation of the expression.

Suppose Mini-language Procedures were extended to include a return statement with the syntax:

```
return identifier;
       expression
```

This statement would only be permitted in a procedure. Its execution would cause control to return to the point at which the procedure was invoked with the value associated with the identifier as the value of the reference to the procedure. To invoke a procedure containing a return statement by a call statement would be meaningless since there would be no way of using the returned value. The Mini-language extension would therefore require a rule that restricted reference to a procedure containing return statements to expressions.

Consider the following example of a value-returning procedure:

```
procedure ADD_ONE (V: value):
begin
   V := V + 1;
   return V;
end;
```

Such a procedure must be invoked in an expression such as:

```
X := A * ADD_ONE(A) + A;
```

If the value of A were 3, then 15 would be assigned to X.

Note that the parameter is declared with *value* mode. Had it been declared with *location* mode, the evaluation of the expression

```
A * ADD_ONE(A) + A
```

would be harder to understand and the outcome less certain. The problem is that, when V has a *location* mode, execution of the ADD_ONE procedure not only calculates a return value but also adds one to the argument. This is known as a *side-effect*. The actual result that is assigned to X in the above example will now depend on the details of the evaluation mechanism of the expression. Depending on these, the expression could be equivalent to one of the following:

```
3 * 4 + 3
3 * 4 + 4
4 * 4 + 4
```

Thus the use of value-returning procedures that have side effects can have implementation defined results and is bad programming practice.

7.5 COROUTINES

invocation & execution of procedures

The invocation and execution of procedures described in this chapter are the classical form common to most standard programming languages. Another form, known as *coroutines*, is much less common and will be described in this section.

The relationship between the part of a program that contains a call statement, often called the *main procedure*, and the subroutine is asymmetric. The flow of control that characterizes this relationship is shown in Figure 7.1. The asymmetry is shown by the fact that the called procedure is always entered at its first statement whereas, when control returns to the main procedure, execution is *resumed* at the point following the call. Thus the subprocedure is in a subservient role to the main procedure.

Coroutines have a more symmetric relationship between the calling and called parts of the program. In normal use, a pair of procedures work together as coroutines. When they are invoked, they do not execute to completion as in normal procedures, but return control after partial execution. At this point execution of one coroutine is suspended and the execution of the other is resumed from the point at which its execution was suspended. This sequence of suspensions and resumptions of control continues as the coroutines work together, as shown in Figure 7.2. In this arrangement, the two coroutines are on the same level and there is no master-slave relationship as there is in normal calling mechanisms.

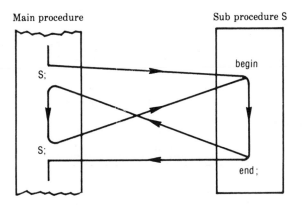

Figure 7.1   Control flow relationship between main procedure and subprocedure

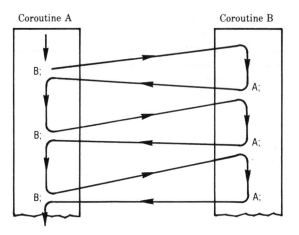

Figure 7.2 Flow of control between a pair of coroutines

Coroutines allow programs with complex sequencing logic to be simplified by allowing the details of the sequencing structure to be separated into separate modules. Coroutines are of use in complex searching processes and in simulation of multiprocessing, discussed in Chapter 15, as well as in the handling of interleaved lists, discussed in Chapter 12.

FURTHER READING

There are several further readings that deserve special note here. Of importance is [Jones and Muchnick 1978]. This discusses the general concept of binding time and the methods of parameter passing in programming languages. It treats most of the issues covered in this chapter and presents the concepts in a clear and effective way.

Readers who wish to explore the origins of call by name may refer to the classic work [Church 1941]. The use of this parameter passing mechanism in Algol 60 is described in [Rutishauser 1977].

Traditionally, as well as in the presentation given above, the arguments of a procedure are always passed in positional order. That is, the arguments given in a procedure call correspond one by one to the corresponding position of the parameters given in the declaration of the procedure itself. An interesting variation of this method of parameter passing is described in [Ichbiah et al. 1979]. This reference describes an alternative mechanism for stating the correspondence between arguments and parameters through the use of a keyword notation, in which the procedure call explicitly names the association between arguments and parameters.

Coroutines were introduced in [Conway 1963]; this paper serves as a good introduction to the use of coroutines in the compiling process.

EXERCISES

Exercise 7.1   Methods of Passing Parameters

Suppose Mini-language Procedures were modified so that a variable declared outside a procedure could be referenced and modified from within the procedure. Consider the following program, written in this variant of Procedures where a parameter mode has been omitted.

```
program
    declare I;
    declare B: array;

    procedure Q(X:      ...      ):
    begin
        I := 1;
        X := X + 2;
        B[I] := 10;
        I := 2;
        X := X + 2;
    end;

begin
    B[1] := 1;
    B[2] := 1;
    I    := 1;
    Q(B[I]);
    output B[1], B[2];
end;
```

Consider the mode of the parameter X of procedure Q to be (1) value, (2) result, (3) value result, (4) location, and (5) name execute the program for each argument passing convention and determine the values output.

Note: One of the executions terminates abnormally; in all others, the results are different.

Exercise 7.2   Pass by Name versus Pass by Value

The short program below incorporates most of the basic pass-by-name and pass-by-value problems. The value returning procedures, INCREMENT_BY_VALUE and INCREMENT_BY_NAME, differ in that their argument is passed by value versus by name. That is the only difference. ADD_BY_VALUE and ADD_BY_NAME differ similarly.

The problem is to determine the values printed in each output statement.

Note: This exercise is adapted from Weil [1965].

```
program
    declare A, B;
    procedure INCREMENT_BY_VALUE (X: value):
    begin
       X := X + 2;
       return X;
    end;
    procedure INCREMENT_BY_NAME (X: name):
    begin
       X := X + 2;
       return X;
    end;
    procedure ADD_BY_VALUE (X: value):
    begin
       return X + X;
    end;
    procedure ADD_BY_NAME (X: name):
    begin
       return X + X;
    end;
    begin
       A := 3;
       B := ADD_BY_VALUE(INCREMENT_BY_VALUE(A));
       output A, B;
       A := 3;
       B := ADD_BY_VALUE(INCREMENT_BY_NAME(A));
       output A, B;
       A := 3;
       B := ADD_BY_NAME(INCREMENT_BY_VALUE(A));
       output A, B;
       A := 3;
       B := ADD_BY_NAME(INCREMENT_BY_NAME(A));
       output A, B;
    end;
```

See 11/17/82
pg. 3

pg. 445
see paper by Weil
"Testing the Understanding
of the Difference Between
call by Name and
call by Value
in algol 60."

Exercise 7.3   Jensen's Device

Passing parameters by name may be used in a programming stratagem known as Jensen's Device. To use the technique, a procedure has two or more parameters that are passed by name. During execution the value of one or more of these parameters is changed. If one of the arguments is an expression that involves the variable that is updated during execution, the expression may be evaluated for many different values of its variables.

A simple example of this procedure is the function procedure:

```
procedure SUM (L_BOUND: value, U_BOUND: value, INCREMENT: value,
               TERM: name, EXPRESSION: name):
   declare TOTAL;

begin
   TOTAL := 0;
   TERM  := L_BOUND;
   while (TERM <= U_BOUND) loop
      TOTAL := TOTAL + EXPRESSION;
      TERM  := TERM + INCREMENT;
   end loop;
   return TOTAL;
end;
```

The invocation of the procedure SUM by

```
SUM (1, 25, 1, I, A[I]);
```

will produce the sum of the first 25 elements of the array A. The invocation

```
SUM (1, 25, 1, I, 1/A[I]);
```

Make extensions
within spirit

will compute the sum of the inverses of the elements.

1. Write an invocation of SUM that will give the sum of the first five powers of three.

2. Write a general purpose routine that will find the maximum value from a set of values obtained by evaluating an arbitrary expression containing a variable that ranges from a given lower bound to a given upper bound in a given step size.

3. Describe the limitations of this technique.

Exercise 7.4 Aliasing

The term *aliasing* is used to describe the situation where a single location, and hence its value, may be accessed through more than one name. Describe:

1. The ways in which aliasing can occur,

2. The implementation problems that aliasing can cause,

3. Some rules for a language without pointers that attempt to prevent aliasing.

Illustrate your answer with examples.

Exercise 7.5 Coroutines

Devise some additional syntax and define the corresponding semantics for the extension of Mini-language Procedure to include coroutines. How could your proposal be generalized to allow any number of intercommunicating coroutines?

Exercise 7.6 Named Parameter Passing

In Ada, the agruments to a subprogram can be given in positional order or by naming the parameters associated with the arguments, or in combination. Named parameters can be given in any order.

For example, with the procedure header

```
procedure PLOT (X, Y: in REAL; PEN_UP: in BOOLEAN);
```

where in denotes an input parameter, we may have the calls:

```
PLOT ( 0.0., 0.0, TRUE);                    -- positional
PLOT ( X => 0.0, Y => 0.0, PEN_UP => TRUE); -- named
PLOT ( PEN_UP => TRUE, X => 0.0, Y => 0.0); -- names reordered
PLOT ( 0.0, 0.0, PEN_UP => TRUE);           -- combination
```

There are basically two positions on this feature:

1. Such a feature is useful and is highly reliable. The programmer does not have to remember the order of parameters. With long parameter lists, the feature is almost indispensable.

2. Such a feature is of dubious importance. The desired effect on readability can be achieved in other ways, for example, writing procedures with fewer arguements or giving mnemonic names to arguments. Furthermore, a change to the names of parameters forces the calls to be changed.

Make your choice, and write a one to three page position paper on your choice.

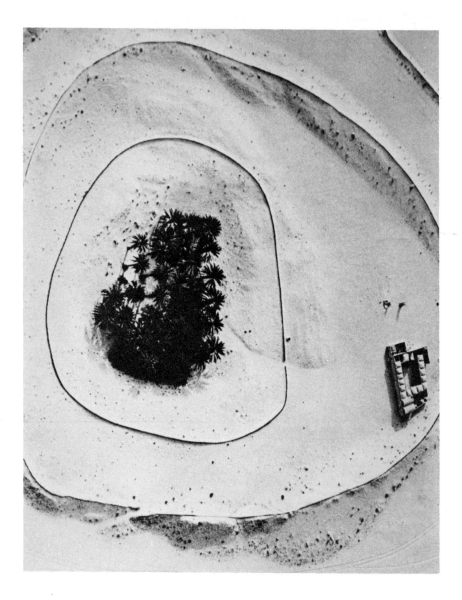

8
Nesting and Scope

Thru pg 238

The association between a parameter and its value holds only within the procedure. Outside the procedure, either the identifier has no meaning, or it is associated with some other object. We say that the identifer is *local* to the procedure.

Identifiers are used in programs to refer to many different kinds of entities. In a large program there can be hundreds, if not thousands, of such identifiers. Since a large program is likely to be the work of many programmers, there must be some method of avoiding incompatible uses of the same identifier without onerous bookkeeping. Identifiers introduced by a programmer should not be required to have the same meaning over the complete program. It must be possible to limit the area of a program in which a particular identifier is associated with a specific entity.

The part of the program over which an identifier refers to the value defined in its declaration is the *scope* of the declaration. The process of matching an identifier reference to its defining declaration is the *resolution* of the reference. An identifier is said to be *known* within the scope of its declaration.

Definition

Mini-language Scope introduced here has rules based on those of Algol and Pascal.

220

8.1   MINI-LANGUAGE SCOPE

As with most of our mini-languages, the program consists of one or more declarations followed by a sequence of statements, as shown in Table 8.1. There are two kinds of declarations: variable declarations and procedure declarations. In any declaration section, a name may be declared only once.

Declarations

A variable declaration introduces one or more integer variables. All variables in a program must be declared.

A procedure declaration introduces a named procedure. A procedure consists of one or more declarations followed by a sequence of statements. All identifiers used within a procedure must also be declared, either in the declarations given with the procedure or in an outer program unit. A program unit is either a procedure (that is, bracketed by the keywords procedure and end) or a main program (that is, bracketed by the keywords program and end).

Statements

Mini-language Scope has assignment, call, input, and output statements, all of familiar form. The expressions that can be used in an assignment statement are extremely simple, and can only consist of operands or the addition of operands.

Scope Rules

A declaration associates certain properties with an identifier; in this mini-language it defines whether an identifier is an integer variable or a procedure. The region of a program over which a particular declaration of an identifier is in effect is the *scope* of the declaration. Within any one declaration section, a particular identifier may only be declared once. A reference to an identifier in a statement sequence must be within the scope of the declaration of that identifier.

A program in Mini-language Scope is made up of blocks. The complete program is itself a block. The part of a procedure declaration from the symbol : to the end symbol that terminates the procedure is also a block. Except for the outermost block, all blocks are contained in at least one other block. The scope of a declaration consists of the block

Table 8.1   Mini-Language Scope

program	::=	`program`
		    declaration-section
		`begin`
		    statement...
		`end;`

declaration-section	::=	[variable-declaration...] [procedure-declaration...]
variable-declaration	::=	`declare` identifier [, identifier]... : `integer;`

procedure-declaration	::=	`procedure` identifier :
		    declaration-section
		`begin`
		    statement...
		`end;`

statement	::=	assignment-statement | call-statement | input-statement | output-statement
assignment-statement	::=	identifier := expression ;
call-statement	::=	identifier ;
input-statement	::=	`input` identifier [, identifier]... ;
output-statement	::=	`output` identifier [, identifier]... ;
expression	::=	[operand +] operand
operand	::=	integer | identifier | (expression)

in which it occurs and all contained blocks that do not have a redeclaration of the same identifier.

Although a particular identifier may not be declared more than once in any one declaration section, it may be declared in other declaration sections. Each such declaration can associate the identifier with different properties. Each declaration has its own scope, which is disjoint from the scopes of all other declarations of the same identifier.

The following program fragment shows how the scopes of different declarations of the same identifier cover different parts of the program:

```
                                            Scopes
                                        A1    A2    A3
 ┌program                                _
 │   declare A: integer;      -- A1       |
 │  ┌procedure B:                        _|     _
 │  │   declare A: integer;   -- A2              |
 │  │   ...                                      |
 │  └end;  -- B                          _      _|
 │  ┌procedure C:                         |
 │  │  ┌procedure E:                     _|           _
 │  │  │  ┌procedure A:       -- A3                    |
 │  │  │  │  ...                                       |
 │  │  │  └end;  -- A                                  |
 │  │  │  ...                                          |
 │  │  └end;  -- E                       _           _|
 │  │  ...                                |
 │  └end;    -- C                         |
 │  ...                                   |
 └end;                                   _|
```

The outer declaration of A has a scope that consists of the outermost block and the procedure C; however, it includes neither the procedure B, where it is redeclared as an integer variable, nor the procedure E, where it is redeclared as a procedure. The gaps corresponding to parts of the text where the identifier has been redeclared are known as *holes in the scope*.

An identifier declared in a block is said to be *internal* or *local* to the block in which it is declared, and *external* or *global* to all inner blocks that do not contain redeclarations of it.

When an identifier is used within a statement sequence, the declaration that defines the identifier can be determined as follows:

■ If the declaration section of the block that contains the statement sequence has a declaration of the identifier, ~~that is,~~ *then, this*
claration is the defining declaration.

■ Otherwise, the blocks enclosing the sequence of statements are examined, and the most local closing block containing a declaration of the identifier defines the given identifier.

A procedure's local variables do not exist until the procedure is invoked. At that time, the variables are created with undefined values. The variables continue to exist until execution of the procedure is completed, at which point they cease to exist.

Examples

Example 8.1 shows the use of nesting and the redeclaration of identifiers. Here a variable named A is declared within the procedure PURELY_LOCAL. Its scope thus consists only of the procedure itself. The variable A is also declared in the main program; its scope does not include the procedure PURELY_LOCAL.

When the program of Example 8.1 is executed, the value of A will be set to 1, and then this value will be output. The procedure PURELY_LOCAL is then called; this procedure sets the local variable to 5 and outputs its value. It thus has no effect on the containing program unit. Finally, the value of A in the main program unit is again printed. Since the value associated with this identifier has not been changed by the call of PURELY_LOCAL, the value 1 will again be printed for the variable A.

Example 8.2 shows a program similar to that of Example 8.1, except that the variable A is not declared as local to the procedure. The effect of the procedure PURELY_GLOBAL in Example 8.2 will be to change the value of A declared in the main program. Thus when this program is executed, the first output statement will print the value 1 and the second output statement will print the value 5. However, in this example, the third output statement will also print the value 5, since the call to PURELY_GLOBAL changes the value of A.

```
program
   declare A: integer;

   procedure PURELY_LOCAL:
         declare A: integer;      local
   begin
      A := 5;
      output A;
   end;
begin
   A := 1;
   output A;
   PURELY_LOCAL;
   output A;
end;
```

Output
```
      A = 1
      A = 5
      A = 1
```

Example 8.1   Use of a local variable

```
program
   declare A: integer;              Global

   procedure PURELY_GLOBAL :
   begin
      A := 5;
      output A;
   end;
begin
   A := 1;
   output A;
   PURELY_GLOBAL;
   output A;
end;
```

Output
```
      A = 1
      A = 5
      A = 5
```

Example 8.2   Use of a global variable

Example 8.3 illustrates the full complexities of Mini-language Scope. The main program unit introduces three variables A, B, and C. Three procedures, Q, R, and S, are also defined within the main program unit. Furthermore, procedure R introduces a local declaration of the variable C, and procedure S introduces local declarations of B and C, as well as an inner declaration of procedure Q.

The way in which this program executes is shown in Table 8.2. The statement numbers correspond to those shown in comments in the program. In order to distinguish the separate uses of the same identifier, the variables are distinguished in Table 8.2 by prefixing their names with the name of the procedure in which they are declared. For example, S.C is the variable C declared in the procedure S. Execution begins at the first statement in the statement sequence of the outermost program unit, line 17.

Where the same identifier is used for more than one object in a program and the rules of scope must be used to determine which object is being referenced, the names of the objects are said to *clash*. The many clashes illustrating the rules of Scope in Example 8.3 make the program difficult to understand and are best avoided.

8.2   THE IDEA OF SCOPE

In mathematical writing, the concept of scope is used extensively. It is common to introduce local definitions to give the current meaning of a symbol. For instance, we may write, "let N be . . ." Such definitions are usually local to a section of text and have no connection to other uses of the symbol N elsewhere in the text. Although there are no formal rules that define the scope of such textual declarations, in a clearly written document there will be no difficulty in understanding. The meaning in programming languages, since compilers have no intuition to rely on, we must be more precise in our definition of scope, hence, for example, the scope rule given for Mini-language Scope.

The idea of a declaration having a scope that is less than the complete program, allows the same identifier to be used for different purposes in separate parts of a program. Consider the program fragment of Example 8.4. We assume that we are writing a program that processes text. This program contains two procedures, GET_SYMBOL and MOVE_LINE_POSITION. Within these procedures a number of variables are declared, and these declarations are assumed to hold for the procedure in which they are given. Notice that two variables, INDEX and LENGTH, happen to have the same identifier in both procedures, although they represent different entities. To reflect this meaning, each of the variables has a scope that consists of a region of text comprising the procedure in which the declaration of the variable is given.

```
program
    declare A, B, C: integer;   -- variables A, B, and C

    procedure Q:
    begin                   -- line 1
      A := A + 2;           -- line 2
      C := C + 2;           -- line 3
    end;

    procedure R:
      declare C: integer;      -- variable R.C
    begin                   -- line 4
      C := 2;               -- line 5   R.C
      Q;                    -- line 6
      B := A + B;           -- line 7
      output A, B, C;       -- line 8   R.C
    end;

    procedure S:
      declare B, C: integer;   -- variables S.B, and S.C
      procedure Q:
      begin                 -- line 9
          A := A + 1;       -- line 10
          C := C + 1;       -- line 11   S.C
      end;
    begin                   -- line 12
      B := 3;               -- line 13
      C := 1;               -- line 14
      Q;                    -- line 15
      R;                    -- line 16
    end;

begin                       -- line 17
  A := 1;                   -- line 18
  B := 1;                   -- line 19
  C := 1;                   -- line 20
  R;                        -- line 21
  S;                        -- line 22
end;
```

Example 8.3   The joys of scope

Table 8.2 Execution of Example 8.3

line	A	B	S.B	C	R.C	S.C	Notes
17	?	?	—	?	—	—	The three local variables of the outermost block have no defined value. No other variables exist.
18	1	?	—	?	—	—	A is assigned 1.
19	1	1	—	?	—	—	B is assigned 1.
20	1	1	—	1	—	—	C is assigned 1.
21	1	1	—	1	—	—	The procedure R is invoked.
4	1	1	—	1	?	—	R's local variable C is created.
5	1	1	—	1	2	—	R's local variable C is assigned 2.
6	1	1	—	1	2	—	The procedure Q is invoked.
1	1	1	—	1	2	—	
2	3	1	—	1	2	—	A is incremented by 2.
3	3	1	—	3	2	—	C is incremented by 2, Q is completed.
7	3	4	—	3	2	—	
8	3	4	—	3	2	—	A=3, B=4, C=2 is printed. R is completed. R's local variable C ceases to exist. Control returns to the main program.
22	3	4	—	3	—	—	Procedure S is invoked.
12	3	4	?	3	—	?	S's local variables B and C are created.
13	3	4	3	3	—	?	S's local variable B is assigned 3.
14	3	4	3	3	—	1	S's local variable C is assigned 1.
15	3	4	3	3	—	1	Procedure Q contained in S is invoked.
9	3	4	3	3	—	1	
10	4	4	3	3	—	1	A is incremented.
11	4	4	3	3	—	2	S's local variable C is incremented. Q completed.
16	4	4	3	3	—	2	Procedure R is invoked.
4	4	4	3	3	?	2	R's local variable C is created.
5	4	4	3	3	2	2	R's local variable C is assigned 2.
6	4	4	3	3	2	2	The procedure Q is invoked.
1	4	4	3	3	2	2	
2	6	4	3	3	2	2	A is incremented by 2.
3	6	4	3	5	2	2	C is incremented by 2. Q is completed.
7	6	10	3	5	2	2	
7	6	10	3	5	2	2	A=6, B=10, C=2 is printed. R is completed. Control returns to S. S is completed. Control returns to main program, which is completed.

```
program
   ...

   procedure GET_SYMBOL:
      declare INDEX, LENGTH, SYMBOL_CODE: integer;
   begin
      -- statements for obtaining the next symbol code;
   end;

   ...

   procedure MOVE_LINE_POSITION:
      declare INDEX, LENGTH, TEMP_POSITION: integer;
   begin
      -- statements for advancing the current line position;
   end;

   ...

begin

   -- statements for main program

end;
```

Example 8.4   Reuse of local variable names

The value of such an idea is immediate. When writing a procedure, a programmer can devise names that are suitable for the computation at hand, without regard to other portions of the program. In a program with a large number of procedures written by several programmers, the programmers can choose names quite freely.

Some languages, for instance, Basic and Cobol, do not have the concept of scope. Whenever a new entity must be declared, the programmer is forced to devise a unique name for the entity. Even in relatively small programs, this forces somewhat awkward naming conventions. Perhaps even more important, the declaration and use of the name may be quite distant. Thus the programmer may have no clear way of showing the locality of effects on the various components of the program. For these reasons, almost all recently designed programming languages have some notion of scope.

Block Structuring

Mini-language Scope is modeled on the idea of block-structured languages, originally introduced with Algol 60. Similar directions have been taken in many other languages, for example, PL/I, Pascal, Algol 68, and Ada.

The essential feature of block structure is a system of program units that delimit the regions of program text and a method for specifying the names that belong to these regions. In Mini-language Scope, we use program or procedure as the opening bracket of a unit and end as the closing bracket. Note that blocks can be nested one inside another.

There are in general two sets of rules for the resolution of name references. These rules correspond to the static and the dynamic structure of the program. We will first discuss the box that corresponds to the static structure of the program, this is sometimes called *lexical scoping*. The term *lexical* refers to the fact that all references can be resolved from the text of the program. The term *static binding* is also used, this indicates that the connection between the declaration and the reference does not change during the execution of the program.

The conventional rules of lexical scoping are:

■ The scope of a declaration includes the block in which it occurs but excludes any block surrounding it.

■ The scope of a declaration includes any block contained within the block in which the declaration occurs but excludes any contained block in which the same identifier is redeclared.

These two rules are a more formal statement of the concept of scope for Mini-languge Scope given in Section 8.1.

One effect of these rules is to prevent access to variables and procedures declared within a procedure from outside the procedure. For example, consider the fragment:

```
. . .
procedure P:
   declare B: integer;
   procedure C:
      . . .
   end;
begin
   -- statements for P
end;
. . .
```

The variable B cannot be referenced outside the procedure P nor can the procedure C be invoked from outside the procedure P. The variable B in P does not exist unless the procedure P has been invoked.

Another consequence is that the redeclaration of an identifier prevents reference to the original entity. For example, consider the fragment:

```
declare X: integer;     -- outer X
procedure A:
   declare X: integer;  -- inner X
   procedure B:
      ...
   begin
      ...   -- the outer X cannot be referenced here
   end;
begin
   ...
end;
```

PL/I provides an escape from this situation by using external names. External variables behave as though they were declared in a conceptual block that contains all the separately compiled procedures of the program.

An external name may be referenced within the scope of any declaration of the same identifier with the attribute EXTERNAL, as in the following fragment:

```
DECLARE X FIXED EXTERNAL;  /* OUTER VARIABLE X */
A:
PROCEDURE;
   DECLARE X FIXED;        /* INNER VARIABLE X */
   B:
   PROCEDURE;
      DECLARE X FIXED EXTERNAL;
      X = 5;  /* REFERENCE TO OUTER VARIABLE X */
      END B;
      X = 5;  /* REFERENCE TO INNER VARIABLE X */
   END;
X = 5;        /* REFERENCE TO THE OUTER VARIABLE X */
```

Global Variables

The use of even a few global variables in a block increases the complexity of the block considerably. An understanding of the computation performed by the block involves considering the use that is made of the global variables in the larger context of the complete program. Changes made to global variables outside the block can affect the correctness of the block itself.

With blocks that are procedures, the dangers of global variables can be seen quite dramatically. Consider the program of Example 8.2. Here we have the sequence of statements:

```
output A;
PURELY_GLOBAL;
output A;
```

Notice that the same output statement appears twice, but the value output by each statement is different. The problem here is caused by the invocation of the procedure PURELY_GLOBAL. The call statement does not even mention the variable A, yet the invocation of the procedure changes the value of this variable. This is known as a *side effect* or a *context effect*.

In a small program like Example 8.2, the danger of side effects may not appear to be particularly serious. But imagine a program with hundreds of statements and many procedure calls, where each procedure exhibits some side effect. Keeping track of the dynamic behavior of such a program is often almost impossible.

8.3 DYNAMIC STORAGE ALLOCATION

In addition to the use of block structure as a means of controlling the scope of declarations, it is also of significance at execution time. Variables are associated with locations in storage, and a consequence of a block structure is that it leads to an efficient technique for storage management. It may be argued that, with the development of inexpensive storage on modern computers, this gain in efficiency may be dubious.

The fact that a variable is not known outside the block in which it is declared means that storage for variables in a block need only be allocated during the execution of the block. Thus storage for the variables is obtained when the block is entered and released when the block is completed. This provides a basis for the sharing of storage between blocks in an easily controlled and well-defined way. This form of storage management is known as *dynamic storage allocation*. It was originally developed for the implementation of Algol 60 and has since been adapted for other block structured languages.

The acquisition of storage on block entry is handled by a special sequence of instructions, known as the *prologue*, generated by the compiler. Corresponding to the prologue, there is an *epilogue* that is executed as the block terminates. The epilogue handles the release of storage that is no longer required. Generally, the simplest way to manage dynamic allocation is through the use of a stack.

The Run-time Stack

The basic idea is to use a region of consecutive locations of storage as a stack. That is, allocated storage will always be added to the top of the stack by incrementing a stack pointer, and released storage will always be removed from the top of the stack by decrementing the pointer. Although this kind of management technique is unable to handle arbitrary allocation and release of storage, the last-in, first-out mode of operation corresponds precisely to the storage requirements of a block structured language.

All the storage required for the fixed size variables of a block is collected together into a single area of storage called an *activation record*. In addition to the storage for variables, an activation record will contain other items concerned with the control of the execution of the program. Such items include:

■ Information about parameters

■ Information about local variables that cannot be determined during compilation, for example, where the bounds of a local array are calculated from the parameters.

■ Temporary storage for expression evaluation

■ Addressing information for nonlocal variables

■ The return address, that is, the point in the calling block to which control returns when the current block terminates

■ A pointer to the activation record of the caller.

The prologue manipulates the stack pointer and the initializes the newly created activation record on the stack. Upon termination, the pointer is reset to its position before the block's invocation and returns control to the caller. Thus, at any time during execution, the run-time stack consists of activation records for all those blocks that have been invoked but have not yet terminated.

As an illustration of the use of the run-time stack, we trace block entries and exits (with their corresponding effects on the run-time stack) of Example 8.3, as shown in Table 8.3.

The rules of scope define a mapping from an identifier reference to a declaration. The environment of a block provides the mapping from the declarations to locations and thus values. The mechanism of providing one or more environment pointers in an activation record is not the only possible implementation. A full discussion of these techniques is beyond the scope of this text; for further information the reader is referred to a compiler text such as [Aho and Ullman 1977].

Arrays and structures whose sizes are unknown during compilation *arrays & structures* can also be handled on the run-time stack. The technique generally employed is to allocate first the part of the activation record whose size is known during compilation. Once this has been done, the size of the array can be calculated and the size of the activation record can be increased by advancing the stack pointer. A pointer to the array is then inserted into the fixed part so that it can be accessed through an address calculated during compilation.

A recursive procedure is one that can have more than one activation record on the run-time stack at some point during execution. Each of these activation records is distinct and each can contain locations for different generations of the local variables. It is of particular importance in dealing with recursive invocations that questions of environment be carefully defined. We shall return to this question in later chapters.

Other Kinds of Storage Management

A block structured language allocates storage for variables as each block is invoked. This is however not true of all languages; there are essentially three different times at which storage can be allocated:

1. When the complete program is loaded into storage. This is the case in Fortran and Cobol, the PL/I storage class STATIC, and Algol *own* variables. PL/I static storage and Algol *own* variables differ from normal block structured storage in that they are preserved when control leaves a block containing them and their values are made available on re-entry.

2. When the block is invoked. This is the type of storage management that we have described in detail in this section. The allocation and release of storage is tied directly to the block structure of the program.

3. Under the direct control of the programmer. This is achieved through the execution of special statements. This case is discussed in Chapter 13.

Table 8.3   Stack Execution of Example 8.3

[SP denotes the stack pointer]

Line 17: The main program is entered. An
activation record containing locations for
variables A, B, and C is created.

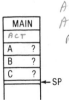

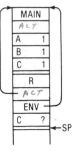

Line 21: Procedure R is invoked.
Line 4: Procedure R is entered. An activation
record containing a location for variable C is
created. This new activation record contains a
pointer to the activation record of the caller.
A reference to the identifier C in this block is
a reference to the current activation record.
However references to the identifiers A and B
are references to these variables in the
previous activation record labeled MAIN.

Line 6: Procedure Q is invoked.
Line 1: Procedure Q is entered. An activation
record for this block is obtained. Since this
block does not have any local variables there is
no need for any storage for them. However, space
for control information such as the return
address is still needed. References to the
identifier A and C are references to the
activation record of the main program. A simple
pointer to the activation record of the caller
does not provide the necessary information and
an additional pointer, labeled ENV, is needed.
This is the *environment* pointer and is used
when the calling procedure does not contain
the called one, for example, when S invokes R.

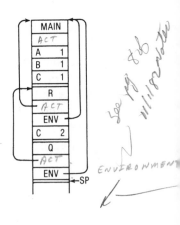

Table 8.3 continued

Line 3: Execution of Q completes and control returns to Line 7. The activation record for Q is removed from the stack.

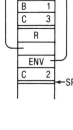

Line 8: Execution of R is completed and control returns to line 22. The activation record for R is removed from the stack.

Line 22: Procedure S is invoked.
Line 12: Procedure S is entered. An activation record containing locations for variables B and C is created. The storage used for this activation record is the space just released from the activation record of procedure R.

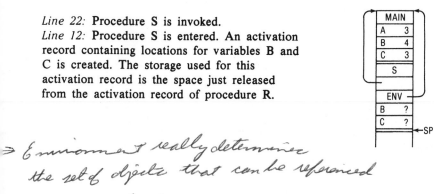

⟹ Enviroment really determines
the set of objects that can be referenced
in a procedure.

Table 8.3   continued

Line 15: Procedure Q internal to S is invoked.
Line 3: Procedure Q is entered. An activation
record for this block is obtained. The
environment for this block consists of the
activation record for S for references to the
identifiers B and C and the activation record
for MAIN for references to the identifier A.
Thus two environment pointers are provided in
the activation record for procedure Q.

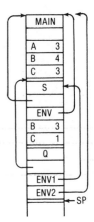

Line 11: Execution of procedure Q is completed
and control returns to line 16. The activation
record for procedure Q is removed from the
stack.

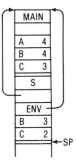

Line 16: Procedure R is invoked.
Line 4: Procedure R is entered. An activation
record containing a location for the variable C
is created. The environment pointer permits
references to A and B in the main program.

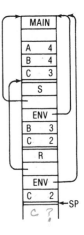

274

Table 8.3   continued

Line 6: Procedure Q is invoked.
Line 1: Procedure Q is entered. An activation record for this block is obtained. This activation record is at a different place on the run-time stack from the previous activation record for this block. Since procedures Q, R, and S are all immediately contained in the main procedure, the activation record for the main procedure is the environment for each of these blocks.
Line 3: Execution of Q is completed and control returns to line 7. The activation record for Q is removed from the stack.

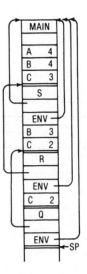

Line 8: Execution of R completes and control returns to the end of procedure S. This terminates S and returns control to the end of the main procedure, which also terminates. As each terminates, its activation record is removed from the stack. The stack is left empty.

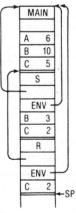

8.4   DYNAMIC SCOPE

In addition to the more usual static rules of scope that we have defined and demonstrated through Mini-language Scope, there are some languages where the resolution of an identifier reference to the defining declaration must be performed dynamically. That is to say, the region of the program over which a particular declaration applies varies during the execution of the program.

Definition The scope rules used by Snobol, APL, and Lisp are essentially the same. These require that a reference to an identifier be resolved to the declaration of that identifer in the most recently invoked, but not yet terminated, block that contains a declaration of the identifier. Thus, the resolution of a nonlocal reference will depend on the sequence of invocations and the resolution can change during execution.

Implementation The implementation of this type of scope rule can be achieved with a run-time stack by including in the activation record a list of all identifiers declared in the block. Resolution is performed by searching the stack for the most recent activation record that contains the desired identifier. In practice, this can be time consuming and more efficient implementations are available. However, it serves well as a model of the process.

Surprises Some surprising effects can result from this kind of scope rule. In particular, an assignment statement does not always change the same variable, and a call statement may invoke a different procedure depending on the state of the run-time stack.

Example For example, suppose that the rules of Mini-language Scope were changed so that name resolution had to be performed dynamically. The execution of Example 8.3 would then proceed differently. In particular, procedure R is invoked both from the main procedure and from procedure S. When R is invoked from the main procedure, the reference to B in line 7 is to the variable B in the main procedure, and the invocation of Q in line 6 is an invocation of the procedure Q that includes lines 1 through 3. When R is invoked from procedure S, the reference to B in line 7 is resolved to a reference to the variable S.B and the invocation of Q in line 6 is an invocation of the procedure Q that includes lines 9 through 11. This is because S's activation record is more recent than that of the main procedure.

Serious consequence A consequence of this kind of behavior is that it is impossible to protect the variables of a block against access by a subroutine. In a statically scoped language, such protection exists where the subroutine is not contained inside the calling block. This danger with dynamic scoping brings into serious question the applicability of dynamically scoped languages to the production of large reliable programs.

FURTHER READING

Certainly the most complete reference on the topics treated in this chapter is given in [Schwenke 1978]. This rather lengthy paper outlines the area traditionally associated with scope, surveys the various mechanisms required in a number of contemporary programming languages, and studies the impact of many of these issues on implementation.

An earlier article [Wulf and Shaw 1973] summarizes the dangers associated with the use of global variables.

Another early work [Johnston 1971] discusses a model in which block structured languages with scope rules may be viewed.

An additional work in this area is [Jones and Muchnick 1978]. This short text defines a small language called Tempo; this language and the authors treatment present an overall view of argument passing and scope, with particular emphasis on the notion of binding times (see Exercise 8.5).

EXERCISES

Exercise 8.1   Revisiting the Joys of Scope

Trace the execution of the following program written in Mini-language Scope.

```
program
    declare A, B, C;
    procedure Q:
    begin
        B := B + 2;
        C := C + 2;
    end;  -- Q
    procedure R:
        declare A;
    begin
        C := 2;
        Q;
        B := A + B;
        output A, B, C;
    end;  -- R
```

```
procedure S:
   declare A, C;
   procedure Q:
      declare C;
   begin
      A := A + 1;
      C := C + 1;
   end;
   begin
      B := 3;
      C := 1;
      Q;
      R;
   end;   -- S
begin
   A := 1;
   B := 1;
   C := 1;
   R;
   S;
end;
```

Exercise 8.2   Static Scope

This is more difficult than Exercise 8.1. Trace the execution of the following program:

```
program
   declare A, B, C;

   procedure P:
      declare C;

      procedure Q:
         declare A, B;
      begin
         A := 3;
         B := C + A;
         output A, B, C;
      end;   -- Q
```

```
            procedure S:
                declare C, D;
                procedure R:
                begin
                    C := A + (B + 3);
                    A := B + D;
                    output A, B, C;
                end;
            begin
                A := A + 3;
                C := 5;
                D := 2;
                Q;
                R;
            end;  -- S
    begin
        C := 2;
        A := A + 1;
        B := A + C;
        R;
        S;
    end;  -- P

    procedure R:
        declare A;
    begin
        A := B + 2;
        B := B + C;
        C := C + 5;
        output A, B, C;
    end;  -- R
begin
    A := 1;
    B := 2;
    C := 3;
    P;
end;
```

Exercise 8.3 Avoiding Side-effects in Functions

Consider a programming language having the usual rules of scope, that is, a block structured language. There are two types of internal procedures allowed in the language: *functions*, which return a value to the point of invocation, and *subroutines*, which do not. The language is defined so that function invocation cannot cause any side effects.

If you were implementing the compiler, how would you make sure that this rule is enforced?

Note: It may be necessary to restrict the types of statements that can appear within the body of a function, either to enforce the rule or to warn programmers who apparently do not understand the rule.

Exercise 8.4   Reaching Above a Local Scope

In accordance with the "usual" block structure rules of scope, a declaration causes a declared identifier to have local scope. The use of an identifier yields a reference to the innermost containing procedure or block in which the identifier is declared.

Suppose we wish to retain these rules but add some way of allowing identifiers to be declared so that they have a nonlocal scope that is derived from a containing block, but not necessarily the innermost containing block. For example, with the structure

```
procedure A:
   declare X;

   procedure B:
      declare X;

      procedure C:
         declare X;
         ...    -- use of X
      end;   -- C
   ...
   end;   -- B
...
end;   -- A
```

we would like some way for the use of X in procedure C to refer to the X in procedure A, rather than be local as it is now, or refer to the X in procedure B as it would if it were not redeclared in procedure C.

1. Suggest an extension or modification to the declaration syntax to accommodate the revised scope rules.

2. What problems, if any, would this extension cause if run-time references were resolved using the usual simple symbol table?

3. Offer arguments for or against the use of these revised scope rules in a programming language.

Exercise 8.5   Binding Time

The term *binding* is used to denote the association of an identifier with a value. Basically there are six times at which binding can occur:

1. Writing of program text
2. Compilation of program text
3. Linking together of separately compiled modules to form a complete program
4. Loading of complete program into machine storage
5. Invocation of a subprogram
6. Execution of a statement.

Give an example of a binding that can occur at each of these times.

Exercise 8.6   Dynamic Scope

Trace the execution of Example 8.2 under the rule of dynamic scope as described in Section 8.4.

Exercise 8.7   Aliasing

Construct an example of a program fragment where an optimizing compiler would be unable to perform an optimization due to the possibility of aliasing.

A Closer Look

9
Higher Level Control Structures

Thru 269

Most programming languages offer control facilities beyond those of the basic sequence, conditional, and loop structures of Mini-language D. These additional control structures are believed to allow the programmer to express algorithms more clearly and naturally.

In this chapter we discuss the meaning and application of these structures. In addition, we discuss the goto statement and the consequences of including it in a programming language. As usual, we begin with a mini-language.

9.1 MINI-LANGUAGE L

The context free syntax of Mini-language L is given in Table 9.1. As in most of our Mini-languages, a program consists of a declaration section followed by a sequence of executable statements. Each of the variables used in a program must be declared exactly once.

The simplest kind of statement in Mini-language L is the assignment statement, whereby an identifier is assigned the value of an expression. An expression consists of a sequence of operands separated by the symbols + or −.

The if statement has the same form and meaning as the if statement in Mini-language D.

The mechanism for repeated calculations is the loop statement:

247

```
loop
   -- statements to be repeated
end loop;
```

The statements within the loop are executed repeatedly until an exit, cycle, or goto statement transfers control out of the loop.

An exit statement has the form

```
exit (i);
```

where *i* is an integer greater than zero. Execution of an exit command causes termination of the *i* enclosing loops. For example, consider the loop:

```
loop
   -- statements to obtain data values
   if (INPUT_VALUE = 0) then
      exit(1);
   end if;
   -- statements to process data values
end loop;
   -- statements following loop
```

This loop continues to obtain and process data until INPUT_VALUE is 0, at which point the exit statement is executed and the loop is terminated by transfering control to the statement following the loop. The value of *i* must be less than or equal to the number of enclosing loops.

Consider next the sketch:

```
begin
   . . .
   loop
      . . .
      loop
         . . .
         exit (2);    -- inner and outer loops terminated
      end loop;
   end loop;
   -- continuation point (a)
   . . .
   exit (1);    -- illegal, no enclosing loop
   . . .
end;
```

Table 9.1 Mini-language L

program	::=	`program`
		   `declaration...`
		`begin`
		   `statement...`
		`end;`

declaration	::=	`declare` identifier [`,` identifier]... `;`
statement	::=	[identifier `:`] simple-statement
simple-statement	::=	assignment-statement | if-statement | loop-statement | cycle-statement | exit-statement | goto-statement | input-statement | output-statement
assignment-statement	::=	identifier `:=` expression `;`

if-statement	::=	`if` condition `then`
		   `statement...`
		[`else`
		   `statement...`]
		`end if;`

loop-statement	::=	`loop`
		   `statement...`
		`end loop;`

cycle-statement	::=	`cycle` (integer `);`
exit-statement	::=	`exit` (integer `);`
goto-statement	::=	`goto` identifier `;`
input-statement	::=	`input` identifier [`,` identifier]... `;`
output-statement	::=	`output` identifier [`,` identifier]... `;`
condition	::=	[condition `and`] comparison | [condition `or`] comparison
comparison	::=	(operand comparison-operator operand)
expression	::=	[expression `+`] operand | [expression `-`] operand
operand	::=	integer | identifier | (expression)
comparison-operator	::=	`=` | `≠` | `<` | `>`

Here execution of

```
exit (2);
```

causes termination of both enclosing loops and execution to continue at point (a). The statement

```
exit (1);
```

is illegally placed since there are no loops bracketing it.
Programs may also contain control statements of the form

```
cycle (i);
```

where i is an integer greater than zero. The execution of a cycle statement is similar to an exit statement, except that the ith enclosing loop is re-executed, that is to say, control is transfered back to the beginning of that loop. For example, in the sketch

```
begin
  ...
  loop     -- beginning of outermost loop
    ...
    loop
      ...
      cycle (2); -- transfer to start of outermost loop
    end loop;
  end loop;

  ...
  cycle (1);  -- illegal, no enclosing loop
  ...
end;
```

execution of the nested cycle statement causes re-execution of the outermost loop. Execution of the statement

```
cycle (1);
```

is illegal, since there are no enclosing loops.
Statements within a program may be prefixed by a label consisting of an identifier:

```
HERE:   A := A + 1;
```

A label prefix is a declaration of the identifier as a label, thus marking a statement in the program to which control can be transfered by a goto statement. Since the label prefix acts as a declaration, a label identifier cannot be the same as an identifier declared as a variable or as any other label.

For example, we may have:

```
HERE:    A := A + 1;
         . . .
THERE:   A := A + 2;

         . . .
         if (X > 10) then
            goto HERE;
         else
            goto THERE;
         end if;
```

Any statement within the program may be labeled, and execution of a goto statement causes execution to continue at the referenced statement. If no label exists, the goto statement is illegal. In particular, a goto statement can transfer control in to and out of loops and to a statement within the then or else parts of an if statement. For example, in the following

```
goto INNER_LOOP;
...
loop
   ...
   loop
      INNER_LOOP: A := A + 1;
      ...
      goto THEN_PART;
   end loop;
   ...
end loop;
if (A = 3) then
   THEN_PART: output B;
end if;
```

both kinds of transfers of control are shown.

Generally speaking, we can state the flow of control rules of Mini-language L as follows:

Flow of Control Rules
Mini-language L

■   Statements in a sequence are executed in the order in which they appear unless a loop, if, goto, exit, or cycle statement is encountered.

■   Execution of a loop statement causes the enclosed statement sequence to be executed repeatedly, until an exit, cycle or goto statement transfers control out of the loop.

■   Execution of an if statement causes the execution of the statement sequence following the then symbol if the condition is true; otherwise the statement sequence following the else symbol, if it exists, is executed.

■   Execution of a goto statement causes control to be passed to the statement labeled by the identifier in the goto statement.

■   Execution of exit (i) causes control to be passed to the statement immediately following the ith loop enclosing the exit statement.

■   Execution of cycle (i) causes control to be passed to the beginning of the ith loop enclosing the cycle statement.

Finally, Mini-language L also includes the usual input and output statements.

We next give two small examples in Mini-language L. Example 9.1 shows the use of a simple one-level exit from a loop. The loop is used to calculate the sum of a number of items. When the value of COUNT is equal to the number of items, the loop is terminated.

Example 9.1
Discussion
Example 9.2

Example 9.2 performs the same calculation as Example 9.1 except that, in Example 9.2, the loop is terminated by a goto statement. When the goto statement is executed, control continues at the output statement prefixed by the label DONE.

9.2   CLASSES OF CONTROL STRUCTURES

We now turn to various classes of control structures.

D-structures

We begin by reviewing the definition of "D-structures," given in Chapter 5 for Mini-language D. A D-structure is any program constructed from only the following one-in, one-out primitive structures:

```
program
    -- This program reads in an integer specifying the number
    -- of integer items and then reads in the items.
    -- It outputs the sum of the integers.

    declare COUNT, NUM_ITEMS, NEXT_ITEM, SUM;
begin
    input NUM_ITEMS;
    COUNT := 0;
    SUM    := 0;
    if (NUM_ITEMS > 0) then
        loop
            input NEXT_ITEM;
            SUM    := SUM + NEXT_ITEM;
            COUNT := COUNT + 1;
            if (COUNT = NUM_ITEMS) then
                exit (1);
            end if;
        end loop;
    end if;
    output SUM;
end;
```

Example 9.1 Use of a simple exit

D Structures

1. Basic actions that can be D-structures themselves
2. Sequences
3. Conditional constructs
4. Loops

D'-structures

D'-structures consist of D-structures plus some extensions built from them; these are:

1. Single branching if statements
2. Multi-way branching case statements
3. Until loops
4. For loops

The set of D'-structures contain the set of Pascal control structures apart from the goto. As defined here, all D'-structures are one-in, one-out structures in the sense that any well-defined loop has one entry and one exit.

```
program
    -- This program reads in an integer specifying the number
    -- of integer items and then reads in the items.
    -- It outputs the sum of the integers.

    declare COUNT, NUM_ITEMS, NEXT_ITEM, SUM;
begin
    input NUM_ITEMS;
    COUNT := 0;
    SUM   := 0;
    if (NUM_ITEMS > 0) then
        loop
            input NEXT_ITEM;
            SUM    := SUM + NEXT_ITEM;
            COUNT := COUNT + 1;
            if (COUNT = NUM_ITEMS) then
                goto DONE;
            end if;
        end loop;
    end if;
    DONE: output SUM;
end;
```

Example 9.2   Use of a simple goto statement

RE₁-structures

An RE_1-structure is composed of basic actions, sequences, if-then-else structures, loop structures, and exit statements that leave a single enclosing loop, that is, exit (1) statements. For example, we may have:

```
loop
    ...
    if c₁ then
        exit (1);
    end if;
    ...
    if c₂ then
        exit (1);
    end if;
end loop;
```

Note that a while loop of the form

```
while (A = B)
    -- statements
end loop;
```

is equivalent to the RE_1-structure:

```
loop
    if (A ≠ B) then
        exit (1);
    end if;
    -- statements to be repeated
end loop;
```

RE_n-structures

An RE_n-structure is composed of basic actions, sequences, if-then-else, and loop structures, together with exit statements of the form, `exit` (i), where i is a positive integer between 1 and n. On execution, the statements within a loop are to be repeated indefinitely until an exit statement is encountered. The execution of the exit statement causes termination of the i enclosing loops.

REC_n-structures

An REC_n-structure is similar to an RE_n-structure, with the inclusion of additional statements of the form, `cycle` (i); . The execution of a cycle statement is similar to an exit command, except that the ith enclosing loop is re-executed.

REC_n-structures and their variants represent conventional programs for which transfers of control can only be made to the end or the beginning of an enclosing control loop.

L-structures

An L-structure is defined as any structure without restrictions on the transfers of control. An L-structure corresponds to a program with free use of labels and goto statements.

This set of control structures embraces most of the control structures found in conventional languages. It is important to note that these control structures do not take into account scope rules.

9.3   THE CONCEPT OF POWER IN CONTROL STRUCTURES

We now consider the relative power of control structures by examining the conversion of a control structure to an equivalent form. Conversions of this type formed the basis of our demonstration of the Boehm and Jacopini theorem in Chapter 5.

The minimum requirement that we place on the conversion of a control structure S into a control structure T is that it preserve the function of the structure, that is:

For every input, T computes the same result as S.

If this condition holds, we say that the two structures are *functionally equivalent*. We also say that a control structure S is *more powerful* than a structure T if the conversion of S to T requires the introduction of new actions, conditions, or variables. Finally, we say that a structure S is *semantically equivalent* to T if the conversion of S to T does not require any new actions, conditions, or variables.

The Boehm and Jacopini theorem on the theoretical completeness of D-structures makes the following points:

1. *Any* L-structure (even including those permitting arbitrary transfer of control) can be converted to a functionally equivalent D-structure,

2. In the functional conversion of an L-structure to a D-structure, a number of boolean variables may have to be introduced.

The importance of result (1) is that it proves that the goto statement is, at least theoretically, not needed to perform computations and that, D-structures are sufficient.

We might now ask: under which conditions is a control structure convertible to a D-structure, without introducing new boolean variables or changing the particular actions and conditions of a program? The answer to this question [Kosaraju 1974] lies in the detection of a loop with two or more distinct exits. In general, an L-structure is convertible to a semantically equivalent D-structure if and only if the structure does not contain a loop with more than one distinct exit. If a structure contains only loops with one exit, conversion can be made by rearrangement and possible duplication of the existing actions and predicates.

For example, consider the program schema of Figure 9.1. This is a typical structure that cannot be converted to a D-structure without new

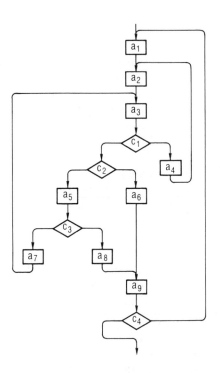

Figure 9.1 An L-Structure not convertible to a D structure without new variables or new actions

variables or actions. Here we have a loop consisting of a sequence with two exits, one through a_6 and the other through a_8. Note that the branch to a_4 is not an exit from this loop, since the flow of control must return to a_3, via a_2.

McCabe [1976] has shown that any program that is not written with just D-structures will contain at least two of the following control situations:

Branching out of a loop
Branching into a loop
Branching into a decision
Branching out of a decision

For example, the path from c_3 to a_8 in Figure 9.1 branches both out of a loop and out of a decision. This result gives a basis for understanding why departures from the pure use of D-structures apparently increase the complexity of programs.

A Hierarchy of Control Structures

There have been numerous attempts to discover the limitations of D-structures as well as to explore the expressive power of other control structures. These results show that there are programs that cannot be converted to D-structure form without changing the length, execution time, or basic actions of a given program. One of the more important results, due to Kosaraju [1974], answers the question: how do the structures given in section 9.2 relate to each other? *pg. 252*

The basic results are outlined in Figure 9.2. A downward line connecting one class of structures to another class means that the upper class is in general only convertible to the lower one with the introduction of new actions and variables. The main results shown in Figure 9.2 may be summarized as:

Summary

- ■ D and D'-structures are semantically equivalent; that is, the basic D-structures can provide a simple means of expressing the extensions embraced by D'-structures.

- ■ D and D'-structures are less powerful than RE_1 or REC_1-structures. Thus to write a program using only D or D'-structures, we may have to introduce new boolean variables and actions to achieve the desired effect.

- ■ RE_n-structures are semantically equivalent to REC_n-structures. Somewhat surprisingly, the addition of the cycle statement does not add to the theoretical power of the repeat-exit control structure.

- ■ If no prior bound is placed on the index n, *any* structure is convertible to an RE_n or REC_n-structure.

- ■ For any finite value of n, there exist L structures that cannot be converted to RE_n or REC_n-structures without the introduction of new actions and predicates.

Implications of the Results

From the programmer's viewpoint, the results suggest that there are control situations where more powerful control structures, (e.g. RE_1 or L-structures) are preferable to D or D'-structures because, for example, they do not require new control variables, conditions, or actions. Aside from questions of efficiency, the results also suggest that the use of stronger control structures like RE_n-structures and their

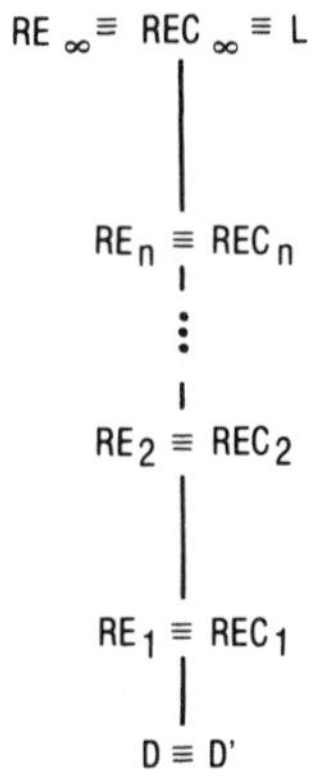

$$RE_\infty \equiv REC_\infty \equiv L$$

$$|$$

$$RE_n \equiv REC_n$$

$$\vdots$$

$$RE_2 \equiv REC_2$$

$$|$$

$$RE_1 \equiv REC_1$$

$$|$$

$$D \equiv D'$$

Figure 9.2 A hierarchy of control structures

variants may obviate the need for goto's and control variables. In the next section, we show an example that, in fact, presents evidence *counter* to these suggestions.

9.4 AN EXAMPLE

When all is said and done, the practicing programmer is primarily interested in solving *problems* using the set of control structures provided by a particular language. Although theorems on the *conversion* of one form of structure to another may be of some practical interest in that they show the situations where the introduction of new variables may be required, conversion is not the basic issue.

Of much greater importance is the question of naturalness of expression. That is, can the control structures of the language under consideration form a natural expression of the algorithm needed to solve the current problem? In particular, are there problems for which D or D'-structures do not provide solutions that are as clear as the more powerful control structures? We now present an example aimed at resolving this issue.

We have chosen a problem that is apparently difficult for D'-structures; its solution seems to require the ability to leave nested loops both to restart and to terminate the loops.

For this problem, we must write a program segment that sets the value of a variable LEGAL_NAME_FLAG to 1 or 0, depending on whether a given PL/I qualified name is a legal or illegal reference.

Data structures in PL/I may be declared with nested components, for example:

```
DECLARE 1 A,
          2 B,
            3 C CHARACTER (5),
            3 D FIXED;

DECLARE 1 X,
          2 B,
            3 C FLOAT,
            3 E FLOAT;
```

A reference to a structure element is legal if, and only if, it designates a unique component of a structure. Using the declarations of A and X, the references A, A.B, A.B.C, A.C, and B.E are all legal. However, both references B and B.C are ambiguous and hence illegal. The reference B.C could refer to either A.B.C or to X.B.C.

To solve this problem, a number of primitives are assumed:

assumed primitives

1. A linked list of entries, called QUALIFIED_NAME, that contains a separate entry for each identifier component of the qualified name to be tested.

2. A linked list of entries called SYMBOL_TABLE, which contains a separate entry for each identifier declared in a program. An identifier declared in more than one structure has an entry corresponding to each occurrence.

3. A function named BASE_ID, which, when applied to QUALIFIED_NAME, yields the rightmost or lowest level entry in the name. For example, the BASE_ID of the qualified name A.B.C is the entry for C.

4. A function named NEXT, which, when first applied to SYMBOL_TABLE, gives the first entry, and on subsequent applications to a symbol table gives succeding entries in the symbol table. Repeated applications thus provide each entry of the symbol table in some undefined order, terminated by a null entry.

5. A function FATHER, which can be applied to either a qualified name entry or symbol table entry. In each case, it yields the next higher order entry in the corresponding linked list, or the null entry if there is no father entry. For example, in the linked list for A.B.C, the father of the entry for C is the entry for B, and the father of the entry for A is the null entry.

Each of these primitives is illustrated in Figure 9.3. Finally, we assume that FALSE and TRUE are constants with the respective values 0 and 1.

$F = o$
$T = 1$

    Example 9.3 shows a solution to this problem using REC_2-structures. This solution makes liberal use of cycle and exit statements for escapes from one and two levels of loops. A _conversion_ of this program to a D or D'-structure is impossible without the introduction of

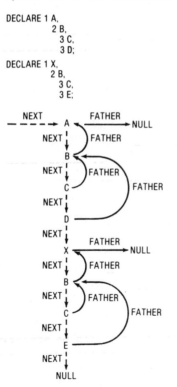

Entry for the Qualified Name A.B.C.

Symbol table for the declarations:

DECLARE 1 A,
    2 B,
      3 C,
      3 D;
DECLARE 1 X,
    2 B,
      3 C,
      3 E;

Figure 9.3 Primitives for the qualified name problem

```
NAME_BASE          := BASE_ID(QUALIFIED_NAME);
DIRECT_HIT         := FALSE;
NUM_PARTIAL_HITS := 0;

loop
   TABLE_ENTRY := NEXT(SYMBOL_TABLE);
   if (TABLE_ENTRY = NULL) then
   -- exit(1);
   end if;
   if (TABLE_ENTRY = NAME_BASE) then
      LOCAL_TABLE_ENTRY := FATHER(TABLE_ENTRY);
      LOCAL_NAME_ENTRY   := FATHER(NAME_BASE);
      SKIP               := FALSE;
      loop
         if (LOCAL_NAME_ENTRY = NULL) then
            if (LOCAL_TABLE_ENTRY = NULL) then
               if (SKIP = TRUE) then
                  NUM_PARTIAL_HITS := NUM_PARTIAL_HITS + 1;
               else
                  DIRECT_HIT := TRUE;
                  -- exit(2);
               end if;
            else
               NUM_PARTIAL_HITS := NUM_PARTIAL_HITS + 1;
            end if;
         else
            if (LOCAL_TABLE_ENTRY ≠ NULL) then
               if (LOCAL_TABLE_ENTRY = LOCAL_NAME_ENTRY) then
                  LOCAL_NAME_ENTRY := FATHER(LOCAL_NAME_ENTRY);
               else
                  SKIP := TRUE;
               end if;
               LOCAL_TABLE_ENTRY := FATHER(LOCAL_TABLE_ENTRY);
               cycle(1);
            end if;
         end if;
         cycle(2);
      end loop;
   end if;
end loop;
if (DIRECT_HIT = TRUE) or (NUM_PARTIAL_HITS = 1) then
   LEGAL_NAME := TRUE;
else
   LEGAL_NAME := FALSE;
end if;
```

Example 9.3   A solution using REC$_n$-structures

Dave
Wheaton

Section 1P 9.4

(Zshow Examples 9.3 ; 9.4 pg 262, §263
Done   ⇒ Follow thru text carefully →
       See

11/15/18 pg 2.5

```
TABLE_ENTRY       := NEXT(SYMBOL_TABLE);
NAME_BASE         := BASE_ID(QUALIFIED_NAME);
DIRECT HIT        := FALSE;
NUM_PARTIAL_HITS := 0;

while (TABLE_ENTRY ≠ NULL) and (DIRECT_HIT = FALSE) loop

   if (TABLE_ENTRY = NAME_BASE) then
      LOCAL_TABLE_ENTRY := FATHER(TABLE_ENTRY);
      LOCAL_NAME_ENTRY  := FATHER(NAME_BASE);
      SKIP              := FALSE;

      while (LOCAL_NAME_ENTRY ≠ NULL) and (LOCAL_TABLE_ENTRY ≠ NULL) loop
         if (LOCAL_TABLE_ENTRY = LOCAL_NAME_ENTRY) then
            LOCAL_NAME_ENTRY := FATHER(LOCAL_NAME_ENTRY);
         else
            SKIP := TRUE;
         end if;
         LOCAL_TABLE_ENTRY := FATHER(LOCAL_TABLE_ENTRY);
      end loop;

      if (LOCAL_NAME_ENTRY = NULL) then
         if (LOCAL_TABLE_ENTRY = NULL) then
            if (SKIP = TRUE) then
               NUM_PARTIAL_HITS := NUM_PARTIAL_HITS + 1;
            else
               DIRECT_HIT;
            end if;
         else
            NUM_PARTIAL_HITS := NUM_PARTIAL_HITS + 1;
         end if;
      end if;

      TABLE_ENTRY := NEXT(SYMBOL_TABLE);
   end if;

end loop;

if (DIRECT_HIT = TRUE) or (NUM_PARTIAL_HITS = 1) then
   LEGAL_NAME := TRUE;
else
   LEGAL_NAME := FALSE;
end if;
```

Example 9.4   A solution using D-structures

new boolean-valued variables. While not intrinsically bad and often making for clearer programs, in this case the additional boolean variables increase the complexity of the program.

However, by starting again from the original problem statement, it is possible to devise a new functionally equivalent solution using D-structures. This solution, shown in Example 9.4, requires neither new variables nor excessive copying of code; its clarity compares very favorably with the solution using REC_2-structures. Thus, the expected superiority of REC_2-structures over D-structures is not supported by the example.

9.5   THE GOTO STATEMENT AND LABEL VALUES

In recent years there has been a great deal of discussion of the goto statement. Although not the first to speak against its use, Dijkstra [1968] provided the first argument against it that was really noticed. It began:

> "For a number of years I have been familiar with the observation that the quality of programmers is a decreasing function of the density of goto statements in the programs they produce."

Reaction was strong. Many people appeared to have misunderstood what Dijkstra was saying. He was not arguing against all transfers of control, which would be ridiculous since the power of a computer stems from conditionals and loops, but rather against the use of undisciplined transfers of control. In this section we examine the properties of the goto statement and label values.

Among the contributions to the debate on the goto statement there was a tongue-in-cheek suggestion in [Clark 1973] that the goto statement could be eliminated in favor of a *come from* statement. For example, in Fortran:

```
10    J = 1
11    COME FROM 20
12    WRITE (6,40) J
      STOP
13    COME FROM 10
20    J = J + 2
40    FORMAT(I4)
```

Here, after executing statement 10, control is transferred to statement 13. Although this was intended as a spoof, there was a large grain of truth contained in it, and it really shows the difficulty with the goto statement.

In a program with many goto statements, we are likely to have this kind of situation:

```
...
goto LA;
...
goto LA;
...
LA:  ...
...
goto LA;
...
```

At any point in a computation, there is a particular value associated with each of the program's variables. The set of these values constitute the *computation state* at that point in the program. Thus, when control is transferred to the statement labeled LA, the computation state will depend on the point from which control came. In order to understand the program, the programmer must be aware of all the possible states and therefore must be able to keep in mind the state at each goto statement. Thus, it is not so much a goto problem as a come from problem.

The computation state is generally referred to as the *environment*. The environment is a mapping from an identifier in a declaration to a location and thus to a value. The action of a goto statement not only involves a transfer of control but also a transfer of environment. A large measure of the complexity of a program with goto statements is due to the difficulty in understanding the possible computation states at various points in the program. While, for transfers of control that remain within a single block, the mapping between identifiers and locations does not change, this is not the case when goto statements are allowed to tranfer control in to or out of blocks. Such transfers increase program complexity greatly.

Consider a cross between the Mini-languages Scope and L, where goto statements can transfer control between procedures. Assume also that the value of a label identifier can be assigned a variable. A label identifier denotes a label constant whose value is a label object, which has two parts:

A label identifier denotes a label constant whose value is a label object which has two parts:

1. The unique statement designated by the label.

2. An environment for the designated statement.

The execution of a goto statement of the form goto X is:

■ The value of X is obtained. If it is not a label value, the program is in error. Note that the mini-language is dynamically typed, that is both integer and label values can be assigned to the same variable at different points in the program.

■ Execution continues from the statement designated by the label value with the environment defined by the label value.

Consider the program shown in Example 9.5. Here, the statement goto A in the procedure P causes control to be transferred to the statement labeled LA. This is because the label value LA was assigned to the variable A before the procedure P was entered. The transfer to LA causes the procedure P to be terminated.

In the program shown in Example 9.6, the execution of the statement labeled LA causes the procedure P to be re-entered. What precisely happens at this point depends on the definition of the environment part of the label value assigned to the variable A inside P. This definition specifies, for example, whether P's variable B has value 3 or is undefined when control arrives at the statement labeled LC. The whole issue of goto's and environment changes is a rather heavy matter, and would take us far beyond our intent.

9.6 CONCLUSIONS

We draw three basic conclusions from our discussion of Mini-languages D and L.

(1) ■ From the programmer's viewpoint, theoretical results based on the conversion of one program form to another, under restrictive conditions, may not be of practical significance.

The formal results discussed earlier in this chapter suggest the limitations of D and D'-structures. The supporting evidence rests mainly on the impossibility of converting (under particular restrictions) control

```
program
   declare A, B;

   procedure P:
      declare B, C;
   begin
      B := 3;
      C := 4;
      goto A;
   end;
begin
   A := LA;
   B := 2;
   P;
   A := 6;
LA:  A := 1;
   output A;
end;
```

Example 9.5   Example of leaving a block by a goto statement

```
program
   declare A, B;

   procedure P:
      declare B, C;
   begin
      B := 3;
      A := LC;
      goto LA;
   LC:  C := 4;
      go to LB;
   end;
begin
   B := 2;
   P;
   A := 6;
LA:  goto A;
LB:  A := 1;
   output A;
end;
```

Example 9.6   Simple example of environment

schema into equivalent forms limited to D or D'-structures. However, the practicing programmer is rarely concerned with converting programs from one form to another. Concern is centered on the naturalness with which a particular set of control structures can express the algorithmic solution to the problem at hand.

For the programmer then, the acid test of the "power" of control structures must involve their use in the solution of specific problems typical of those met in programming. Of course, the potential strengths and weaknesses indicated by the theoretical results will guide the choice of particular test problems. For example, the Qualified Name problem of Section 9.4 was originally chosen to illustrate the weakness of D and D'-structures in dealing with exit problems. To make the comparison, separate solutions to the same problem were *independently* programmed using the control structures under investigation.

Inevitably, the conventions of a programming language dictate the way that the solution to a problem is expressed. Developing each solution from the original problem statement will ensure that the peculiarities of one set of control structures do not become obstacles to the clear expression of another solution using a different set. Each Qualified Name solution was shaped by the particular characteristics of the control structure being used. Had the solution based on the REC_2-structure been *converted* into one using D'-structures, we would have had to introduce additional complexity as well as several new variables. The result of this comparison shows that it is easy to gain the wrong impression by considering theoretical results that are based only on conversion under restricted conditions.

$\mathcal{V}$· ■ The need for higher level (above D or D') control structures remains unproven.

There have been many, many works suggesting new control structures, higher than D and D'. These higher control structures are generally techniques for implementing exits from containing structures. In our opinion, such exits reduce clarity. The basic function of a control structure is to provide clarity by operational abstraction. Thus, the reader of a program should be able to take a level at a time, without having to bother with the inner details to find the exit conditions. For this reason, one-in, one-out structures like D and D' provide very effective abstractions.

We believe that there is no good evidence for the need of these higher forms. For these higher forms to be advantageous, the gain in naturalness, clarity of expression, and efficiency in solving problems must be sufficient to offset the additional complications introduced to both the language and its compiler.

3- ■   The utility of the goto is seriously questioned.

In some ways it is strange that the discussion of the goto statement has been included with that of the higher level control structures. On the one hand, the goto statement is the most powerful control structure from the point of view of the Kosaraju hierarchy presented earlier. On the other hand, as Dijkstra [1968] says, "The goto statement as it stands is just too primitive; it is too much an invitation to make a mess of one's program."

Generally the arguments advanced in favor of the use of the goto statement are for clarity and efficiency. Knuth [1974] says that "Sometimes it is necessary to exit from several levels . . . and the most graceful way to do this is a direct approach via the goto or its equivalent." Here, its equivalent would appear to be a more disciplined form such as an exit statement. While one example does not make a theorem any more than one swallow makes a summer, our example discussed in Section 9.4 does not seem to support this contention. The use of a disciplined form of exit statement is preferable to the use of the goto statement for the same purpose.

The argument for efficiency, that the goto statement allows for more efficient programs, is frequently made. That is, by clever use of the goto statement a more efficient algorithm can be constructed. However, in almost every large program, efficiency obtained by clever use of control structures is a tiny fraction of the overall cost. While no optimizing compiler can be expected to perform *macro-efficient* optimizations like converting a linear search into a binary one, redundant tests and repeated actions are typical of the *micro-efficient* conditions that can be eliminated by good optimizing compilers, rare though they may be at the present time. It is this type of optimization that is the province of the compiler and not that of the programmer, who should be primarily interested in developing *clear* macro-efficient programs. Indeed, it is becoming clear that general optimization can be done automatically with greater effect when the program is built from D-structures.

Finally, we admit that any recommendation for a good set of control structures is subjective. However, we must conclude from this examination that D-structures and their variants, with all their simplicity, lead the practicing programmer toward clear and effective solutions.

FURTHER READING

Two readings relevant to this chapter stand out. The first is [Kosaraju 1974], where the results on control structures are carefully explained. Beware though, this paper is surely for those with a mathematical mind.

The second reading [Knuth 1974] presents arguments that we have criticized here. Though this paper summarizes well the arguments given by those supporting the use of higher order control structures, a counter view is expressed in [Ledgard and Marcotty 1975].

EXERCISES

Exercise 9.1　Programming in Mini-language L

In Exercise 3.2, we defined a program to compute the number of each digit required for typesetting a book. Solve this problem in Mini-language L, without using goto's.

Exercise 9.2　Mechanical Restructuring

It is often a tedious exercise to convert a program from one form into another, and about as much fun as maintaining someone else's program. But there are rewards, so here goes.

a. Take the program of Example 9.3, which contains cycle and exit statements, and construct its flowgraph.

b. Convert the flowgraph to D-structure form using the restructuring algorithm given with the Bohm and Jacopini proof in Chapter 5.

c. Take the flowgraph obtained after conversion and write the corresponding program.

d. Compare the program obtained in (c) with the program shown in Example 9.6.

Exercise 9.3　Use of Various Control Structures

In [Knuth 1974] there is a text processing example.
Suppose that we are processing a stream of text character by character and that we want to read and print the next character. However, if the character is a slash (/), we want to *tabulate* instead

(that is, to advance the output to the next tab-stop position on the current line); moreover, two consecutive slashes means a *carriage return* (that is, to advance the output to the beginning of the next line). After printing a period (.), we also want to insert an additional space in the output.

The following code adapted from Knuth clearly does the trick.

```
input X;

if (X = SLASH) then
    input X;
    if (X = SLASH) then
        return the carriage;
        goto DONE;
    else
        tabulate;
    end if;
end if;

output X;
if (X = PERIOD) then
    output SPACE;
end if;

DONE: ...
```

Write two other solutions to this program, one using only D or D'-structures and the other using only the control structures of Mini-language L (but without goto's).

In both cases, you should strive for the clearest possible program. You will probably find it best to start from the problem statement rather than to try to convert the above program. Finally, compare your solution with the one shown above.

Exercise 9.4   Use of Various Control Structures

The meaning of the informally expressed program shown below should be quite clear, even though it is unstructured.

```
Set MAX to N
If N <= 1 go to DONE
Set I to 1
```

```
LOOP:     Set J to 1
          Set FLAG to false

COMPARE:  If TABLE[J] < TABLE[J+1] go to INC
          Set TEMP to TABLE[J]
          Set TABLE[J] to TABLE[J+1]
          Set TABLE[J+1] to TEMP

INC:      Set J to J+1
          If J < MAX go to COMPARE
          If FLAG is false go to DONE
          Set I to I + 1
          Set MAX to MAX-1
          If I < (N+1) go to LOOP

DONE:     Exit
```

a. Rewrite this program using only the control structures of Mini-language D. To do this you may need additional boolean variables. Preserve the form of the algorithm as much as possible.

b. Rewrite the program using only the control structures of Mini-language L, but no goto's. Again, preserve the form of the original algorithm as much as possible.

c. Write the clearest functionally equivalent program to the given program, using any control structures you wish. The form of the original algorithm may be changed provided that the new version performs the same net computation. If you feel that cycle and exit statements will help you to produce the clearest program, then use them.

Exercise 9.5   The Zahn Control Structure

The Zahn control structure [see Knuth 1974] is a loop to be repeated until one of a number of events occurs.   When this happens, the loop is terminated. Exit from the loop invokes a specific action determined by the event that caused the exit. A possible syntax for this in Mini-language L would be:

```
zahn-statement ::=    loop until event [or event]...
                          begin
                              statement...
                          end;
                      then
                          event => statement...
                          [ event => statement... ]...
                      end loop;

loop-statement ::=    event ;
                 |    statement

event           ::=    identifier
```

Write a program to solve the Qualified Name problem given in Section 9.4 using Mini-language L extended to include the Zahn structure.

Lecture, 11/17
11/22 pg3

Exercise 9.6 Environment

pg264

In Section 9.5 we describe the semantics of the goto statements and label values. The exact behavior of the program shown in Example 9.6 depends on the way in which the environment component of a label is defined. There are several possible definitions for this, for example:

pg267

E1. The environment component of a label value consists of a snapshot of the environment made at the time of the assignment of a label value to a variable. This snapshot records the locations and values of all identifiers in the environment and is used to reestablish the environment when a goto statement is executed.

E2. The label value has no environment component. The environment that exists following the execution of a goto statement is the current environment of the statement to which control is transferred.

E3. The environment upon exit from the block containing the label value assignment to the environment is established by the goto statement.

pg267

Execute the program shown in Example 9.6 under each of these definitions. Comment on the implementation consequences of each.

Great care must be exercised to be assured of correct results. Unusual things could happen

10
Definition of New Data Types

thru 292

A high level programming language seeks to develop tools that represent the objects and operations of an application properly. Different areas of application, for example, data processing, graphics, operations research, or text preparation, require abstractions through data types that are not directly available in general purpose languages like Fortran, PL/I, or Basic. With these languages, the programmer must make *mental* associations between the objects and operations of the application's real world and the structured data objects that represent them in the program.

To make application programming easier, special purpose languages have often been developed to suit some well-defined application area, such as machine tool control. This approach has the drawback that, because of limitations on the size of a language, not all the objects and operations that would be potentially useful in writing programs for a single application area can be included in the language. More importantly, almost every application involves more than one application domain, and planning to live with any predetermined number of special purpose features will restrict the usefulness of the language.

Another approach has been taken in the more recent languages such as Pascal, Simula 67, Algol 68, Euclid, Alphard, Clu, and Ada. To various extents, these languages enable the application programmer to define particular abstract objects and operations, that is, to define

275

new data types. The application program can then be written using newly defined types and their operations. In essence, the programmer can create a dialect of the original language that more closely matches the application.

In this chapter, the beginnings of a user-defined type mechanism is explored using Mini-language Typedef. This mechanism is like that provided in Pascal. Important extensions of this facility available in other languages are then discussed.

10.1   MINI-LANGUAGE TYPEDEF

The syntax of Mini-language Typedef is given in Table 10.1. Mini-language Typedef has many features similar to the Mini-languages presented in previous chapters. As with previous Mini-languages, a program in Typedef consists of a declarative part followed by a sequence of statements.

All identifiers in a Typedef program must be declared exactly once. There are two kinds of declarations, type declarations and variable declarations. A variable declaration associates one or more identifiers with the type integer or with a type that has been defined in a type declaration. Integers have the usual meaning and operations.

The statements in Mini-language Typedef are quite straightforward. In an assignment statement, the variable and the expression must have the same type.

The major item of interest in Mini-language Typedef, however, lies in the declaration of new types. For example, we may have:

```
type DAY:  (MON, TUE, WED, THU, FRI, SAT, SUN);
type COIN: (PENNY, NICKEL, DIME, QUARTER, HALF_DOLLAR, DOLLAR);
```

The first declaration introduces a type named DAY. Just as we can say

```
declare COUNTER: integer;
```

to declare a variable COUNTER of type integer, we can say

```
declare TODAY:    DAY;
declare NEW_COIN: COIN;
```

to declare a variable TODAY of type DAY and also a variable NEW_COIN of type COIN.

Similarly, just as a variable of type integer can only take integer values, a variable of type DAY can only take one of the seven values

Table 10.1   Mini-language Typedef

```
program                 ::=   program
                                  type-declaration...
                                  variable-declaration...
                              begin
                                  statement...
                              end;
```

type-declaration   ::=   `type identifier : type-definition ;`

variable-declaration   ::=   `declare identifier [ , identifier ]... : type ;`

type   ::=   `integer` | type-definition | identifier

type-definition   ::=   enumeration-type | range | array-type

enumeration-type   ::=   (identifier [, identifier]...)

range   ::=   value .. value

value   ::=   integer | identifier

array-type   ::=   `array [ range ] of` identifier

```
statement               ::=   assignment-statement | loop-statement
                            | if-statement | input-statement
                            | output-statement
```

assignment-statement   ::=   `variable := expression ;`

```
if-statement            ::=   if comparison then
                                  statement...
                            [ else
                                  statement... ]
                              end if;
```

```
loop-statement          ::=   while comparison loop
                                  statement...
                              end loop;
```

input-statement   ::=   `input variable [ , variable ]... ;`

output-statement   ::=   `output variable [ , variable ]... ;`

comparison   ::=   (operand comparison-operator operand)

expression   ::=   [operand arithmetic-operator] operand

```
operand                 ::=   integer | identifier | variable | (expression)
                            | succ( expression ) | pred( expression )
```

variable   ::=   identifier | identifier [expression]

arithmetic-operator   ::=   + | – | * | div

comparison-operator   ::=   < | = | ≠ | >

MON through SUN. In this language, type describes a class of values. The two types introduced above are called *enumeration types* since the type declarations explicitly enumerate the class of values.

One of the properties of every enumeration type is that the values are ordered. In particular, the values are assumed to be enumerated in increasing order. For the type DAY, the first value is MON, the last is SUN.

As emphasized in Chapter 6, a data type implies more than a class of values. There is also a class of operations that can be performed on the values. In Typedef, the operations for an enumeration type are predefined by the language. Variables declared with the new types behave much like variables declared of type integer. They can be assigned to variables of the same type and have values assigned to them from constants belonging to that class of values. For example, we may have

```
TODAY    := MON;
NEW_COIN := NICKEL;
```

but not:

```
SUN   := MON;     -- only variables can be assigned values
TODAY := 1;       -- types do not match
TODAY := NICKEL;  -- types do not match
```

Variables of the same type can be compared with each other and with values of the type. Thus if variable TODAY has the value MON, we may have the following comparisons:

```
(TODAY = TUE)   -- comparison is false
(TODAY ≠ FRI)   -- comparison is true
```

However, the arithmetic operators can only operate on integer values and are not available for variables of enumeration values. The operators +, – and * are conventional; the div operator provides integer division.

The functions succ and pred are two predefined operations that only apply to enumeration values. They yield respectively the next and previous values of an enumeration value in the declared ordering. For a given enumeration type, the first value in the type definition has no predecessor, and the last value has no successor. For example, we can have the expressions

```
succ(MON)        -- value is TUE
succ(succ(MON))  -- value is WED
```

but not:

```
succ(SUN)     -- value is undefined
pred(TODAY)   -- undefined, value of TODAY is MON
```

The input and output facilities of Mini-language Typedef also apply to values of enumeration types. When applied to an enumeration variable, an input statement gets the next item in the input stream, checks that it is the character representation for a value of the enumeration type of the variable, and sets this value to the corresponding variable. Similarly, an output statement prints the character representation corresponding to the enumeration value of the variable.

Finally, for simplicity, an identifier can only appear in one enumeration type. Thus the pair of declarations

```
type TRAFFIC_LIGHT: (RED, AMBER, GREEN);
type FLAG_COLOR:    (RED, WHITE, BLUE);
```

is not allowed.

Restricted sequences or subranges of both integer and enumeration types can be defined by a range type. A range is specified by its *bounds*, its lowest and highest values. The purpose of range types is to control the set of values that a variable may take during execution. For example, we may have:

```
type YEAR_NUM  : 1776..2001;
type COLUMN_POS: 1..72;
type WEEKDAY   : MON..FRI;         How does system know this
type WEEKEND   : SAT..SUN;
```

Both the lower and upper bounds of a range must be of the same type and must be stated in increasing order.

The operations that are valid over variables of a range are those of the type of its bounds. For example, the following range definitions are illegal:

```
type A: 1..PENNY;        -- bounds not of the same type
type B: DOLLAR..PENNY;   -- bounds not in increasing order
```

A range type is thus characterized by three properties: *Range Characteristics*

■   *The containing type:* For instance, the containing type of YEAR_NUM is integer; the containing type of WEEKDAY is DAY.

■   *The bounds of the range:* For instance, 1776 and 2001 are the bounds for the type YEAR_NUM.

■   *The range size:* This is the number of elements in the range type. For instance, the range size of WEEKDAY is 5.

Variables of a range type are declared just as for variables of other types. Examples are:

```
declare WORK_DAY:  WEEKDAY;
declare THIS_YEAR: YEAR_NUM;
```

A range variable behaves much like a variable of the containing type. The only difference is that a range variable is constrained during execution to hold only scalar values that belong to the range. While the value of a range type is a subset of the containing type, the operations of a range type are those that are applicable to the containing type. Thus, the succ and pred functions, comparison operators, and input-output operations apply to range values exactly as they apply to values of the containing type. For range types whose containing type is integer, the arithmetic operators apply as well. In Typedef, expressions including variables and constants of various types are allowed, provided that operations are applied only to values for which the operation is defined. For instance, consider the following:

```
(TODAY = MON)   -- valid only if TODAY is of type DAY

X + Y           -- valid only if X and Y are of type integer
                -- or ranges thereof
```

The context in which expressions appear may require the result value to be restricted to a specified range. For example, the left side of an assignment statement may be a variable declared with a range constraint. In such assignments, the evaluation of the expression on the right must yield a value within the range of the variable. Any attempt to assign a value that lies outside of the declared range will result in an execution error. Examples of range variable assignments in Mini-language Typedef are:

```
WORK_DAY  := SUCC(TUE);    -- always valid
THIS_YEAR := THIS_YEAR + 50;  -- can lead to an execution error
```

In general, exceeding a declared range can only be detected during execution. However, it is important to note that sensible use of ranges allows system detection of range errors. Without a range specification, there would be no hint of wrong-doing until some doubtful results appear in the program output.

Finally, the types definable in Mini-language Typedef include array types. For example, we may declare the array variables

```
declare INPUT_VALUES: array [1..72] of integer;
declare COIN_VALUE   : array [PENNY..DOLLAR] of integer;
```

or alternatively, use:

```
type INPUT_LINE  : array [1..72] of integer;
type MONEY_VALUES: array [PENNY..DOLLAR] of integer;

declare INPUT_VALUE: INPUT_LINE;
declare COIN_VALUES: MONEY_VALUES;
```

As for range types, the bounds of an array type must belong to a declared enumeration type or to the predefined type integer.

The components of an array are denoted by naming the array and giving an expression specifying an individual element. For example, we may have:

```
INPUT_VALUE[2]     -- the second input value
INPUT_VALUE[I]     -- the I-th input value
COIN_VALUE[PENNY]  -- the value of the PENNY
```

Any attempt to use a subscript outside the bounds declared for the array variable results in an execution error.

As a simple illustration of the power of user-defined types, we present two example programs. Both perform the same transformation of data.

The first program is given in Example 10.1. This program uses typical language characteristics of languages without enumeration types and type definition mechanisms. The second program is given in Example 10.2. (The need to define a STOPPER in Example 10.2 is discussed in an exercise at the end of this chapter.)

These examples illustrate the basic idea that a program can introduce a type to describe a class of values needed for an application.

```
program

    -- This program reads in six integer values, respectively
    -- representing the number of pennies, nickels, dimes, quarters,
    -- half-dollars, and silver dollars in coinage.
    -- The program outputs the total value of the coins in dollars
    -- and cents.

    declare NEXT_COIN, COIN_COUNT, TOTAL_VALUE,
            NUM_CENTS, NUM_DOLLARS: integer;
    declare COIN_VALUE: array [1..6] of integer;

begin

    COIN_VALUE[1] :=   1;
    COIN_VALUE[2] :=   5;
    COIN_VALUE[3] :=  10;
    COIN_VALUE[4] :=  25;
    COIN_VALUE[5] :=  50;
    COIN_VALUE[6] := 100;

    TOTAL_VALUE := 0;

    NEXT_COIN := 1;

    while (NEXT_COIN ≠ 7) loop
       input COIN_COUNT;
       TOTAL_VALUE := TOTAL_VALUE + (COIN_VALUE[NEXT_COIN]*COIN_COUNT);
       NEXT_COIN := NEXT_COIN + 1;
    end loop;

    if (TOTAL_VALUE = 0) then
       output TOTAL_VALUE;
    else
       NUM_DOLLARS := TOTAL_VALUE div 100;
       NUM_CENTS   := TOTAL_VALUE - (NUM_DOLLARS*100);
       output NUM_DOLLARS, NUM_CENTS;
    end if;

end;
```

Example 10.1   Counting money

Read carefully

```
program
    -- This programs reads in six integer values, respectively
    -- representing the number of pennies, nickels, dimes, quarters,
    -- half-dollars, and silver dollars in coinage.
    -- This program outputs the total value of the coins in dollars
    -- and cents.

    type COIN:
          (PENNY, NICKEL, DIME, QUARTER, HALF_DOLLAR, DOLLAR, STOPPER);
    type MONEY_VALUES: array [PENNY..DOLLAR] of integer;

    declare COIN_COUNT, TOTAL_VALUE,
          NUM_CENTS,  NUM_DOLLARS: integer;
    declare NEXT_COIN : COIN;
    declare COIN_VALUE: MONEY_VALUES;
begin
    COIN_VALUE[PENNY]        :=   1;
    COIN_VALUE[NICKEL]       :=   5;
    COIN_VALUE[DIME]         :=  10;
    COIN_VALUE[QUARTER]      :=  25;
    COIN_VALUE[HALF_DOLLAR]  :=  50;
    COIN_VALUE[DOLLAR]       := 100;

    TOTAL_VALUE := 0;
    NEXT_COIN := PENNY;

    while (NEXT_COIN ≠ STOPPER) loop
       input COIN_COUNT;
       TOTAL_VALUE := TOTAL_VALUE + (COIN_VALUE[NEXT_COIN]*COIN_COUNT);
       NEXT_COIN := succ(NEXT_COIN);
    end loop;

    if (TOTAL_VALUE = 0) then
       output TOTAL_VALUE;
    else
       NUM_DOLLARS := TOTAL_VALUE div 100;
       NUM_CENTS   := TOTAL_VALUE - (NUM_DOLLARS*100);
       output NUM_DOLLARS, NUM_CENTS;
    end if;
end;
```

Example 10.2   Counting money using the type COIN

Read Carefully

10.2   TYPE DEFINITIONS

In Mini-language Typedef all programmer-defined types are introduced by type declarations of the form:

    type identifier : type-definition ;

The identifier specifies a name for the type. The type definition specifies the class of values and, implicitly, the operations defining ways in which the values can be used. Except for subranges of other defined types, every type definition introduces a distinct type.

   With this discussion in mind, we recall the basic definition of a type given earlier:

> A type characterizes a set of values *and* the set of operations that are applicable to the values.

   The type definitions given in Mini-language Typedef allow the specification of the set of values for a type, however, they do not allow for the specification of new operations that are particular to the type. We will return to this question later in the chapter. In programs written in statically typed languages, like Typedef, all variables have an associated type that is specified when the variable is declared.

   One of the key issues in programming is the certainty with which we can draw conclusions about a program. Consider the following declarations:

    declare TODAY   : DAY;
    declare NEW_COIN: COIN;
    declare COUNTER : integer;

It would be meaningful to have the statements,

    TODAY   := TUE;
    NEW_COIN := NICKEL;
    COUNTER := COUNTER + 1;

but not meaningful to have the statements:

    TODAY   := NICKEL;   -- NICKEL is not a day
    NEW_COIN := TUE;   -- TUE is not a coin
    COUNTER := TODAY + 1; -- addition is not legal for days

As a result of the use of the types DAY and COIN, the compiler enforces more restrictive type checking than is possible with only the primitive types of a language. There is thus a greater certainty that the program is correct, because there will be no violation of type properties during execution.

As mentioned earlier, an enumeration type is defined by enumerating its values. Such types can be used as freely as integers, and often with greater clarity. For example, we may declare a table itemizing the number of hours worked on each day of the week as:

```
HOURS_WORKED: array [MON..FRI] of integer;
```

Furthermore, we may have a loop iterating over Monday through Friday, as in:

```
CURRENT_DAY := MON;
while (CURRENT_DAY ≠ SAT) loop
   -- what to do for each value of CURRENT_DAY
   CURRENT_DAY := succ(CURRENT_DAY);
end loop;
```

Note the clarity of this loop compared with the following:

```
DAY_INDEX := 1;
while (DAY_INDEX ≠ 6) loop
   -- what to do for each value of DAY_INDEX
   DAY_INDEX := DAY_INDEX + 1;
end loop;
```

Table 10.2 shows the definition of a number of enumeration types. The use of such types can add considerably to the clarity of a program. However, the rather limited type definition mechanism of Typedef still has some problems. In particular, all enumeration types have an ordering forced on them even when, as in CONTROL_CHAR or COLOR, this ordering does not correspond to anything meaningful in the real world. Later we will see how more advanced languages can avoid this problem.

Table 10.2   A Sampler of Enumeration Types

```
type DAY:            (MON, TUE, WED, THU, FRI, SAT, SUN);

type COIN:           (PENNY, NICKEL, DIME, QUARTER,
                      HALF_DOLLAR, DOLLAR);

type DIRECTION:      (NORTH, EAST, SOUTH, WEST);

type OP_CODE:        (ADD, SUB, MUL, LDA, STA, STZ);

type HALF_DAY:       (AM, PM);

type FILE_STATUS:    (OPEN, CLOSED);

type ARMY_RANK:      (PRIVATE, CORPORAL, SERGEANT, LIEUTENANT,
                      CAPTAIN, MAJOR, COLONEL, GENERAL);

type CONTROL_CHAR:   (NULL, END_OF_TRANSMISSION, ENQUIRE, BELL,
                      BACKSPACE, LINE_FEED, CANCEL, ESCAPE);

type PEN_STATUS:     (DOWN, UP);

type SHAPE:          (TRIANGLE, QUADRANGLE, PENTAGON, HEXAGON);

type DRIVING_CODE:   (NORMAL, LIMITED, SPECIAL, VIP);

type COLOR:          (RED, BLUE, GREEN, BROWN);
```

10.3   DEFINITION OF STRUCTURED TYPES

The type definition mechanism for array types in Mini-language Typedef can be readily extended to include the type definition of record structures like those in Mini-language Type.

Record types are similar to record structured variables in Mini-language Type, in that records are used to model some composite entity in an application. The important difference is that record types enable the programmer to separate the abstraction process of representing a real world object by a collection of data items from the declaration of variables that reference the abstraction.

A record type can be defined by associating a new type name with a description of the fields in the record structure. A simple record type definition is given below:

```
type COMPLEX_INTEGER: record
                  REAL_PART: integer;
                  IMAG_PART: integer;
             end record;
```

The component types need not be restricted to the predefined types, such as integer, but may be any other type defined in a program. The following sequence of declarations is thus perfectly acceptable:

```
type MONTH_NAME: (JAN, FEB, MAR, APR, MAY, JUN,
                  JUL, AUG, SEP, OCT, NOV, DEC);

type YEAR_NUMBER: 1776..2001;

type DAY_NUMBER:  1..31;

type DATE: record
              MONTH: MONTH_NAME;
              DAY  : DAY_NUMBER;
              YEAR : YEAR_NUMBER;
           end record;
```

This set of declarations provides the basis on which the following are built:

```
type EMPLOYEE_NUM: integer;

type MARITAL_STATUS: (SINGLE, MARRIED, DIVORCED, WIDOWED);

type EMPLOYEE: record
                  ID   : EMPLOYEE_NUM;
                  STATUS: MARITAL_STATUS;
                  BORN : DATE;
                  HIRED : DATE;
               end record;
```

Note that in the last record type definition, the two fields **BORN** and **HIRED** are actually two record components of type **DATE**.

Just as for other types, variables may be declared as having a record type. Example record variable declarations are:

```
declare PERSON: EMPLOYEE;
declare BIRTH_DATE, TODAY: DATE;
```

One advantage of record type definitions, in this case, is that it is clear to the user that the variables **BIRTH_DATE** and **TODAY** have identical types, that is, identical structure and component types.

Just as for array type variables, record type variables inherit the operations for record types, for example, component selection. Thus **TODAY.MONTH** refers to the MONTH component of TODAY. In some languages, global operators, that is, operators that apply to the entire structure, are allowed. For example, if E and F have the same record type,

    (E = F)

will be true only if all corresponding components in E and F have identical values, and

    E := F;

will assign the value of F to E.

10.4   USER DEFINED OPERATORS AND TYPE ENCAPSULATION

Typedef

Mini-language Typedef embodies several of the basic ideas for a data type definition mechanism. However, the mini-language lacks some critical features that are available in several languages. These allow the programmer to exercise the full power of a type definition mechanism. They include the ability to define operations as part of the type definition and to make the type definition into a module that is separate from the program.

User Defined Operations

Consider a program that is manipulating data of the type DATE, defined in the previous section. Although the declaration part of the program shows that the program concerns *dates*, the executable part may contain statements such as

    TOMORROW.DAY := TODAY.DAY + 1;

and much of the abstraction is lost because it is written, not in terms of dates, but in terms of fields or components of a type named DATE. It is not clear to the reader that TOMORROW gets the right value during execution; all assignments to the individual fields of TOMORROW must be inspected. If for any reason the definition of the type named DATE has to be changed, the entire executable part of the program must be scanned for further changes. For large programs, this process is unreliable.

Suppose we want to rewrite this program in a manner that better emphasizes the abstraction of a *date.* What we would like to write is something like

```
input TODAY;
TOMORROW := NEXT_DATE(TODAY);
output TOMORROW;
```

In order to write such a program we need to be able to define a new operation, the function NEXT_DATE for a type DATE. This is not possible in Mini-language Typedef, where all operators are predefined. Instead, we need to program new operators for user-defined types, as well as for predefined types. This is part of the general principle of *type encapsulation*, that is, the packaging of operators and values to form a type. One method of encapsulating types is through a function and procedure facility. In our case, we need to be able to write a function that takes a DATE as an argument and returns a DATE as a result.

A function implementing the NEXT_DATE operator for DATE might read:

```
function NEXT_DATE(D: DATE) return DATE:
   declare NEXT: DATE;
begin
   NEXT.DAY := NEXT_DAY(D);
   if (NEXT.DAY < D.DAY) then
      NEXT.MONTH = NEXT_MONTH(D.MONTH);
   else
      NEXT.MONTH = D.MONTH;
   if (NEXT.MONTH < D.MONTH) then
      NEXT.YEAR := D.YEAR + 1;
   else
      NEXT.YEAR := D.YEAR;
   return NEXT;
end;
```

It is only during the writing of an operator such as this that the actual structure of the type DATE needs to be defined. The operator NEXT_DATE is defined through the use of the operators NEXT_DAY and NEXT_MONTH over the field types. The definition of the structure of DATE is paralleled by the definition of its NEXT_DATE operator.

An alternative approach would be for it to be possible to define an infix operator, such as +, to mean adding a number of elapsed days to a date to get a new date. So, instead of using the operator NEXT_DATE, we could write:

```
TOMORROW := TODAY + 1;
```

This would mean defining another type of overloading to the + operator. This might be done with a definition of the form:

```
operator + (DAY: DATE, INCREMENT: integer) return DATE:
   -- body of operator
end;
```

Note that this does not define a + operator between two dates, which does not correspond to reality, but between a DATE value and an integer value. In order to permit an expression of the form,

```
1 + TODAY
```

a companion operator,

```
operator + (INCREMENT: integer, DAY: DATE) return DATE:
begin
   return (DAY + INCREMENT);
end
```

would also have to be defined.

Complete Type Encapsulation

By careful programming, knowledge of a type representation can be restricted to its own operators, as indicated above. Such practice makes a program easier to understand and maintain.

Although use of functions and procedures can provide good facilities for abstractions, it does not guarantee the integrity of these abstractions. Nothing prevents a main program from accessing the fields of a DATE and changing them arbitrarily. This may be convenient, but it may also lead to serious troubles. For instance, the main program could set a date variable to the thirty-first day of February, which is not a valid date. Furthermore, it is not known how the operations over a date would behave on such data, since they were written with real dates in mind. Programming errors of this kind can be especially difficult to correct. Thus, some safeguards are needed to preserve the integrity of these abstractions.

In Ada (most notably), Alphard, Euclid, and Clu the definition of a data representation for a new type and the definition of new operations are grouped in a program module. This module can be separated from the main program, and thus the representation can be "hidden" from the main program. The module includes specifications of what can be known about itself from outside of the module. Some parts of the data type representation may remain private to the module and be used exclusively for internal computations needed to implement the operations. Similarly, operations needed to implement the visible operations may be hidden from the user.

For example, consider Example 10.3 where the type DATE is sketched as an Ada *package*. The only items that may be known outside of the package are declared in the module header, in the span of the text between the package and private keywords. That is, the type name DATE, and the fact that the operator NEXT_DATE takes a DATE value and returns a DATE value. Note that the internal representation of type DATE is kept private to the package. A user cannot make use of the fact that a date may be represented by a record structure and cannot access any field of a DATE.

The combination of information-hiding mechanisms with data type definition mechanisms promotes abstraction by enforcing a clear separation between type implementation and type usage. This separation represents a clear conceptual advantage for program design. It also facilitates validation and maintenance. Changes in a data type representation need only affect the type definition module, while changes to the main program or to other modules remain localized.

```
package D is
    type DATE is private;
    function NEXT_DATE(D: DATE) return DATE;
private
    type DATE is
        record
            -- internal structure of a date that is
            -- kept hidden in the module
        end record;
end;

package body D is
    -- local declarations and types

    function NEXT_DATE(D: DATE) return DATE is
        ...
    end;

    -- definition of other operations
begin
    -- code to initialize data abstractions
end;
```

Example 10.3   An Ada package

The preceding paragraphs have sketched a type definition mechanism combining the type definition facility of Typedef, a function and procedure facility, modular grouping, and information hiding mechanisms. Some languages implement this scheme to various degrees. Pascal and Algol 68 lack the module and information control facilities. Pascal lacks the means of defining operators. Simula 67 provides a powerful modular facility called a "class" but access to module components cannot be restricted. Alphard, Clu, Euclid, and Ada offer all the abstraction mechanisms described above. However, these languages differ in the extensions and complexities of the basic mechanism.

Conclusion

Type definition mechanisms enable the user to bring the programming environment closer to the application than many languages usually allow. The early stages of program design may require more effort and discipline to select the abstractions of applications that need to be implemented in order to solve the application problem. However, when compared to other languages, languages with type definition mechanisms promote the development of self-documenting code and security. The clear separation between the definition and use of a type facilitates validation and maintenance of programs.

FURTHER READING

Of the topics treated in this text, few have received more attention in the literature than the idea of abstract data types and the definition of new types.

A key work in this area is [Hoare 1972]. This work discusses both the notion of simple types as well as composite types. The properties of types are well expressed in the work [Guttag 1977].

In the area of type encapsulation facilities, there are numerous relevant works. The early work [Liskov and Zilles 1976] discusses a model for type definitions. Other related works are [Mailloux 1968] and [Demers et al. 1977].

A good discussion of some of the problems in the area of data abstraction can be found in [Gries and Gehani 1977].

Of all of the language facilities for encapsulated types, the design of the package facility in Ada clearly stands out. The rationale for this design is given in [Ichbiah et al. 1979].

EXERCISES

See 11/22/82 pg 2

Exercise 10.1 The Stack Data Type

277

Define an extension to Mini-language Typedef that adds a stack structure to the base language in the same way that an array is part of the language. This definition should include the operations that are to be available in the language for access and manipulation of stacks. *Look Up 370 Notes for Stacks*

Exercise 10.2 Programming Using Type Definitions

Complete the program sketched in Example 10.3 in one of the following languages: Pascal, Simula 67, Algol 68, Euclid, Alphard, Clu, or Ada.

Exercise 10.3 Enumerated Types

In Section 10.2 we show a program fragment for performing a computation by iterating over the days of the week:

```
CURRENT_DAY  :=  MON;
while (CURRENT_DAY ≠ SAT) loop
   -- what to do for each value of CURRENT_DAY;
   CURRENT_DAY  :=  SUCC(CURRENT_DAY);
end loop;
```

If we attempt to modify this program to iterate over Monday through Sunday, a problem arises. Describe this problem. A rather unsatisfactory solution to the problem is the use of STOPPER in the definition of the type COIN in Example 10.2. Propose changes to Mini-language Typedef that would avoid this problem entirely.

Exercise 10.4 Definitions of Record Types

Write down the context-free productions needed to add the record type definitions like those given in Example 10.3 to Mini-language Typedef.

Exercise 10.5   "Extensible" Languages

Opinions differ on what *extensible* means when applied to programming languages. At the trivial level only simple text substitution is allowed, while the very ambitious allow elaborate new data types and operations on them to be defined.

Describe what you feel an extensible language should offer. Aim for an intermediate level of complexity between the two extremes: simple enough for competent programmers to understand and use without heroic efforts, yet complex enough to add nontrivial power and capability to the language.

Illustrate your ideas with examples showing the syntax and semantics of your extensions. Your ideas must be implementable without recourse to magic, but do not describe implementation strategy. You may assume that the base language has a reasonable assortment of data types and control structures, that is, that one can write nontrivial programs in the base language without extending it.

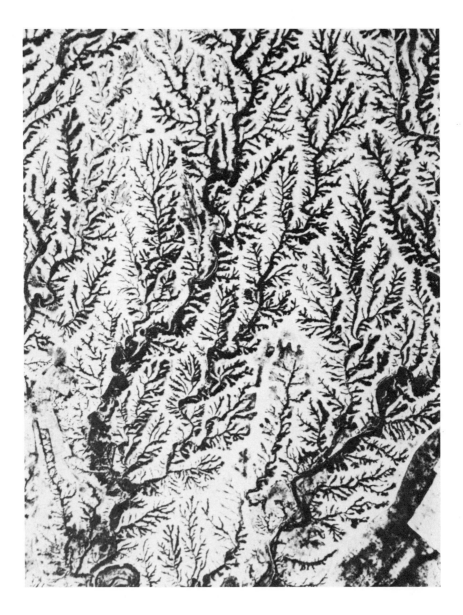

11
An Applicative Language: Functions and Recursion

Thru 323

We now turn to a mini-language that is very different from the other mini-languages given in this text. This mini-language is devoted to functions and their application to produce values. Perhaps the most striking feature of this mini-language is the absence of commands, for example, assignment and repetition, that are common to the other mini-languages.

The material in this chapter has roots from several sources. The most notable is the programming language Lisp. Other roots are the work of Landin [1965] and the lambda-calculus [Church 1941].

11.1 MINI-LANGUAGE APPLY

A program in Mini-language Apply consists of an expression, optionally followed by a sequence of function definitions. The syntax of the language is defined in Table 11.1.

Execution of the program consists of evaluation of an expression and the printing of its value. This may involve invocation of the functions specified by the function definitions.

A function definition associates a name with a function that maps one or more arguments into a single value. Within the function definition, the arguments are denoted by identifiers. The value returned by the function is specified by an expression. The expression may contain identifiers denoting the parameters of the function and references to other functions. All functions referenced must either be explicitly defined or be built-in functions of the language.

For example, consider the function definition:

```
where DOUBLE(X) is
    X + X
```

This definition specifies a function named DOUBLE. The function has one parameter, denoted by the identifier X. The value returned by the function is the sum of X and X. Execution of the simple program

```
program
    DOUBLE(6) + 3
    where DOUBLE(X) is
        X + X
end
```

will cause the application of the function DOUBLE to the argument 6 and add 3 to the result. Finally, the number 15 is printed.

Expressions

The expressions in Mini-language Apply are of two varieties: simple expressions, whose values can be computed directly, and selector expressions, whose values depend on the truth of one or more conditions. The value of an expression is either an integer, one of the truth values, true or false, or a list of integer values. A special value null denotes a list with no components. For example, we may have the following simple expressions:

```
6           -- an integer
true        -- a truth value
'1,2,3,4'   -- a list with four integers
null        -- the empty list
```

Table 11.1   Mini-language Apply

program	::=	program
		    expression
		    [function-definition]...
		    end

function-definition	::=	where identifier (identifier [,identifier]...)is expression
expression	::=	simple expression
	|	selector-expression
simple expression	::=	[operand +]... operand
	|	[operand -]... operand
	|	[operand *]... operand

selector-expression	::=	select
		    condition => expression
		    [condition => expression]...
		    [else => expression]
		    end select

condition	::=	function-application | comparison
comparison	::=	(operand comparison-operator operand)
operand	::=	identifier | integer
	|	truth-value | integer-list
	|	function-application | (expression)
function-application	::=	function-name(expression [,expression]...)
function-name	::=	identifier
	|	first | last | tail
	|	stem | append | length
integer-list	::=	null | ' integer [, integer]... '
truth-value	::=	true | false
comparison-operator	::=	< | = | ≠ | >

Values can also be computed through the application of a function to arguments. For example, we may have:

```
DOUBLE(1)                -- a simple function application
DOUBLE(1) + DOUBLE(2)   -- an addition of two computed values
```

Assuming that the function named DOUBLE is as specified above, these expressions have the values 2 and 6 respectively.

A number of functions are predefined within the language. These functions are given as follows:

Predefined Functions

1. `first` — This function takes a list as an argument and returns the first component of the list. If the list is empty, an execution error results.

2. `last` — This function takes a list as an argument and returns the last component of the list. If the list is empty, an execution error results.

3. `tail` — This function takes a list as an argument and returns the list obtained from the argument by removing its first component. If the argument is a list with one component or is empty, the empty list is returned as a result.

4. `stem` — This function takes a list as an argument and returns a list obtained from the argument by removing the last component of the list. If the argument is a list with one component or is empty, the empty list is returned as a result.

5. `append` — This function takes two arguments, a list and an integer, and returns a list constructed by appending the given integer to the end of the given list. If the first argument is an empty list, the value of the function is a list consisting of a single element, the second argument.

6. `length` — This function takes a single argument, a list, and returns an integer, whose value is the number of elements in the given list.

Table 11.2 illustrates the application of each of these functions to various arguments.

As mentioned above, within the body of a function definition, an identifier is used to denote the value of a parameter. For example, we

Table 11.2 Examples of Application of the Predefined Functions

Expression	Value
first ('1,2,3,4')	1
first ('5')	5
first (null)	*error*
last ('1,2,3,4,5')	5
last ('5')	5
last (null)	*error*
tail ('1,2,3,4,5')	'2,3,4,5'
tail ('5')	null
tail (null)	null
stem ('1,2,3,4,5')	'1,2,3,4'
stem ('5')	null
stem (null)	null
append ('1,2,3,4', 5)	'1,2,3,4,5'
append ('5', 1)	'5,1'
append (null, 1)	'1'
length ('1,2,3,4,5')	5
length ('1')	1
length (null)	0

may have the expressions:

```
X + X            -- computes twice X
X + G(X+1)       -- computes X plus the result of G(X + 1)
tail(X)          -- computes the tail of a list
append(L, last(M)) -- appends a copy of the last element of
                 -- list M to the list L
```

The value of each of these expressions depends, of course, on the values of the arguments corresponding to the parameters X and M.

The second form of expression in Mini-language Apply is the selector expression consisting of a sequence of conditions, each associated with a corresponding expression. When a selector expression is evaluated, each of the conditions is evaluated in sequence until one of the conditions evaluates to true. When a true condition is found, the value of its associated expression is the value of the selector expression.

For example, consider the following selector expression:

```
select
    (X < Y) => 1
    (X = Y) => 2
    (X > Y) => 3
end select
```

Depending on whether X is less than, equal to, or greater than Y, the value of this expression will be respectively 1, 2, or 3.

Normally, a selector expression will be terminated by an else part. The expression following the else symbol is returned as the value of the expression if none of the previous conditions evaluates to true. For example, consider the following expression:

```
select
    (X > 5) => X
    else    => X + 1
end select
```

Here if X is greater than 5, the value of X itself is returned. Otherwise, the value of X + 1 is returned. Evaluation of a selector expression for which no condition is true results in an execution error.

The conditions forming a selector expression can be comparisons in which two operands are compared using one of the comparison operators. This is the case in the two examples given above. A condition can also be a function application where the value returned by the function is either true or false.

The body of a function may reference not only the names of other functions but also its own name. Thus a function may be defined recursively. This recursive invocation causes no problem. When the body of a function is evaluated, evaluation proceeds normally. If it happens that evaluation of the function body requires re-application of the function itself, the function is simply reapplied to the new arguments before the evaluation of the initial application is completed.

Don't understand return true or false

Examples

Consider the program:

```
program                    3 + 6
    F(2) + F(6)
    where F(X) is
        select
            (X > 5) => X
            else    => X + 1
        end select
end
```

In the evaluation of the expression F(2) + F(6), the function F is invoked twice giving the values 3 and 6. ✓
In the example,

```
program
    G(3)
    where G(X) is
        select
            (X > 5) => X
            else    => X + G(X + 1)
        end select
end
```

G is a function defined recursively. If its parameter X is greater than 5, then the X is returned as the value of the function; otherwise, G is applied to the argument X + 1 and the value of this application is added to X. The evaluation of the expression G(3) gives the value 18. The evaluation process may be viewed as the following steps: ✓

Depth of Call	Value
0	G(3)
1	3 + G(4)
2	3 + 4 + G(5)
3	3 + 4 + 5 + G(6)
4	3 + 4 + 5 + 6

Thus the function G is called four times, and on the fourth call it returns the simple value 6. The final sum, 18, is the result of evaluating G(3). ✓

The next example,

Depth of Call	Value
0	Length ('1;2,3,4')
1	1 + Length ('2,3,4')
2	1 + 1 + Length ('3,4)
3	1 + 1 + 1 + Length (
4	1 + 1 + 1 + 1 + Length
5	1 + 1 + 1 + 1 + 0

4

```
program
   LENGTH('1,2,3,4')
   where LENGTH(L) is
      select
         (L = null) => 0
         else        => 1 + LENGTH(tail(L))
      end select
end
```

contains a definition of the function LENGTH, which is the same as the predefined function length. This shows that, even though the function length is predefined, it can also be defined in the language. The result of executing this program is 4. ✓

The name of a function may also be used as an argument to another function. Consider the following example:

```
program
   G(DOUBLE, 2) + G(TRIPLE, 3)

   where G(P, X) is
      P(X) + P(1)

   where DOUBLE(X) is
      X + X

   where TRIPLE(X) is
      X + X + X
end
```

Here the function G has two parameters, P and X. It returns the value of an expression in which P is applied twice, once to X and once to the integer 1. For correct execution, the argument, corresponding to the parameter P, must be the name of a function. In evaluating the expression

```
G(DOUBLE, 2) + G(TRIPLE, 3)
```

the function G is invoked twice. The parameter P takes on two different values, DOUBLE and TRIPLE. When the expression

```
P(X) + P(1)
```

is evaluated during the first invocation of G, it is the equivalent of evaluating

```
DOUBLE(2) + DOUBLE(1)
```
$2+2 \quad + \quad 2_{-1+1}$ $= 6$

and, in the second invocation, it is equivalent to:

```
TRIPLE(3) + TRIPLE(1)
```
$3+3+3 \quad 1+1+1$ $\dfrac{12}{18}$

The result of executing this program is 18.   ✓

11.2   FUNCTIONS

The dominant feature in Mini-language Apply is that a program is written entirely as the definition and application of functions. Functions have a long history in mathematics and it is from this concept that functions in programming languages have been developed.

A function f is a mapping or rule of correspondence between one object x, the *argument*, and another unique object y, the *value*, of the function. Thus we can say that f transforms x into y, or that y is the result of applying f to x. This is generally written:

$$y = f(x)$$

Generally, functions may only be applied to certain kinds of objects and will only produce certain kinds of objects as a result. The set of objects to which a function may be applied is the *domain* of the function. The set of objects that can result from the application is the *range* of the function. In describing a function, it is common to specify the types of the domain and range. For example

```
DOUBLE:   integer  →  integer
length:   list  →  integer
append:   list, integer  →  list
```

specify the types of the functions DOUBLE, length, and append.

Operations used in expressions are also functions. Thus an alternative notation for writing the expression

```
A + B
```

would be:

```
+ (A, B)
```

In Mini-language Apply, the type of the + operator is:

```
+: integer, integer → integer
```

The type of a function in Mini-language Apply is not defined explicitly in a declare statement as in other mini-languages. Nevertheless, a mismatch of types will lead to an execution error. For example, if the function G defined by

```
where G(P, X) is
    P(X) + P(1)
```

were invoked by the expression

```
G(1, 2)
```

there would be an execution error when the parameter P was applied to the parameter X, because the constant 1 is an integer, not the name of a function.

One of the fundamental and useful properties of using pure functions is a principle generally known as *referential transparency*. Given an expression of the form

$$F(X_1, X_2, ..., X_n)$$

where F is a function and X_1 through X_n denote arguments, we can always replace the expression by a value. The replacement of the expression by its value is entirely independent of the context in which the function application appears. For example, given the definition of DOUBLE shown earlier, an expression including

```
... DOUBLE(2) + DOUBLE(3) ...
```

may be directly replaced by the value 10, no matter what context surrounds the expression. Even when an expression appears with identifiers denoting arguments, for example

```
DOUBLE(X)
```

we may still perform the same abstraction. That is, the above expression always returns a value that is twice its argument. With the property of referential transparency, all we need to know in order to abstract the value of an expression is knowledge of the values of its components. This property is true of all of the examples in Mini-language Apply.

The two major differences between programming in a conventional procedural language like Cobol or Pascal and in an applicative language are: *Δ between Pascal & Applicative Language*

■ The applicative language has no concept of sequence of operations or flow of control. The whole program execution consists of the evaluation of an expression.

■ The applicative language has no assignment statement. Values are communicated entirely through the use of parameters.

To illustrate the difference between programming in a procedural language and programming in an applicative language, we consider the well-known problem of writing a program to solve the *Eight Queens problem*.

Eight Queens Problem

The Eight Queens problem is stated as follows. We wish to write a program to determine an arrangement of eight queens on a standard chessboard in such a way that no queen can capture any other. A chessboard can be viewed as an 8 by 8 array of squares, and one queen can capture another if they are both in the same row, same column, or on the same diagonal.

For example, consider:

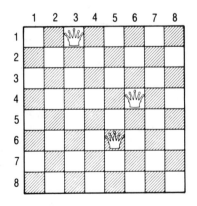

The queen in row 1, column 3, board[1, 3] can capture any other queen in row 1 or column 3. She can also capture the queen in board[4, 6]

because they are on the same diagonal. The queen in board[6, 5] cannot be captured by either of the other queens. We wish our program to indicate either that no solution is possible, or to find one of the possible configurations in which the eight queens can be placed.

The straightforward approach would be for the program to form every possible way of arranging eight queens on the board and testing each of these as a solution. The difficulty with this approach is the large number of trials that must be made. There are about $4.4*10^9$ ways of placing eight queens on the board, and if we assume that we can generate and check a possible solution in 100 microseconds, it will take about 122 hours to check every possibility. It is obviously necessary to find a shortcut. Our solution, based on [Wirth 1971], is designed to reduce time by eliminating impossible arrangements before they are fully generated.

First of all, we eliminate all configurations with more than one queen in any column. The strategy is to start by placing a queen at board[1, 1]. Since this queen is the only one, she is safe. The next step is to find a safe position in column 2 where the second queen can be placed. Another queen is placed at board[1, 2]. Since this queen can be attacked, the row number is incremented by 1 and the queen is tested on that square. This process continues, successively advancing a queen until a safe position in a column is found. If a configuration arises in which no queen can be placed safely in a given column, the queen already positioned in the previous column is advanced to the next row. The entire process is continued until a complete configuration is found.

One small point: two queens lie on the same downward diagonal if the difference between the row and column coordinates is the same. Similarly, two queens lie on the same upward diagonal if the sum of their row and column positions are identical.

A solution to the eight queens problem in the procedural language Pascal is given in Example 11.1. In this solution an array named CONFIGURATION is used to store the row positions of the queens safely placed in each of the columns 1 through 8.

Boolean valued arrays are also introduced. For each column 1 through 8, the array SAFEROW has the value TRUE or FALSE depending on whether the given row has another queen positioned somewhere in the same row. Similarly, each entry of the arrays SAFEDOWNDIAG and SAFEUPDIAG has the value TRUE or FALSE according to whether another queen exists on the corresponding upward or downward diagonal.

In the program in Example 11.1, assignment is used to set the components of the arrays describing the status of the board. Notice also that looping statements are used to iterate over the various board configurations. Finally, notice that the procedures and functions used in this program employ a number of global variables, in this case, the variables describing the status of the board.

A substantially different solution to the Eight Queens problem is given in Example 11.2. This solution to this problem is written using Mini-language Apply. Notice here that there is no use of assignment, no looping control structures, and no global variables. Rather, the solution consists of a single expression

```
QUEENS('1')
```

followed by a sequence of function definitions.

In this program, the board configuration is represented by a list of integers giving the row positions of the queens safely placed in each column that has been processed. The initial invocation of QUEENS is with an integer list that represents the first step toward a solution, placing the queen in the first column in row 1. This list is similar to the array CONFIGURATION in Example 11.1.

The solution of Example 11.2 compares quite favorably with the Pascal solution, despite the meager facilities of Mini-language Apply. Both programs find the same board configuration as their solution to the problem:

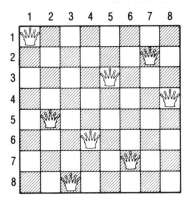

Functions in a Procedural Language

You may have noticed the use of a function in the Pascal solution to the eight queens problem. The function, ISSAFE, is a function in the same sense as those used in Mini-language Apply. Generally, however, the

```
program QUEENS (INPUT, OUTPUT);
   var I,
       ROW, COL:  INTEGER;
       CONFIGURATION: array [ 1 .. 8 ] of INTEGER;
       SAFEROW      : array [ 1 .. 8 ] of BOOLEAN;   Safe to put a Queen On
       SAFEDOWNDIAG : array [-7 .. 7 ] of BOOLEAN;
       SAFEUPDIAG   : array [ 2 .. 16] of BOOLEAN;
procedure CLEARTHEBOARD;
   var  I: INTEGER;
begin
   for I := 1 to 8 do
      SAFEROW[I] := TRUE;
   for I := -7 to 7 do
      SAFEDOWNDIAG[I] := TRUE;
   for I := 2 to 16 do
      SAFEUPDIAG[I] := TRUE
end;
procedure SETQUEEN(ROW, COL);
begin
   SAFEROW[ROW]             := FALSE;
   SAFEDOWNDIAG[ROW - COL] := FALSE;
   SAFEUPDAIG[ROW + COL]   := FALSE;
   CONFIGURATION[COL]       := ROW
end;
procedure REMOVEQUEEN(ROW, COL);
begin
   SAFEROW[ROW]             := TRUE;
   SAFEDOWNDIAG[ROW - COL] := TRUE;
   SAFEUPDIAG[ROW + COL]   := TRUE;
   CONFIGURATION[COL]       := 0
end;
procedure ISSAFE(ROW, COL): BOOLEAN;
begin
   if SAFEROW[ROW] and SAFEDOWNDIAG[ROW - COL]
   and SAFEUPDIAG[ROW + COL] then
      ISSAFE := TRUE
   else
      ISSAFE := FALSE
end;
```

Example 11.1   Pascal solution to the Eight Queens problem

```
begin
   CLEARTHEBOARD;
   COL := 1;
   ROW := 1;

   repeat
      while (ROW < 9) and (COL < 9) do
         if ISSAFE(ROW, COL) then
            begin
               SETQUEEN (ROW, COL);
               COL := COL + 1;
               ROW := 1
            end
         else
            ROW := ROW + 1;

      if (ROW = 9) then
         begin
            COL := COL - 1;
            ROW := CONFIGURATION[COL];
            REMOVEQUEEN (ROW, COL);
            ROW := ROW + 1
         end
   until (COL = 9)

   for I := 1 to 8 do
      WRITE (CONFIGURATION[I])
end.
```

Example 11.1   continued

really, the

facility for functions in a procedural language is not quite so pure as that in Mini-language Apply. There are often three major differences:

Δ Functions in Apply & Other Procedural Languages

(1) In some languages, the value of the argument to the function may be altered during a call to the function.

(2) In most languages, execution of the body of the function may result in a change in the value of a variable that is global to the function body.

(3) In every language that we know of, the body of a function may reference variables whose values are global to the function body, even if they are not changed.

```
program
  QUEENS('1')
  where QUEENS(CONFIGURATION) is
    select
      IS_COMPLETE(CONFIGURATION)  => CONFIGURATION
      else                        => QUEENS(GET_ANOTHER(CONFIGURATION))
    end select
  where IS_COMPLETE(CONFIGURATION) is
    select
      (length(CONFIGURATION) = 8)  => IS_SAFE(CONFIGURATION)
      else                         => false
    end select
  where GET_ANOTHER(CONFIGURATION) is
    select
      (last(CONFIGURATION) = 9)   => ADVANCE(stem(CONFIGURATION))
      IS_SAFE(CONFIGURATION)      => START_NEW_COL(CONFIGURATION)
      else                        => ADVANCE(CONFIGURATION)
    end select
  where ADVANCE(CONFIGURATION) is
    append(stem(CONFIGURATION), (last(CONFIGURATION) + 1))
  where START_NEW_COL(CONFIGURATION) is
    append(CONFIGURATION, 1)
  where IS_SAFE(CONFIGURATION) is
    select
      (length(CONFIGURATION) = 0) => true
      else  => CHECK_NEW_QUEEN(stem(CONFIGURATION),
                               last(CONFIGURATION),
                               length(CONFIGURATION))
    end select
  where CHECK_NEW_QUEEN(CONFIGURATION, ROW, COL) is
    select
      (length(CONFIGURATION) = 0) => true
      POSSIBLE_CAPTURE(last(CONFIGURATION), length(CONFIGURATION),
                       ROW, COL) => false
      else => CHECK_NEW_QUEEN(stem(CONFIGURATION), ROW, COL)
    end select
  where POSSIBLE_CAPTURE(ATTACK_ROW, ATTACK_COL, ROW, COL) is
    select
      (ATTACK_ROW = ROW)                      => true
      ((ATTACK_ROW - ATTACK_COL) = (ROW - COL)) => true
      ((ATTACK_ROW + ATTACK_COL) = (ROW + COL)) => true
      else                                    => false
    end select
end
```

Example 11.2 Mini-language Apply solution to the Eight Queens

```
       REAL A, B, C, F, G
       COMMON A

          A = 10.0
          B = 3.0
10        C = F(B) + G(B)
          WRITE (2, 200) C

          A = 10.0
          B = 3.0
20        C = G(B) + F(B)
          WRITE (2, 200) C

200       FORMAT (F5.2)
       END


       REAL FUNCTION F(X)
       REAL A, X
       COMMON A
       A = A + 1.0
       F = A * X
       RETURN
       END


       REAL FUNCTION G(X)
       REAL A, X
       COMMON A
       A = A + 2.0
       G = A * X
       RETURN
       END
```

Example 11.3   Fortran functions with side effects

The first two properties allow functions with side effects to be written in procedural languages. That is, functions can change the value of variables that exist outside the function.

Example 11.3 demonstrates this problem with a very simple Fortran program. The expressions in the statements labeled 10 and 20 are identical except for the order in which the functions F and G are invoked.

Using a left-to-right evaluation, the values printed for C (72 and 75) are not the same. Here, the familiar commutative property of addition is lost because of the assignment to a global variable in COMMON.

Certainly many programmers would be surprised to learn that

    F(B) + G(B)

is not equivalent to:

    G(B) + F(B).

Since Fortran employs conventional mathematical notation, it is dangerous to write functions that violate the properties of established mathematical systems.

The case against side effects becomes even more severe when we need to modify a program. Change is a daily occurrence in programming. Someone may find a more efficient algorithm, an error may be detected, or revised specifications may be given. If a piece of code to be changed has side effects, then those effects must be accounted for. This requires delving deeply into the entire program for a clear understanding of what effects a function has on other parts of the program. Adding a few extra lines of code for that desirable change may kill the correctness of another piece of code. As a result, another change may be needed to right matters, and so on.

Even if this process succeeds, it is not likely to add to the clarity or flexibility of the program. Had the original program been written without side effects, the function could be changed *without* looking at the rest of the program.

In short, the design of a good facility for functions is an important part of most programming languages. Any deviation from their normal mathematical properties should be handled with great care.

11.3 RECURSION

We have already seen in this chapter an example of a recursive definition:

```
where LENGTH(L) is
   select
      (L = null) => 0
      else       => 1 + LENGTH(tail(L))
   end select
```

We have also seen recursive definitions in Chapter 2.

Loosely speaking, a recursive definition is one in which the object being defined is used as part of the definition. For example, the word *descendant* may be defined as:

A descendant of a person is an offspring or a descendant of an offspring of the person.

In this definition, *all* the descendants of the person are simply and precisely accounted for. A nonrecursive definition of descendant that attempts to take all possibilities into account is the following:

A descendant of a person is a son or daughter, or a grandson or granddaughter of the person, or a great-grandson or great-granddaughter of the person, etc.

In this case, the definition is longer than the recursive definition and avoids infinite length through the use of "etc." Dictionaries try to avoid obvious recursion by defining a descendant as:

One who has a specific person among one's ancestors.

However, an ancestor is defined as:

One from whom a person is descended.

Thus the recursion is still present, though indirectly.

It is unfortunate that recursion is so little understood in many programming circles. In Mini-language Apply, the idea is particularly important. All iteration is handled by recursion, since there is no flow of control. Mathematically, recursive definitions are often more succinct than iterative ones, and this applies in programming as well.

Consider, for example, the following Pascal function TOTAL, which takes a vector A and integer N as arguments and returns the sum of the first N elements of A:

```
function TOTAL(A: VECTOR;  N: INTEGER): INTEGER;
   var
      PARTIALSUM, I: INTEGER;
begin
   PARTIALSUM := 0;
   for I := 1 to N do
      PARTIALSUM := PARTIALSUM + A[I];

   TOTAL := PARTIALSUM
end;
```

The equivalent function in Mini-language Apply is as follows:

apply

```
where TOTAL(A, N) is
   select
      (N = 0)   => 0
      else      => first(A) + TOTAL(tail(A), N-1)
   end select
```

Here the array is represented by a list. The recursive definition in Apply is simpler because it avoids the use of the extra variables, such as PARTIALSUM and I.

Models for Recursion

There appear to be three predominant models for understanding recursion:

3 Predominant Models for understanding Recursion :

- ■ The replacement of recursion by an equivalent iteration.

- ■ The use of push-down stacks. This is often used in explaining the implementation of a programming language.

- ■ The mathematical concept of fixed points.

We believe that fixed points provide the clearest approach to understanding recursion.

A recursive definition has the form:

$$q = \ldots q \ldots q \ldots$$

Here we have a definition of some entity q in which the same entity q is used in the definition. In reality, such definitions do not define anything. Rather, they are *equations*, and there must exist some entity that when used for q satisfies the equation.

For example, consider the following recursive definitions:

1. $y = y^2 - 12$

2. identifier ::= letter | identifier letter

3. $L = (a, L)$

4.
```
where F(N) is
   select
      (N = 0)   =>  1
      else      =>  N * F(N - 1)
   end select
```

What are the "solutions" to these equations? The type of object defined depends on the defining equation:

1. the integers 4 and -3

2. the infinite set of identifiers { A B ... Z AA AB ... }

3. the infinite binary list (a, (a, (a, ...)))

4. the function for computing the factorial of its argument

Notice that in each case, the solution "satisfies" the equation.

In obtaining a solution to equation (4), we will treat F as representing an object, a function object, in just the same way that y in equation (1) represents an object, an integer object. The type of F is:

integer → integer

We are looking for some function that, when substituted for F, leaves it unchanged. Such a function is said to be a *fixed point* of the definition.

Let's try the function INCREMENT, which adds one to its argument, as a fixed point of the definition. By replacing F by INCREMENT in our equations, we have:

```
INCREMENT(N)
   =  select
          (N = 0) => 1
          else    => N * INCREMENT(N - 1)
      end select

   =  select
          (N = 0) => 1
          else    => N * N
      end select

   ≠  INCREMENT(N)
```

Thus INCREMENT is not a solution of the equation.

Now let's try the function FACTORIAL. We have:

```
FACTORIAL(N)
   =  select
          (N = 0) => 1
          else    => N * FACTORIAL(N - 1)
      end select

   =  FACTORIAL(N)
```

Thus FACTORIAL works and is a fixed point of the equation.

This view leads to an important point. In programming languages there are really no such entities as *recursive functions*. There are recursive definitions or equations whose solution yields a function. A function is a bona fide entity, and it is not *recursive*. Thus we should not say that F is a recursive function. Instead, we should say that the function F is defined recursively, and has a solution that is the factorial function. After all, the factorial function simply maps a number N into $N * (N - 1) * \ldots * 1$.

A Strange Function

To emphasize this last point, consider the program:

```
program
    F(14)
    where F(N) is
        select
            (N > 100) => N - 10
            else      => F(F(N + 11))
        end select
end
```

If we attempt to step through the execution of this program as it evaluates the expression F(14), we have:

```
F(14) = F(F(25)) = F(F(F(36))) = F(F(F(F(47)))) =  ...
```

There seems to be no way of getting the result easily.

Suppose we now approach the problem as one of finding the fixed point of the recursive definition. There are many functions that we could try without success. However, we will try, for no more logical reason than that we already know the answer, the function NINETY_ONE:

```
where NINETY_ONE(N) is
    select
        (N > 100) => N - 10
        else      => 91
    end select
```

Substituting this into the recursive definition of F, we have:

```
where
NINETY_ONE(N) is
   select
      (N > 100) => N - 10
      else      => NINETY_ONE(NINETY_ONE(N + 11))
   end select
```

Now

$$\text{NINETY\_ONE(NINETY\_ONE(N + 11))} \quad \text{for N} \le 100$$

is

$$\text{NINETY\_ONE(NINETY\_ONE(N))} \quad \text{for N} \le 111$$

which is always 91. Thus the NINETY_ONE function *is* a fixed point of the recursive definition of F. Hence the recursive definition was really a definition of the NINETY_ONE function. Now what is F(14)? Sure, 91.

At this point you may very well feel that this discussion only serves to verify that the function NINETY_ONE is, in fact, a fixed point of the recursive definition. While the preceding discussion will not in general help you to find the fixed point of a recursive definition, it does illustrate the idea of the fixed point, an important concept in *understanding* recursion.

Understanding Recursion

Consider, for example, the recursive definition:

```
where REVERSE(L) is
   select
      (L = null)     => null
      (length(L) = 1) => L
      else           => append(REVERSE(tail(L)), first(L))
   end select
```

If we read this definition, we know from its name that it has something to do with lists and putting their components in reverse order. Let us assume, for the moment, that the function does compute a list with its elements exactly in reverse order. Thus our first step in understanding recursion is to develop a clear mental picture of what we assume the definition defines.

Our second step is to test our mentally assumed fixed point against the definition at hand. To do this, we read the recursive definition and constantly test the definition against the assumed fixed point. In the above case, our thinking may go as follows:

a. If the parameter is null, then certainly its reverse is null, and thus the answer given in the recursive definition is correct, at least for this case.

b. If the parameter is a list of length 1, then the list has only one element and the reverse of the list is clearly itself. Thus, the recursive definition gives assumed fixed point in this case also.

c. Now for the real mental leap. If the list is not null and does not have one element, then the else clause applies. In this case, our definition calls on us to apply the reverse function to the tail of L. Assuming our fixed point is correct we can easily imagine reversing the second, third, and so on elements of L. Our definition then asks us to form a single list by appending the first element of L to the end of the list formed by reversing the tail of L. With a little thought, we see that this is exactly the reverse of a list with two or more elements.

Of course, our job is not complete. Having verified that our definition returns the correct answer in all cases stated in the definition, we must finally check that all of the possible input values are covered. In our case above, we see that lists of length zero and one are covered in the first two cases, and lists of two or more elements are covered by the else clause. Thus our definition is also complete.

Finally, note that the above discussion presents a model of recursion that can be interpreted statically, that is, without the need for simulating nested recursive calls or employing pushdown stacks.

11.4   FUNCTIONS AS OBJECTS

The definition of the function

```
where F(Y) is
     Y + 3
```

is really the equivalent of saying that:

F is the function of Y that is Y + 3

It is a declaration of the identifier F as having a constant meaning or value, just as the Mini-language Ref declaration

```
declare MAX_COL: integer constant = 72;
```

associates the identifier MAX_COL with a constant value.

We are familiar with the idea of functions having constant meanings, since that is how they generally appear in mathematics. In the expression

$$(x + y) * (x + z)$$

the x and y are regarded as variables that can take on a range of values. The operators + and * however, always have the same meaning, like the numerals 3, 5, or 7.

In most programming languages, functions are usually treated as restricted objects that can only be used in certain contexts. For example, in most languages functions cannot be passed as arguments to subroutines. This would be useful, for example, in writing a numerical integration routine where a parameter could be the function that calculates the value of the mathematical function being integrated.

Functions Whose Values Are Functions

We are familiar with functions whose values are integers, lists, or other simple values. We have already seen a function whose parameter is itself a function. We will now see how functions can have values that are functions in their own right.

The plus function is a function of two variables. Thus we can write (2 + X) as +(2,X). Suppose we introduce a new function +' that takes a single argument, for example, +'(2). The value of the function +' is defined to be a new function of a single argument that adds a constant to it. Thus, the value of +'(2) is a function that adds two to its argument. In other words, its value is the function:

```
X  →  X + 2
```

Similarly, the value of +'(5) is the function:

```
X  →  X + 5
```

The type of both functions is:

```
integer  →  integer
```

Hence the type of the function +ʹ is:

integer → (integer → integer)

With only a minor change to the syntax of the Mini-language Apply, we can write a definition of this function as follows:

```
where PLUS_PRIME(X) is
    G
    where G(Y) is
        X + Y
```

As part of our modification to Mini-language Apply, we now allow the expression in a function definition to refer to an identifier that does not occur in the parameter list. In the function G, the identifier X refers to the parameter of PLUS_PRIME, which contains G. Thus we have slyly introduced a kind of variable into Apply.

A variable, such as X, whose value is established outside the function definition is known as a *free variable* and corresponds to a global variable in procedural languages. A variable that is not a free variable is a parameter, also known as a *bound variable*.

Bound

The function PLUS_PRIME consists of a simple expression that names its internal function G. This function is the *value* returned by PLUS_PRIME. This is analogous with a function that consists of the simple expression 5. Evaluation of this function returns the integer object 5. In the case of PLUS_PRIME, it is a function object that is returned, one of the class of integer → integer function objects.

A function object consists of two parts, the body of the function that defines how to calculate the result, and a free variable list that provides the values needed to complete evaluation of the function body.

In the case of evaluating the expression

```
PLUS_PRIME(K)
```

we would have:

```
body:  K + Y
free variable list:   K
```

Here Y is the parameter of the function object. The free variable list of the function object corresponds to the environment part of a label value as described in Chapter 10.

Uses for Function Objects

We have already mentioned the use of parameters that are functions in numerical integration programs. Generalized sort routines can also use such parameters in order to obtain access to functions that compare and interchange the objects being sorted. In this way, the sort routine does not need to have the definition of the objects and can be used for any set of objects.

In artificial intelligence research, much work is being done to devise new ways of representing knowledge. While much can be done through records that contain conventional values, such as integers and character strings, in certain areas it is more convenient to represent knowledge as functions and procedures. For example, the representation of certain classes of patterns can best be done by executable functions that return a truth value that reports if the pattern has been recognized. The inclusion of such functions in a data base is an application of functions as data objects.

While certain languages already allow functions to be treated as objects, much research is still needed in this area.

FURTHER READING

The basis of Mini-language Apply is taken from Lisp [see McCarthy et.al. 1960]. More recent work on the applicative type of languages is contained in [Burge 1975, Backus 1978, and Henderson 1980].

A foundation work for treating functions as objects is the lambda-calculus. The original work [Church 1941] and the work in [Curry and Feys 1958] are definitive references on this topic, although certainly hard to read. Numerous applications of the lambda-calculus and derived formal systems can be found. The most famous of these is the work by Landin [1964]. Other implications are given in [Stoy 1977].

An interesting informal account of recursing and the application of function objects is given in [Hofstadter 1979].

EXERCISES

Exercise 11.1   Removing Duplicates from a List

In Mini-language Apply, a list can have duplicate elements, for example:

```
'1, 2, 3, 1, 2, 3, 4'
'2, 2, 3, 3, 2'
```

Write a function named REDUCE that takes a list as an argument and returns the list without duplicate elements. For example,

```
REDUCE('1, 2, 3, 1, 2, 3, 4')
```

has the value '1, 2, 3, 4' and

```
REDUCE('3, 2, 3, 3, 2')
```

has the value '3, 2'.

Exercise 11.2   Sorting — see 11/22/82 pg 4, Fair amount of frustration

Write a program in Mini-language Apply that will rearrange a list of integers into ascending order.

Exercise 11.3   Finding a Fixed Point

Consider the following definition:

```
where H(X) is
    select
        (X > 0) => 1 + H(X - 1)
        else    => 0
    end select
```

What is the fixed point of H? Once you find it, write a simpler definition of H.

Exercise 11.4   Self-Application

Is X(X) ever meaningful, that is, does it ever make sense to apply an object to itself?

Exercise 11.5   Ackermann's Function

Trace the execution of the following Apply program:

```
program
    ACKERMANN(2, 3)
    where ACKERMANN(M, N) is
        select
            (M = 0) => N + 1
            (N = 0) => ACKERMANN(M-1, 1)
            else     => ACKERMANN(M-1, ACKERMANN(M, N-1))
        end select
    end
```

Exercise 11.6   Applicative versus Conventional Languages

The nodes in a graph may be labeled with integers, and a connection from one node to another may be given as a pair of integers. In a graph with four nodes, the nodes may thus be denoted as 1, 2, 3, 4. A connection from node 1 to node 3 may be given as (1 3).

A graph is said to be connected if there is a path from each node to every other. Thus the connections

(1 2) (2 3) (3 4)

or

(1 3) (3 1) (2 4) (3 2)

describe a connected graph, whereas

(1 3) (3 1) (2 4)

does not.

Write one program in Mini-language Apply and another in a conventional language (for example, Fortran, Pascal, or Mini-language Typedef) to determine if a graph is connected. You may give the input data in any suitable form.

Enhancement

12
Input and Output

Input and output are generally found to be among the least satisfactory aspects of a programming language. This is probably because the clean abstract view of the world presented by a programming language must meet the practical compromises of the real world. In the early days of high level languages, the compiler generated code that interacted directly with the input-output hardware; as a result, the peculiarities of the hardware were reflected directly in the language.

Currently, many of these rather unpleasant details are screened from the programming language by the operating system. By providing a standard interface between the abstract machine of the language and the abstract machine represented by the operating system, it is possible to achieve a considerable measure of implementation independence.

While every programming language provides facilities for input and output of data, there seems to be little agreement on standard methods for doing it. For example, Fortran uses a format statement approach, Snobol uses a pattern matching operation for input and a special print operation for output, and Ada uses the procedure approach for defining specialized input and output operations.

The methods mentioned above are used primarily for communication between programs and humans. For example, a user may be entering data from results of tests, or may be reading a report summarizing the test results. A second class of input-output issues arises when communication is internal to the machine. For example, data may be read from a secondary storage device or may be stored on magnetic tape. This type of transmission is fundamentally different from the first.

Because of the profusion of input-output methods, their occurrence in every programming language, and the need for standardized, straight-forward techniques to specify them, a mini-language devoted exclusively to input-output has been devised. Mini-language Format is based on the familiar format statement in Fortran. This mini-language gives rise to a discussion of methods for human input and output. Finally, we briefly treat methods for machine input and output.

For this mini-language the common definition of input and output statements given for the other mini-languages does not apply.

12.1   MINI-LANGUAGE FORMAT

The syntax of Mini-language Format is given in Table 12.1.

We assume that we have two devices, one for input and one for output. Each of these can be viewed as a device containing an infinitely long piece of paper allowing 72 characters per line and 55 lines per page. For input we shall look at the characters typed, from left to right and line by line. For output, we shall print characters in the same conventional order.

The layout of characters on the input or output device is specified through format declarations. Given that the device is positioned at some point on a line, a format declaration specifies the text to follow, on a character by character basis. Actual input-output is initiated with an input or output statement referencing a particular format declaration. During execution of the input-output statement, a correspondence is established between items in the statement and fields in the format declaration.

Consider the following sequence:

```
format NEXT_NUM: 2D;

...

input  N  using NEXT_NUM;
output N  using NEXT_NUM;
```

When the input statement is executed, a value from the input device is obtained and assigned to the variable N. The value is specified as having the form indicated by 2D. The item specification 2D indicates that the next two characters are to represent a number having one or two digits. Either, but not both, of the characters may be blank.

Similarly, when the output statement is executed, two characters will be printed on the output device. These characters represent the

Table 12.1   Mini-language Format

program	::=	program
		    variable-declaration...
		    format-declaration...
		begin
		    statement...
		end;

variable-declaration	::=	declare identifier [, identifier]... ;
format-declaration	::=	format identifier : field [, field]... ;
field	::=	integer item-specification
item-specification	::=	B | L | D | C
statement	::=	assignment-statement | loop-statement | input-statement | output-statement | if-statement
assignment-statement	::=	identifier := expression ;
loop-statement	::=	for identifier := expression to expression loop statement... end loop;

if-statement	::=	if comparison then
		    statement...
		[else
		    statement...]
		end if;

input-statement	::=	input [identifier [, identifier]...] using identifer ;
output-statement	::=	output [output-item [, output-item]...] using identifier ;
output-item	::=	expression | ' character... '
expression	::=	[operand arithmetic-operator] operand
comparison	::=	(operand relational-operator operand)
operand	::=	integer | identifier | (expression)
character	::=	letter | digit | special-character
arithmetic-operator	::=	+ | – | * | div
relational-operator	::=	< | = | ≠ | >
special-character	::=	b | + | – | * | / | : | ; | _ | . | , | $ | % | =

value of N. If the value of N can be specified with one digit, then the digit is right-justified in the space where the two characters are to be printed.

In general, each input statement specifies a list of variables to be input, and the external form of the variables is specified in the named format declaration. Similarly, an output statement generally contains a list of expressions and character strings whose values are to be output, and the printed form of each expression or string is specified in the associated format declaration. Every correct expression in Mini-language Format has an integer value.

For the output of expressions, the integer value is right-justified. For the output of strings, the characters are left-justified. When the value cannot fit within the specified space, an execution error will result.

For example, consider the following output statement and associated format declaration:

```
format HEADER: 25C;
...
output 'HUMAN FACTORS LIMITED' using HEADER;
```

Here a text string HUMAN FACTORS LIMITED is output with a field specification of 25C. The format specification, 25C, indicates that 25 characters are reserved for the output of a string. Since the string is shorter than 25 characters, the string is left-justified within the reserved space. The remainder of the space is filled with blanks.

Aside from the specification of the arrangement of integer and string values, format declarations can also specify the configuration of blank spaces and blank lines. For example, consider the following statements and associated format declaration:

```
format NEXT_LINE: 1B, 3D, 1B, 3D, 1L;
...
input  A, B  using NEXT_LINE;
output A, B  using NEXT_LINE;
```

The input statement reads in the values of A and B as follows:

```
1B   -- skip 1 character
3D   -- assign the integer in the next 3 characters to A
1B   -- skip 1 character
3D   -- assign the integer in the next 3 characters to B
1L   -- skip the rest of the line
```

Similarly, consider the effect of the output statement:

```
1B  -- print 1 blank
3D  -- print the value of A in the next 3 character positions
1B  -- print 1 blank
3D  -- print the value of B in the next 3 character positions
1L  -- skip to the next line
```

We may now summarize the actions to be taken on input and output:

1. For each input or output statement, the named format declaration is examined.

2. If the next field in the format declaration specifies a spacing action, the appropriate spacing action takes place.

3. If the next field specifies a sequence of digits, the corresponding input or output item must be a numeric item, and the input or output of this value takes place.

4. For output statements, if the next field specifies a character string, the corresponding output item must be a character string, and the output action takes place.

5. Input or output terminates when the last field in the format declaration is processed.

In all cases, the number of items to be input or output must match the number of format fields in the named format declaration.

An input action results in an execution error if a numeric field does not contain an integer. An output action results in an execution error if there is not enough space for an output item. A summary of input and output actions is given in Table 12.2.

We now turn to more mundane parts of our mini-language. As in most of our mini-languages, a program consists of a sequence of declarations followed by a sequence of executable statements. All variables used in a program must be declared exactly once, and each format specification named in an input or output statement must also be declared.

In addition to input and output statements, the executable statements in Mini-language Format include:

- an assignment statement

- an if statement

Table 12.2   Summary of Input-Output Actions

Let X be the next item on the input or output list, and n be the value of the integer in the corresponding format field.

Format Spacing:	*Action on Input*	*Action on Output*
nB	The next n characters from the input device are skipped.	The next n characters sent to the output device are printed as blanks.
nL	The remaining characters on the current line and the next $(n-1)$ lines from the input device are skipped.	The remaining characters on the current line and the next $(n-1)$ lines sent to the output device are printed as blanks.
Data:		
nD	The next n characters from the input device will be treated as a number and assigned as the value of X. If the next n characters are not a well-formed number, input action is in error. Leading or trailing blanks are allowed, however, embedded blanks are not.	The digits of the value of X will be printed on the output device. If the value of X can be specified by fewer than n digits, the number will be right-justified with leading zeroes suppressed. If there is not enough space specified for the value of X, the output action is in error.
nC	Not allowed.	The characters of X will be printed on the output device. If X has fewer than n characters, the characters will be left-justified. If X has more than n characters, the output action is in error.

■   a for loop, whereby an enclosed sequence of statements is executed repeatedly.

The definition of a for loop specifies a control variable that is to be assigned a sequence of values, starting from the value of one expression and increasing by one at each iteration until the value of a second expression is reached. The control variable in a for loop may not be updated within the loop, and on termination of the loop, the value of the control variable is undefined.

Finally, a few brief notes. Input or output statements need not contain data items, in which case only a spacing action may be specified in the format declaration. The character strings given in an output statement may include letters, digits, blanks, and a number of special characters as defined in Table 12.1.

Examples

In Example 12.1 we see a very simple program in Mini-language Format. Here a single line of text is output, in this case, a sequence of six integer values.

In Example 12.2, if the first line on the input device contains an integer N in its first three characters, and the next N lines contain two (to be appropriately spaced) columns of integers, then the two columns are printed in reverse order on the output device.

12.2 VARIETIES OF INPUT-OUTPUT SPECIFICATIONS

There appear to be three dominant strategies for handling the formatting of input or output data. These three approaches can be summarized as follows:

1. *Remote Format specifications:* Format specifications are based upon the idea that an input or output statement has an associated but separate format declaration. This declaration specifies the layout of data values and the use of spacing.

This method is used in Mini-language Format as well as in Fortran and PL/I. The central idea here is that every input or output action is associated with a construct describing the layout of the associated characters in the external medium.

```
program
   declare A, B, I;
   format TWO-NUMS: 4D, 4D;
begin
   A := 11;
   B := 22;
   for I := 1 to 3 loop
      output A, B  using TWO_NUMS;
   end loop;
end;
```

Output

```
11  22  11  22  11  22
```

Example 12.1   A simple output of a line of integers

```
program
   declare A, B, NUM_LINES, LINE_COUNT;
   format IN_LINE: 3D, 1L;
   format NEXT_LINE: 2B, 3D, 2B, 3D, 1L;
begin
   input NUM_LINES  using IN_LINE;
   for LINE_COUNT := 1 to NUM_LINES loop
      input  A, B   using NEXT_LINE;
      output B, A   using NEXT_LINE;
   end loop;
end;
```

Input

```
3
   1    2
  11   22
 111  222
```

Output

```
   2    1
  22   11
 222  111
```

Example 12.2   A simple column reversal program

2. *Picture specifications:* With picture specifications, the layout of characters is associated with a particular data item. Each piece of data has an associated picture clause describing the form that such an item would have on an input or output device.

Thus, the character layout of an item is not associated with an actual input or output statement, but rather with a declaration of the item itself. This view appears in Cobol and PL/I.

3. *Specialized procedures:* Here the layout of data for different kinds of data items is defined in specialized procedures. For example, we may have a procedure to output integers, another procedure to output real numbers, and another procedure to output character strings.

With this technique of input and output, there is no notion akin to a format or picture declaration. The spacing and layout of data is handled entirely by the particular procedure invoked. This method is used in Pascal, Simula 67, and Ada.

Even within these three major approaches, there are, of course, considerable differences in language details. Nevertheless, the method for input and output in most programming languages follows one of these three general approaches.

In the following discussion, we consider a common problem, the generation of a simple report. Table 12.3 illustrates a simple price list giving two columns of data. The first column indicates the quantity of the item sold, and the second column indicates the price of the corresponding quantity, assuming a fixed unit price. Our problem is to generate this price list, exactly as shown in Table 12.3.

12.3   REMOTE FORMAT SPECIFICATIONS

Remote format specifications are based on the idea that the layout of data on an external device can be described separately from the input or output statement initiating the input-output. Typically such schemes describe not only the form of data but also the configuration of blank spaces and blank lines. To describe the layout, special description characters are introduced and numbers are used to indicate repeated specification characters.

Table 12.3   A Simple Price List

```
                     PRICE LIST
                     ----------



ITEM CODE : 1234
ITEM      : EASY APPLICATOR
UNIT PRICE: $4.36



QUANTITY      PRICE
--------      -----

     1        $ 4.36
     2        $ 8.72
     3        $13.08
     4        $17.44
     5        $21.80

     6        $26.16
     7        $30.52
     8        $34.88
     9        $39.24
    10        $43.60

    11        $47.96
    12        $52.32
    13        $56.68
    14        $61.04
    15        $65.40

    16        $69.76
    17        $74.12
    18        $78.48
    19        $82.84
    20        $87.20
```

For example, in Fortran we can have the format specifications:

```
I3      -- space for a 3 digit integer, right-justified
2X      -- 2 blank spaces

F6.2    -- space for a 5 digit fixed point number with a decimal
        -- point 2 digits from the right
A10     -- space for 10 characters
```

Notice that the letters I (for integers), X (for blanks), F (for fixed point numbers), and A (for characters) indicate the type of the field.

This is the method used in Mini-language Format. Example 12.3 shows a solution to our price list problem using Mini-language Format. A number of comments about this approach are in order.

First, each format statement is associated with a name, which can be referenced by various input and output statements. Thus, it is possible to give some mnemonic significance to a format description.

Because formats are identified by name, it is also possible to refer to the same format specification in different input or output statements. In Example 12.3, the format specification named TITLE_LINE is referenced in two output statements, one giving the title and the other its underline. This kind of reuse of a format specification can enhance both maintenance and readability.

One of the debits of this approach is, of course, that the remoteness of the format specifications may cause difficulties in understanding programs with a good deal of input and output. Often, the reader of a program will have to turn to a different section of the program in order to discover the exact layout of characters. One could in turn argue that format declarations should really be *statements*, which could then be placed near the corresponding input or output statements. This alternative has problems in that format information might detract from the readability of the algorithm specified by the other statements.

The design of the compiled code for the output of a list of values according to a format list frequently makes use of the idea of *coroutines* (described in section 7.5). This provides a convenient way of stepping through the data item list and the format list in parallel.

One small but interesting problem occurs in Mini-language Format when no data items are printed but some control over blank spacing or blank lines is needed. For example, consider the output statement:

```
output using TRIPLE_SPACE;
```

```
program

    declare GROUP, UNIT_PRICE, QUANTITY, PRICE, DOLLARS, CENTS;

    format LINE_SKIP   : 1L;
    format TRIPLE_SPACE: 3L;
    format TITLE_LINE  : 25B, 10C, 1L;
    format ITEM_INFO   : 28C, 1L;
    format COL_HEADER  : 8C, 6B, 5C, 1L;
    format ITEM_LINE   : 2B, 2D, 9B, 1C, 2D, 1C, 2D, 1L;

begin
    output using TRIPLE_SPACE;

    output 'PRICE LIST'  using TITLE_LINE;
    output '----------'  using TITLE_LINE;

    output using TRIPLE_SPACE;

    output 'ITEM CODE  : 1234'            using ITEM_INFO;
    output 'ITEM       : EASY APPLICATOR' using ITEM_INFO;
    output 'UNIT PRICE : $4.36'           using ITEM_INFO;

    output using TRIPLE_SPACE;

    output 'QUANTITY', 'PRICE'  using COL_HEADER;
    output '--------', '-----'  using COL_HEADER;

    UNIT_PRICE   := 436;
    for GROUP    := 0 to 3 loop
       output using LINE_SKIP;

       for QUANTITY := (GROUP*5) + 1 to (GROUP*5) + 5 loop
          PRICE      := QUANTITY * UNIT_PRICE;
          DOLLARS    := PRICE div 100;
          CENTS      := PRICE - (DOLLARS * 100);
          output QUANTITY, '$', DOLLARS, '.', CENTS  using ITEM_LINE;
       end loop;
    end loop;
end;
```

Example 12.3   Generation of a price list using format specifications

This problem can occur in Fortran when READ and WRITE reference format statements but have no associated list of statements and expressions. This suggests that the syntax of the input or output statements could be better formulated to avoid the anomaly. For example, we might have adopted a syntax along the lines:

```
output format-identifier [ using output-item-list ];
```

In this case we would have output statements like:

```
output TRIPLE_SPACE;
output TITLE_LINE using 'PRICE LIST';
```

We leave this matter unresolved.

12.4 DATA DESCRIBED WITH PICTURE SPECIFICATIONS

The central idea behind picture specifications is that the physical layout of the data is described along with other declarative information for the data. For example, in the declaration of an integer variable one also specifies how the integer variable is to be represented outside the program. Typically the control of blanks and new lines is also associated with data. Thus the description of data is grouped with corresponding information about leading and trailing spaces as well as blank lines.

Picture specifications are best known in Cobol, where input and output is an important application area. In Cobol the items comprising a unit of printed information are collected into a record-like structure. Each item in the structure is associated with a picture clause describing its external form. Like Mini-language Format, special characters are used to indicate the type of information, and thus a picture clause indirectly defines the type of any variable.

A program along these lines is given in Example 12.4; another solution to our problem of generating a price list. In this program we have altered the syntax of Mini-language Format in order to present the solution; these changes should cause no problem.

In this example, the basic unit of input or output is assumed to be a *line*. Each line is broken into fields. Each field has a name, as well as a picture clause describing the external appearance of the field.

```
program
   declare GROUP, UNIT_PRICE, QUANTITY;

   line LINE_SKIP:
      FILLER: picture 72B;
   end line;

   line TITLE:
      LEFT_PADDING : picture 25B;
      CAPTION      : picture 10C;
      RIGHT_PADDING: picture 37B;
   end line;

   line ITEM_INFO:
      TEXT   : picture 28C;
      PADDING: picture 44B;
   end line;

   line COL_HEADER:
      QTY_HEADER   : picture 8C;
      FILLER       : picture 6B;
      PRICE_HEADER : picture 5C;
      RIGHT_PADDING: picture 53B;
   end line;

   line ITEM_LINE:
      LEFT_PADDING : picture 2B;
      QUANTITY     : picture 2D;
      FILLER       : picture 9B;
      PRICE        : picture $DD.DD;
      RIGHT_PADDING: picture 53B;
   end line;
```

Example 12.4   Generation of a price list using picture specifications

```
begin
   write LINE_SKIP;
   write LINE_SKIP;
   write LINE_SKIP;
   TITLE.CAPTION := 'PRICE LIST';
   write TITLE;
   TITLE.CAPTION := '----------';
   write TITLE;
   write LINE_SKIP;
   write LINE_SKIP;
   write LINE_SKIP;
   ITEM_INFO.TEXT  := 'ITEM CODE  : 1234';
   write ITEM_INFO;
   ITEM_INFO.TEXT  := 'ITEM       : EASY APPLICATOR';
   write ITEM_INFO;
   ITEM_INFO.TEXT  := 'UNIT PRICE : $4.36';
   write ITEM_INFO;
   write LINE_SKIP;
   write LINE_SKIP;
   write LINE_SKIP;
   COL_HEADER.QTY_HEADER   := 'QUANTITY';
   COL_HEADER.PRICE_HEADER := 'PRICE';
   write COL_HEADER;
   COL_HEADER.QTY_HEADER   := '--------';
   COL_HEADER.PRICE_HEADER := '-----';
   write COL_HEADER;
   UNIT_PRICE := 436;
   for GROUP   := 0 to 3 loop
      write LINE_SKIP;
      for QUANTITY := (GROUP*5) + 1 to (GROUP*5) + 5 loop
         ITEM_LINE.QUANTITY := QUANTITY;
         ITEM_LINE.PRICE    := UNIT_PRICE * QUANTITY;
         write ITEM_LINE;
      end loop;
   end loop;
end;
```

Example 12.4 continued

For example, consider the following:

```
line ITEM_INFO:
   TEXT   : picture 28C;   -- space for 28 characters
   PADDING: picture 44B;   -- 44 remaining blank spaces
end line;
```

Here the line of text named ITEM_INFO is defined as having two fields: TEXT for containing a text string, and PADDING for containing blank spaces. The two fields comprise a complete line.

With this scheme, any nonblank item must be assigned a value before printing. In the above case, TEXT must be assigned a string of text, whereas PADDING is assumed to be all blanks. The setting of such values is typically done through assignment statements, for example:

```
ITEM_INFO.TEXT := 'ITEM CODE  : 1234';
```

Here we use the conventional notation for assignment to components of records.

The actual input or output of data is handled by input-output statements naming only the unit to be input or output, in this case by naming the entire line structure. For example, to output the contents of ITEM_INFO we simply use the statement:

```
write ITEM_INFO;
```

One advantage of the picture specification approach is that all the information about a line of text is contained in a single structure. Since both the type and layout of data are specified together, all that one needs to know about a unit of information can be examined quite simply.

Another advantage of this approach is that "insertion" characters are included in the description of data. For example, consider the following:

```
PRICE: picture $DD.DD;
```

Here the characters $ and . are considered as insertion characters that are placed within the numeric value as printed. Thus, for example, the number

436

will be printed as:

    $ 4.36

We assume here that numbers with decimal points are treated as exact numeric quantities.

Finally we note a clear disadvantage with this approach as given: the description of data must often be accompanied by considerable, apparently extraneous, information. For example, in the description of COL_HEADER, we see the need to describe four different fields, two of which are all blank, but all of which must be associated with a name and picture clause. Such descriptions are cumbersome.

12.5 INPUT AND OUTPUT VIA SPECIALIZED PROCEDURES

The last approach we discuss here is that of using specialized procedures for input and output. This approach has emerged in more recent languages, such as Simula 67, Algol 68, Pascal, Ada. The general idea is that for each type of data, and thus for each conceptually different layout operation, a dedicated procedure is used. For example, if we wish to output an integer, a procedure for printing integers is invoked. This procedure may have a parameter indicating the character width of the integer. As with all approaches, there are considerable variations within the general theme.

Consider the following sequence of procedure calls:

```
PRINT_STRING ('ITEM CODE  : 1234');
ADVANCE_LINE (1);
```

Here the procedure PRINT_STRING takes an argument that is a character string and prints the string on an output device. The following procedure ADVANCE_LINE fills the rest of the printed line with blank spaces and advances to the next line.

The exact control of spacing for data items is usually handled with parameters specifying appropriate field widths. For example, consider the following procedure call:

```
PRINT_INTEGER(DOLLARS, 2);
```

Here an integer is printed in a two-digit field. In the case where only one digit is required, the digit is right-justified.

Our third program for generating a price list is given in Example 12.5. Again we have modified the syntax of Mini-language Format to illustrate this technique for input and output.

The use of specialized procedures for input and output has a number of key advantages. Most importantly, we can dispense with explicit format or picture specifications and include input-output within an already accepted feature of programming languages procedures. Thus a programmer does not need to learn any additional language features. Furthermore, the details of printing can be summarized in terms of a familiar abstraction, the call to a procedure.

Another advantage with this approach is that the user will generally want to define special input and output procedures particularly suited to an application. Such procedures fit nicely with any that might be predefined in the language.

We observe several problems with the approach taken in Example 12.5. For one, the sequence of procedure calls to perform a given input or output action can be quite lengthy, as compared with the terse forms used with format specifications. While repeatedly calling procedure after procedure can be quite tedious, it may be argued that the intent is just as clear as referring to remote format or picture specifications.

The subject of specialized procedures brings up two rather interesting extensions to this approach that can add simplicity to the specification of input and output, but at the cost of adding some complexity to the mechanism for procedures. These two extensions are overloading and default parameters.

Overloading of Subprograms

There are situations where we want to define the same conceptual operation on arguments of different types. A typical case is a print operation for printing different types of values.

Consider the procedure headers

```
procedure PRINT (X: integer);
procedure PRINT (X: real);
procedure PRINT (X: string);
```

for printing the string representation of an integer, a floating point number, or a string, respectively.

The actions of each procedure will differ since they are dependent on the format for printing the three kinds of values. The use of two or more subprograms with the same name but different types of parameters is called *overloading*.

```
program

   declare GROUP, UNIT_PRICE, QUANTITY, PRICE, DOLLARS, CENTS;
begin
   ADVANCE_LINE (3);
   PUT_SPACES (25);
   PRINT_STRING ('PRICE LIST');
   ADVANCE_LINE (1);
   PUT_SPACES (25);
   PRINT_STRING('----------');

   ADVANCE_LINE (4);
   PRINT_STRING ('ITEM CODE  : 1234');
   ADVANCE_LINE (1);
   PRINT_STRING ('ITEM       : EASY APPLICATOR');
   ADVANCE_LINE (1);
   PRINT_STRING ('UNIT PRICE : $4.36');

   ADVANCE_LINE (3);
   PRINT_STRING ('QUANTITY      PRICE');
   ADVANCE_LINE (1);
   PRINT_STRING ('--------      -----');
   ADVANCE_LINE (1);

   UNIT_PRICE := 436;
   for GROUP := 0 to 3 loop
      ADVANCE_LINE (1);

      for QUANTITY := (GROUP*5)+ 1 to (GROUP*5)+ 5 loop
         PUT_SPACES (2);
         PRINT_INTEGER (QUANTITY, 2);
         PRICE    := QUANTITY * UNIT_PRICE;
         DOLLARS := PRICE div 100;
         CENTS    := PRICE - (DOLLARS * 100);
         PUT_SPACES (9);
         PRINT_STRING ('$');
         PRINT_INTEGER (DOLLARS, 2);
         PRINT_STRING ('.');
         PRINT_INTEGER (CENTS, 2);
         ADVANCE_LINE (1);
      end loop;
   end loop;
end;
```

Example 12.5 Generation of a price list using specialized procedures

Overloaded subprograms can be called in the conventional manner, for example:

```
PRINT (I + 1);          -- print an integer
PRINT (SQRT(Y));        -- print a floating point number
PRINT ('THIS MESSAGE'); -- print a string
```

The key idea here is that these three subroutine calls are really calls to three different subroutines, each with the name PRINT. The choice of which particular subroutine PRINT is to be invoked by the call is determined by the type of the argument. The subroutine is chosen so that the type of its parameter matches the type of the argument. In most languages, this choice can be made by the compiler.

We note in passing that this use of overloading is similar to the use of + as an operator both for integer addition and floating point addition as discussed in Chapter 6.

Default Parameters

Next consider the following procedure calls:

```
PRINT (I, 3):  -- I is printed with a 3 character field width

PRINT (I);     -- I is printed with a standard field width
```

Here we have two calls to the procedure PUT, and in each case the value of an integer is printed. In the first case, a three-digit field width is specified. In the second case, no second argument is given and the integer is printed with a standard field width. The field width in the procedure is said to be a *default parameter* in the sense that if it is not provided in the call, a standard value is provided in the body of the procedure.

Default parameters can be handled by the use of overloading. For example, with two procedures defined by the headers

```
procedure PRINT (X: integer);  -- uses the standard width
procedure PRINT (X: integer; WIDTH: integer);
```

both of the above calls can be accommodated. Hence their inclusion in a language is questionable.

12.6 COMMUNICATION WITH THE OUTSIDE WORLD

Older programming languages often refer to specific devices but more modern languages generally deal with the more abstract notion of a *file*. A file can be a source or a sink of data and act as a value in a language just like an array or record. In Pascal there are file variables. The correspondence between the abstract file of a program and the physical file or *data set* of the operating system is established by system control statements outside the language. Since these statements are also outside the program, this correspondence can be changed without recompiling the program.

The actual physical connection between the data set and the file is established only at the time the file is *opened* and is broken when the file is *closed*.

Some languages provide special statements for the opening and closing of files. In others, the file is opened when it is first used and closed when the program terminates. At the time of opening the file, checks are made that the data set connected to the file match some of the requirements of the program.

For example, we may have:

access mode:
  read only (card reader, magnetic tape)
  write only (line printer, card punch, magnetic tape)
  read/write (disk or drum, terminal)

There are two distinct ways in which a program can transfer data to and from a file. One mode of transfer takes place without any conversion, that is, the internal representation of the data in the program is identical with its representation in external storage. This type of storage is not meant for data for human consumption, but is intended as a *backing store* to hold temporary results further processed later in the program. In the other mode of transfers, there is a conversion of representation, for example from a two's complement binary representation to a string of decimal characters preceded by a sign. This is the mode discussed in the earlier sections of this chapter.

Finally, there are two fundamental forms of file organization, sequential and random. A sequential file may be accessed as input only in the order in which the data were written, from first to last. The basic operation is the next operation, which gives the next data item in order. The files in the earlier part of this chapter are sequential files. Random files are accessed in an order that is not only different from that in which they were written but in an unpredictable order. The statements for this kind of access must provide a *key* by which the referenced record can be identifed.

Between these two extreme forms of access, there are many intermediate ways of file organization. Like other topics in this text, a full discussion of the subject of file organization goes beyond the scope of this book. Such topics include the language aspects of dealing with such input-output problems as graphics and real-time data acquisition.

FURTHER READING

Of all of the topics covered in this text, the topic of input-output has received least attention. Works devoted primarily to this area are particularly sparse.

As typical language examples, format statements are described in Fortran and PL/I, picture clauses in Cobol, and specialized procedures in Algol 68 and Simula 67.

The use of specialized procedures for input-output as used in Ada is described in [Ichbiah et al. 1979]. Here extensive use is made of overloading and default parameters.

EXERCISES

Exercise 12.1   Table Generation

The object of this exercise is to compare the three methods of output specification described in this chapter. Write three versions of a program defined below using the output specification techniques shown in Examples 12.3, 12.4, and 12.5 to print the temperature conversion table defined below. When you have completed the three programs, compare their clarity and ease of writing.

The program is to output a simple table. The table consists of two columns labeled Fahrenheit and Celsius. The Fahrenheit temperatures are listed for every degree from 32 through 212. The corresponding Celsius temperatures are printed as integers. There is a blank line left after every five degrees. After every 50 degrees, 10 blank lines are output and the column headings are repeated. The Celsius equivalent of t degrees Fahrenheit is $5(t-32)/9$. The first few lines of the table are:

Fahrenheit	Celsius
----------	-------
32	0
33	1
34	1
35	2
36	2
37	3
38	3

Exercise 12.2   Programming in Mini-language Format

Write a program in Mini-language Format that reads a number N from the input device and then prints a pattern of the form shown below.

```
      1
     2 2
    3   3
    .     .
   .       .
  N         N
```

The pattern should be centered on the output device. You may assume that the value of N will be less than 20.

Exercise 12.3   Programming in Mini-language Format

Printing tables and reports is certainly one of the most important applications of input-output. Write a program to solve the following problem.

January 1, 1901 was a Tuesday. The objective of this exercise is to write a Mini-language Format program that takes as input the number of a month (from 1 to 12) and the number of a year (from 1901 to 2000), and prints a calendar for the month. For example:

```
                    JANUARY

         S  M  T  W  T  F  S
         --------------------
                1  2  3  4  5
         6  7  8  9 10 11 12
        13 14 15 16 17 18 19
        20 21 22 23 24 25 26
        27 28 29 30 31
```

Exercise 12.4   Printing Pictures

Suppose that output consists of pictures printed on a two-dimensional coordinate system. If the pictures are limited to straight lines, circles, and arcs of circles, define a set of formatting features for a programming language suitable for drawing pictures.

Exercise 12.5   Backing Storage

Design additional syntax and semantics for Mini-language Format for input and output of data on a file that is to serve as a backing store for temporary results. Such transmission is to take place without any conversion, and the data is represented in the file in the same way that it is represented in machine storage during execution. The new facilities should allow both sequential and random order access to the data.

Exercise 12.6   Using Money

Examples 12.3, 12.4, and 12.5 use three basic approaches for reading and writing data: format specifications, picture specifications, and specialized procedures.

Suppose that input and output of amounts of money were important enough in the design of a special purpose language that they should be built into the language. Describe a *good* set of primitives for this using each of the three approaches. You will need to handle dollar signs, commas in numbers, and decimal point notation for cents.

13
Dynamically Varying Structures

thru 372

One area of programming languages with many divergent views is the area generally included under the term *data structures*. By a data structure we mean a collection of data that bear some relation to each other and are organized so as to represent these relationships. The organization reflects real world relationships and thus must be able to change dynamically. For example, we may describe the nodes in a network, the components of a data base, the items in a linked list, or the members of a family tree.

The naming, searching, deleting, sharing, and updating of items in a data structure are all critical issues. Mini-language Structures is an attempt to deal with some of these issues. In our opinion, the concept of a data structure is still quite vague and none of the existing facilities for data structures is satisfactory. A good attempt to provide such a facility has been made in the language Ada, and the Mini-language Structures is based on this work.

13.1 MINI-LANGUAGE STRUCTURES

Along with integers and strings, the types in Mini-language Structures include classes of objects called *structures*. A *structure type* is declared by a structure declaration that gives the name of the type being declared and also the name and type of each structure component. All structure types must be declared, and inter-dependent definitions are allowed.

For example, we may have the structure declarations:

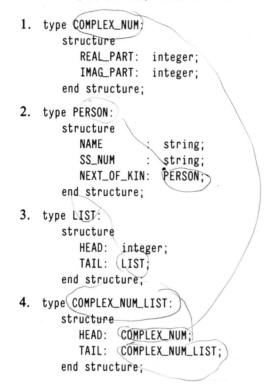

```
1.  type COMPLEX_NUM:
        structure
            REAL_PART:  integer;
            IMAG_PART:  integer;
        end structure;

2.  type PERSON:
        structure
            NAME          :  string;
            SS_NUM        :  string;
            NEXT_OF_KIN:  PERSON;
        end structure;

3.  type LIST:
        structure
            HEAD:  integer;
            TAIL:  LIST;
        end structure;

4.  type COMPLEX_NUM_LIST:
        structure
            HEAD:  COMPLEX_NUM;
            TAIL:  COMPLEX_NUM_LIST;
        end structure;
```

Examples of each of these structures are shown in Figure 13.1. Here an
arrow is used to refer to a component that is itself a structure.

The first declaration above declares a very simple structure with
two integer components. This structure is analogous to a record
structure in Mini-language Type. The essential difference is illustrated
in the second example. Here we see a structure type named PERSON,
which has a string component, an integer component, and a third
component that is of type PERSON itself. This is a recursive definition
and defines a potentially infinite class of objects, one such object is
illustrated in Figure 13.1. The apparent infinite recursion is handled in
Mini-language Structures by a special object called null. The value of
null designates an object with no components. Each defined structure
types includes the null object as one of its values.

The third structure declaration defines a type called LIST. A list
denotes a series of objects, each with a head and a tail component,
terminated by the null object.

Table 13.1   Mini-language Structures

program	::=	program
		   structure-declaration...
		   variable-declaration...
		begin
		   statement...
		end;

structure-declaration	::=	type identifier : structure-definition ;

structure-definition	::=	structure
		   identifier: type;
		   [identifier: type;]...
		end structure

variable-declaration	::=	declare identifier [, identifier]... : type;
type	::=	identifier | string | integer
statement	::=	assignment-statement | loop-statement | if-statement | input-statement | output-statement
assignment-statement	::=	variable := expression ; | variable := new identifier (expression [, expression]...) ;

if-statement	::=	if comparison then
		   statement...
		[else
		   statement...]
		end if;

loop-statement	::=	while comparison loop statement... end loop;
input-statement	::=	input variable [, variable]... ;
output-statement	::=	output variable [, variable]... ;
comparison	::=	(operand comparison-operator operand)
expression	::=	[expression +] operand
operand	::=	null | integer | string | (expression) | variable
variable	::=	identifier | variable.identifier
string	::=	' character... '
character	::=	letter | digit | b
comparison-operator	::=	< | = | ≠ | >

(1) An object of type COMPLEX_NUM

REAL_PART	2
IMAG_PART	1

(2) An object of type PERSON

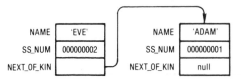

(3) An object of type LIST

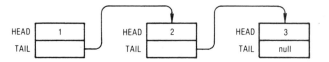

(4) An object of type COMPLEX_NUM_LIST

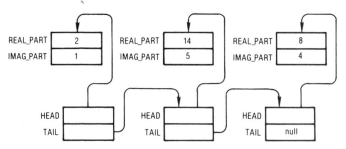

Figure 13.1   Illustrations of structures

The fourth structure declaration defines another class of lists called COMPLEX_NUM_LIST. The HEAD of each component of such a list is a COMPLEX_NUM object. This structure declaration illustrates the definition of structures that require more than one structure declaration for their specification. One member of this class of objects is also illustrated in Figure 13.1.

```
declare HIS_NAME: string;
declare NUM_HITS, NODE_VALUE: integer;
```

```
declare ADAM, EVE, LAST_BORN: PERSON;
declare L: LIST;
declare NEXT_NUM: COMPLEX_NUM;
declare ITEM: COMPLEX_NUM_LIST;
```

There are important differences between the semantics of these declarations of structure variables and declarations of record variables in Mini-language Type. In Type, an identifier declared to be of a record type x has the mode reference-to-x and is identically equal to a location that can contain record objects of type x. This meaning of declarations was discussed in Chapter 4. In Mini-language Structures, an extra level of referencing is inserted. The identifier ADAM declared above is not identically equal to a location that can contain a PERSON object but to a location that can contain a reference to a PERSON object. This object does not exist until it is constructed, as described below, and the contents of the location associated with ADAM are initially undefined.

Components of structure variables can be designated by naming the variable itself, followed by a dot and the name of one of its components. As nested structures are allowed, nested components are designated by giving the name of the appropriate component at each level of nesting. For example, we may have the variables:

```
ADAM.SS_NUM          -- a component of type string
ADAM.NEXT_OF_KIN     -- a component of type PERSON
ITEM.HEAD.REAL_PART  -- a component of type integer
```

Several kinds of assignment statements are allowed in Mini-language Structures. The first is the simple assignment of an arithmetic or string value, for example:

```
NUM_HITS  :=  NUM_HITS + 1;
HIS_NAME  :=  'GEORGE WASHINGTON';

NEXT_NUM.REAL_PART  :=  2;
NEXT_NUM.REAL_PART  :=  NEXT_NUM.REAL_PART + 1;
```

All values assigned to a variable must be of the same type as that declared for the variable.

Of more interest to us here is the assignment of structure objects to structure variables. A null value can be assigned to a structure variable by simply giving null as the assigned expression, as in:

```
LAST_BORN          :=  null;
ADAM.NEXT_OF_KIN   :=  null;
L.TAIL             :=  null;
```

A special kind of assignment is used to create a structure object. The assigned expression is prefixed by the symbol new followed by the name of the structure type and a parenthesized list of expression values, one for each component of the structure. For example, we may have:

```
NEXT_NUM   :=  new COMPLEX_NUM(2,1);
ITEM       :=  new COMPLEX_NUM_LIST(NEXT_NUM, null);
ADAM       :=  new PERSON('ADAM', '000000001', null);
```

Such statements specify the dynamic creation of an object of the type specified by the structure identifier and assigns this value to the variable given on the left hand side of the assignment. The assigned value is a *reference* to the dynamically created object.

During the creation of a structure object, the components of the object are given values from the parenthesized list of expressions following the symbol new. If any of these expressions refers to a previously created object, the value of the expression is a reference to the previously created object. For example, the variables NEXT_NUM and ITEM created above may be represented as in:

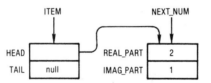

Assignment of one structure variable to another structure variable is also allowed. In this case, after the assignment, both variables will refer to the same dynamically created object. For example, if the above sequence were followed by the assignment:

```
LAST_BORN  :=  ADAM;
```

then both ADAM and LAST_BORN would refer to the same object, as illustrated in:

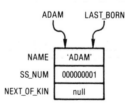

Finally, Mini-language Structures includes the following more traditional statements:

- If statements
- Loop statements
- Input statements
- Output statements

The input and output statements handle only integer and string values.

Examples

Consider Example 13.1. The first statement

```
LAST_BORN  := null;
```

sets the value of the variable LAST_BORN to reference a null object. The birth of the first member of our family is accomplished with the operation new:

```
ADAM       := new PERSON('ADAM', '000000001', null);
LAST_BORN  := ADAM;
```

The first statement above creates a new object with three components and the variable ADAM is set to reference this new object. The second statement assigns a reference to the same newly constructed object to LAST_BORN. Notice that the third component of the object referenced by ADAM is null.

Next, consider a new birth given in the statements:

```
EVE  :=  new PERSON('EVE', '000000002', ADAM);
ADAM.NEXT_OF_KIN  :=  EVE;
LAST_BORN         :=  EVE;
```

The first statement creates yet another object. The second statement results in setting the third component of the object associated with ADAM as a reference to EVE. The third statement updates the value of LAST_BORN.

Now that we have two persons in our family, we can see the development of dynamic relationships during program execution. The third components of ADAM and EVE now refer to each other and LAST_BORN has been maintained as a reference to the person who was last born.

```
program
   type PERSON:
      structure
            NAME        :  string;
            SS_NUM      :  string;
            NEXT_OF_KIN:  PERSON;
      end structure;

   declare ADAM, EVE, LAST_BORN: PERSON;
begin
   -- initial state, no one on earth
   LAST_BORN  :=  null;

   -- birth of Adam
   ADAM        :=  new PERSON ('ADAM', '000000001', null);
   LAST_BORN  :=  ADAM;

   -- birth of Adam's spouse
   EVE   :=  new PERSON('EVE', '000000002', ADAM);
   ADAM.NEXT_OF_KIN  :=  EVE;
   LAST_BORN         :=  EVE;
end;
```

Example 13.1   The beginning of a genealogy

Next consider Example 13.2. After execution of the first six statements, the structure of Figure 13.2 is obtained. The following statements read in an integer representing a node value and then print the number of times the node value occurs in the tree list.

13.2   DYNAMICALLY VARYING DATA STRUCTURES

The general notion of data structures is quite diffuse and almost impossible to treat with a single mini-language.

Often we need to model large amounts of data and express quite complex relationships between the data items. Whether it be the symbol table of a compiler, the connections in a rail network, the accounting system in an organization, Census Bureau information, or simply a binary tree of alphabetically ordered keys, there is an inherent variety and complexity in the kinds of problems that data structures are meant to solve. To deal with this complexity, programmers should be able to work at a very high level of abstraction, often far removed from the details of a machine implementation.

```
program
   type TREE:
      structure
         NODE:  integer;
         LB  :  TREE;
         RB  :  TREE;
      end structure;

   type TREE_LIST:
      structure
         HEAD : TREE;
         TAIL : TREE_LIST;
      end structure;

   declare NODE_VALUE, NUM_HITS: integer;
   declare A, B, C: TREE;
   declare L, P   : TREE_LIST;
begin
   A := new TREE(1, null, null);
   B := new TREE(2, null, null);
   C := new TREE(3, null, null);

   L := new TREE_LIST(C, null);
   L := new TREE_LIST(B, L);
   L := new TREE_LIST(A, L);

   input NODE_VALUE;
   P := L;

   NUM_HITS := 0;
   while (P ≠ null) loop
      if (P.HEAD.NODE = NODE_VALUE) then
         NUM_HITS := NUM_HITS + 1;
      end if;
      P := P.TAIL;
   end loop;

   output NUM_HITS;
end;
```

Example 13.2   Searching a linked list

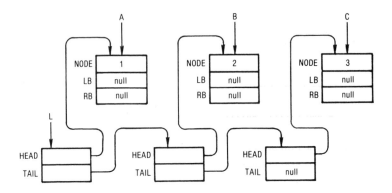

Figure 13.2   Development of a tree list

From a language viewpoint, the concept of such data structures brings in some critical new issues. The first is that the storage requirements for a program cannot be determined simply from the number of variables and the nature of their types. For example, consider the following sequence:

```
L := new LIST(1, null);
L := new LIST(2, L);
L := new LIST(3, L);
L := new LIST(4, L);
```

Here we see the development of a single list structure named L. Over the course of execution, the size of L grows progressively. Generally, the actual number of elements cannot be predicted until execution is completed. Thus, we see a need to allocate storage dynamically. This is in sharp contrast with the variables introduced in previous mini-languages.

A second issue with such structures is that the components of a structure may relate to previously defined structures, and these relationships may themselves change during program execution. In the above sequence of statements, the interrelation of the list elements changes as each statement is executed.

Perhaps the most central issue in the use of data structures is the sharing of information. For example, consider the program of Example 13.3. The structure set up by this program is shown in Figure 13.3. Here both L and M are lists, some of whose components are identical.

```
program
    type LIST:  structure
                    HEAD: integer;
                    TAIL: LIST;
                end structure;
    declare L, M: LIST;
begin
    L := new LIST(1, null);
    L := new LIST(2, L);
    M := new LIST(3, L);
    L := new LIST(4, M);

    output L.TAIL.HEAD, M.HEAD;    -- values are 3 and 3
end;
```

Example 13.3   Building a list in Mini-Language Structures

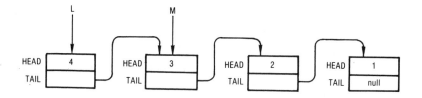

Figure 13.3   A list structure with shared components

In particular, both

```
L.TAIL.HEAD
M.HEAD
```

denote the same value, the integer 3. Finally, note that even if the list L
is assigned a completely new value, as with the statement

```
L := new LIST(5, null);
```

some elements originally in L will still be accessible via the list named
M. This brings up another difficult issue, namely, when do the objects of
a structure become inaccessible?

13.3 POINTERS

In many higher level languages (and in most lower level languages) data structures are developed with some kind of mechanism for pointers. A *pointer* is an object that gives the address of, or refers to, another object.

Working with pointers is full of hazards for the unwary. The object associated with a pointer may change during program execution. Although complex structures may be developed, the programmer must always keep in mind whether a variable refers to an object directly or indirectly through a pointer. Where a complex data structure is involved, a clear understanding of a program that uses pointers is difficult to obtain. The complex relationships that pointers are intended to represent are often very difficult to fathom.

Nevertheless, there is still a fundamental question: do we need the notion of a pointer in order to understand the use of data structures? For example, consider the statements that establish the list structure illustrated above. Here the value of M.HEAD is 3. Now suppose we execute the statement:

```
L.TAIL.HEAD := 6;
```

The value of M.HEAD will now be 6. Notice that M does not appear in this assignment statement, but its value is changed nevertheless.

This is a situation in which the program behavior can be readily understood in terms of the concepts of a pointer. This is especially true when we have the sharing of structure information. Thus, we see that even in Mini-language Structures, in which pointers are not explicit, the idea of a pointer is quite central to understanding actions performed in the language.

Many programming languages make the notion of a pointer explicit. For example, consider the following Pascal declarations:

```
type ITEM = ↑LIST;
     LIST = record
                HEAD: INTEGER;
                TAIL: ITEM
            end;
var  L, M, NEXT: ITEM;
```

Here a pointer type is explicitly indicated with an ↑ . In Pascal, the type of object to which a pointer points must be explicitly indicated, in this case a list. The Pascal statements corresponding to the structures of Figure 13.3 are given in Example 13.4.

Each call to the procedure NEW allocates space for the type of object referenced by the pointer given as an argument and assigns a reference to the new object to the pointer. In subsequent statements, all references to the objects pointed to by L or M must be explicitly indicated. For example, we have:

```
L     -- denotes the pointer value of L
L↑    -- denotes the object pointed to by L
```

In comparison with Mini-language Structures, we see here a very straightforward set of conventions in which pointers are explicitly identified. Unlike Mini-language Structures, however, the Pascal programmer must always be aware of the notion of a pointer, even in the case where knowledge that a value is a pointer is somewhat superfluous. While both views are valid and a final resolution of this issue is not clear, we generally support the suppression of pointers.

13.4 DESIGN CRITERIA FOR DATA STRUCTURES

Facilities for defining dynamically varying collections of data are not a part of every language. For example, neither Fortran nor in Basic has a facility corresponding to that given in Mini-language Structures. With such languages, the reader is forced to use alternative constructs in order to deal with structured data. Typically, arrays are used with indices to simulate pointers. Clearly, if the development of dynamically varying data structures is an important application domain, such languages are difficult to use.

To discuss the various design issues in data structures, we will compare the facilities given in Mini-language Structures with those in Pascal. This is taken further in Examples 13.3 and 13.4.

Definition of Data Structures

A definition of a data structure defines the objects to be manipulated and, implicitly, the ways in which they can be referenced.

In Mini-language Structures, the definition of data structures is handled by a type declaration in which each of the components of the structure is identified. This requires that the structure be defined to have a specific form since arbitrarily connected structures are prohibited. The development of chained structures is handled by the use of recursion in

```
program BUILDLIST (INPUT,OUTPUT);
   type ITEM =  ↑ LIST;
        LIST =  record
                     HEAD: INTEGER;
                     TAIL: ITEM
                end;
   var L, M, NEXT: ITEM;
begin
   NEW (L);
   L ↑ .HEAD := 1;
   L ↑ .TAIL := nil;
   NEXT     := L;

   NEW (L);
   L ↑ .HEAD := 2;
   L ↑ .TAIL := NEXT;
   NEXT     := L;

   NEW (M);
   M ↑ .HEAD := 3;
   M ↑ .TAIL := NEXT;
   NEXT     := M;

   NEW (L);
   L ↑ .HEAD := 4;
   L ↑ .TAIL := NEXT;

   WRITE (L ↑ .TAIL ↑ .HEAD, M ↑ .HEAD)
      { output values are 3 and 3 }
end
```

Example 13.4   Building a list structure in Pascal

the definition of the structure. The apparent infinite recursion indicated in Example 13.3 is prevented by associating a null object with each defined structure.

In Pascal, the mechanism for defining structures is analogous to that of Mini-language Structures. Here, however, an intermediate type must be used to indicate a pointer to another structure, which is in fact the normal record structure in Pascal. This intermediate type slightly obscures the definition of the object being defined, but makes the existence of pointers explicit, as well as clearing up any ambiguity about possible infinite recursion.

Operations over Structures

There are two general kinds of operations relevant to the use of structures. First are those provided within the language. Second are the higher level operations more suitable to the domain these structures are intended to represent.

In Mini-language Structures, the primitive operations over structures are basically those of creation, assignment, and component selection. Assignment of structures is handled just as assignment of variables that can take single values. References to components of structures are specified by the dot notation used for record structures. With the dot notation the use of pointers is suppressed and the dereferencing operation (see Chapter 4) is implicit. Consider the variable M.HEAD in Example 13.3. Here, although M can be viewed as a pointer to a structure, if a component of that structure, HEAD, for instance, is referenced, it is as if M points to the component instead of the whole structure. This implicit dereferencing appears to be generally what is meant when the components of the structure are referenced. Thus Mini-language Structures presents a conceptually simple mechanism for handling the components of structures.

In Pascal, on the other hand, the use of pointers is made explicit. Each reference to the component of a structure must be handled by giving an up-arrow explicitly dereferencing the pointer to the named structure to one of its components. The extensive use of the up arrow-in Pascal is somewhat annoying. While it does make explicit the fact that an object is really a reference to a structure, the repeated use of the up-arrow somewhat detracts from the readability of the intended operations.

For higher level operations, for example, a subprogram to reorder the components of a list, Mini-language Structures and Pascal both require the use of functions and procedures. Thus the user has no way of explicitly defining higher level operations on the structures other than through the mechanism of subprograms. The general issue of defining such operations is treated in Chapter 10 on type definitions.

Construction of Data Structures

In Mini-language Structures the construction of new structures is handled with the new operation. Values must be given for each component of a structure and the component type must be stated. Notice that only one instance of a structure can be generated by a single statement. More complex structures must be built via repeated assignment statements, each with a new operation.

In Mini-language Structures both the allocation of space for the structure and the setting of the pointer value are handled implicitly. Thus, the user can think more directly in terms of the actual kinds of objects being generated.

In Pascal, on the other hand, objects of structures are not created directly. The Pascal procedure NEW must be applied to an object with a pointer type. This procedure call allocates the space for the object and sets a pointer value to this storage area. The actual setting of components of structures must be handled via direct record assignment to each component. This method suffers from the fact that objects are not treated as a whole, but only on a component-by-component basis. Furthermore, the pointer set by the procedure NEW must be explicitly dereferenced when any component of the structure is initialized.

Both languages treat the selection of components of structures in a manner analogous to that of selecting the components of a record valued variable. Pascal, however, has a drawback from our point of view, in that the pointer to the structure object must always be explicitly dereferenced before a component can be selected.

When dealing with data structures, especially large ones, it is frequently the case that different types of objects must be connected into the structure at a particular point. There is thus a need for *union* types as described in Section 6.4. Furthermore, there will be a need to make a test the type of a given object. That is, it must be possible to define predicates that test which type the current value of a union variable belongs. to. Union types and such tests are still very uncommon in modern programming languages.

In Pascal, for example, the type of an object is part of the specification of a procedure. Procedures that operate on multiple types are not allowed, and thus the writing of any generalized procedures is prohibited.

The development of data structures is becoming an increasingly important application domain for computers. Development of large information bases and the applications of computers to much more sophisticated information processing areas is becoming more and more widespread. The issue of dynamically varying data structures as discussed here is only a part of the problem. In this chapter in particular, we have barely scratched the surface.

13.5   DYNAMIC ALLOCATION OF STORAGE

In Mini-language Structures, storage is allocated for structure objects through a special form of the assignment statement. It is thus under the direct control of the programmer. This differs from the allocation pattern for variables in block structured languages, where the activation record forms the model. This pattern was described in Section 8.3.

The space for variables of a block structured language is created when the block is invoked and destroyed when the block terminates. The lifetime of an object thus directly follows the dynamic block structure of the language and may be implemented with an execution stack. The lifetime of an object that is created explicitly by the execution of a special statement does not follow the block invocation pattern. A structure object can exist from one block invocation to the next. Thus a method of storage management that is separate from the execution stack is required for languages where the programmer has explicit control of storage allocation.

In some languages, for example Pascal and PL/I, specific statements are provided for the release of storage allocated for an object. Suppose a destroy statement were added to Mini-language Stuctures, where the form of the statement is:

```
destroy identifier ;
```

Execution of the statement would have the effect of destroying the object referenced by the identifier and setting the value of the identifier to undefined. The problem here is exemplified by the statement sequence:

```
L := new LIST(1, null);
L := new LIST(2, L);
M := new LIST(3, L);
L := new LIST(4, M);
destroy L;
```

The complete list referenced by L has now been destroyed and the value of L is undefined. However, the variable M now references a location that no longer exists. It has become a *dangling reference.* While it is easy to see what is happening in this short fragment, in a larger program invalid references of this sort are very difficult to detect.

An alternative is, as in the original definition of Mini-language Structures, to provide no explicit means for the destruction of an object. Then, for example, if the statement

```
L := new LIST(1, null);
```

which creates a new object and assigns a reference to L, were immediately followed by the statement

```
L := new LIST(2, null);
```

this would create a second LIST object and supplants the reference to the first object by a reference to the second one. The original object can no longer be referenced and there is no way of regaining access to it. The storage occupied by the object is no longer usable and can be returned to the system for potential reallocation. In some languages, such as Lisp and Algol 68, this is done by a special support routine, known as a *garbage collector*, which searches currently allocated storage for objects that are no longer accessible and destroys them. Such support can require a considerable execution overhead.

FURTHER READING

Much of the original work in recursive data statements was done by Hoare [1974]. A good discussion of the issues presented in this section is given in [Ichbiah et al. 1979]. In the rationale for the Ada programming language, a number of issues and problems associated with dynamic types are discussed.

EXERCISES

Exercise 13.1   Programming in Mini-language Structures

Write a program in Mini-language Structures that will read a sequence of numbers, terminated by zero, and put them into a binary tree. When all the numbers have been read, print the numbers in ascending order.

Exercise 13.2   Explicit Versus Implicit Pointers

In Chapter 4, we described Mini-language Ref with explicit pointers. Consider a variant of Mini-language Structures with reference variables instead of recursive structure definitions. Thus the declaration for the type PERSON would be:

```
type PERSON:
   structure
      NAME         : string;
      SS_NUM       : string;
      NEXT_OF_KIN : ref PERSON;
   end structure;
```

This variant requires an explicit dereferencing operator.

Compare the use of explicit versus implicit pointers on the clarity and ease of programming, including comparative examples from both variants of Mini-language Structures.

Exercise 13.3   Storage Management

Mini-language Structures provides no way for the programmer to return storage no longer required to the system. Instead, the implementation must detect and reclaim storage through the use of some *garbage collection* routine. Explain how such a routine could be implemented.

Exercise 13.4   The Dangers of Explicit Pointers

It has been suggested by Hoare that there is an analogy between pointers in a data structure and goto statements in a program. Both are primitive tools capable of increasing the complexity of the program. Provide arguments and examples that support this position and examine how recursive data structures, as used in Mini-language Structures overcomes the problem.

Exercise 13.5   Notation for Pointers

Pascal uses an up-arrow (↑) for dereferencing a pointer and producing the object pointed to. For example, if P is a pointer to an integer, P ↑ denotes the integer. At first glance you might prefer a down arrow to suggest the idea of following down a pointer. Or are there yet better notations?

Propose a notation for declaring and using pointers, and discuss its impact on program readability.

Exercise 13.6   Queues

A *queue* is a list of items where items may be inserted at one end, the *rear* of the queue; and deleted at the other, the *front* of the queue. Write a program in Mini-language Structures that will simulate passengers waiting at a bus stop. The input consists of a sequence of integer pairs. The first integer is a code representing an action. The sequence is terminated by three zeros. The code can be a 1, denoting the arrival of a bus at the stop; a 2 representing the arrival of a group of passengers at the stop; or a 0, marking the termination of the simulation. If the code is a 1 then the second integer represents the number of people for which the bus has room. If the code is a 2 then the second integer represents the number of passengers who join the queue waiting for the bus. The people are assumed to form a single line, entering the line at the rear and leaving the line at the front to get on the bus. If a bus arrives with room for n people, the first n people in the queue get on the bus. If there are less than n people in the line, they all get on the bus, which does not wait for more people to arrive. The program must model the queue with a dynamic data structure and; each time the program reads a pair of integers, it should print out a trace of the action and, after modifying the queue accordingly, a count of the number of people in the queue.

14
Exception Handling

There are "exceptional" conditions that can arise in every program. Input data may contain values that are out of range, a hardware unit may fail, a table may become full, or the wrong reel of tape may be mounted.

To think of all exceptional conditions as errors is too limiting. There are exceptional conditions whose occurrences, though rare, are required for the proper termination of the program. For example, the end of the input file may mark the end of the input phase of a program and the beginning of its computation phase. Unfortunately, there is no generally accepted distinction between exceptional and normal conditions. What is normal in one context, may be exceptional in another.

For our purposes here, we define an *exception condition* as:

> A condition that is detected by an operation, that cannot be
> resolved within the local context of the operation, and must
> be brought to the attention of the operation's invoker.

The action of bringing the condition to the invoker's attention is called *raising* the exception. The corresponding action by the invoker is called *handling* the exception.

Generally, once an exception condition is raised, it must be handled; otherwise, the program is in error. Some languages provide default actions for conditions that are not handled by the program.

Since exception conditions are linked to particular operations, they are *synchronous* in the sense that they can only occur at specific points in the program. For example, a subscript error can only occur during array manipulation. *Asynchronous* events, such as an interrupt caused by a user pressing the break key on a terminal, can occur at any point during a program's execution. The handling of asynchronous events is discussed in Chapter 15. In this chapter, we discuss only synchronous conditions.

14.1   MINI-LANGUAGE EXCEPTIONS

As illustrated in Table 14.1, our mini-language for this chapter contains many features that have appeared in other mini-languages. As usual, the first part of a program consists of a sequence of one or more variable declarations, and each variable in a program must be declared exactly once. Each identifier may represent either a single integer value or a vector of integer values. Integer values may contain at most eight decimal digits. The number of components in arrays is 100, with a subscript range of 1 through 100.

Mini-language Exceptions has a simple procedural mechanism. Each procedure has a name and a body. The body simply consists of a sequence of statements and may also have an exception part, described below.

Most of the statements of this mini-language are familiar, they include:

- Assignment statements
- Loop and if statements
- Call statements
- Input and output statements

In addition, there is a raise statement whose meaning will be explained below.

Exceptions

There are a number of specific situations that can cause exceptions. These exceptions are described in Table 14.2. When one of these situations arises during program execution, the corresponding exception condition is raised. For example, if no value has been assigned to the variable INDEX, then evaluation of the expression

INDEX + 1

Table 14.1 Mini-Language Exceptions

program	::=	program
		    variable-declaration...
		    procedure...
		begin
		    statement...
		    [exception-handler]
		end;

variable-declaration	::=	declare identifier [,identifier...]: integer [array];

procedure	::=	procedure identifier :
		    statement...
		    [exception-handler]
		end;

statement	::=	assignment-statement | loop-statement | if-statement | call-statement | raise-statement | input-statement | output statement

exception-handler	::=	exception
		    when exception-name => statement...
		    [when exception-name => statement...]...

exception-name	::=	identifier | overflow | undefined_value | data_error | subscript_error | end_of_input
assignment-statement	::=	variable := expression ;
loop-statement	::=	while comparison loop statement... end loop;

if-statement	::=	if comparison then
		    statement...
		[else
		    statement...]
		end if;

call-statement	::=	identifier ;
raise-statement	::=	raise exception-name ;
input-statement	::=	input variable [, variable]... ;
output-statement	::=	output variable [, variable]... ;
comparison	::=	(operand comparison-operator operand)
expression	::=	[expression +] operand
operand	::=	integer | variable | (expression)
variable	::=	identifier | identifier [expression]
comparison-operator	::=	< | = | ≠ | >

Similar to PL/1

causes the suspension of normal execution and the raising of the undefined_value condition.

Each of the conditions defined in Table 14.2 can also be raised by the execution of a raise statement. For example, execution of the statement

```
raise overflow;
```

causes the overflow condition to be raised, just as it is when overflow occurs during computation. The raise statement can also be used to raise programmer-defined conditions, thus allowing a subroutine to report the occurrence of an exceptional condition. For example, the statement

```
raise TABLE_EMPTY;
```

would raise the TABLE_EMPTY condition and could be used to indicate that there were no entries in a table. This is a condition defined by the programmer for the particular program. The appearance of the identifier TABLE_EMPTY in the raise statement defines it to be a condition. Whether this would be an error situation would depend upon the context in which it was used.

In Mini-language Exceptions, the user may define how a condition is to be handled. The response can range from printing the values of one or more variables, to taking elaborate steps to deal with the cause of the exception. If the programmer does not specify how an exception condition is to be handled, the program is in error and is terminated. This applies to both predefined and user-defined conditions.

A response to an exception condition is defined by an exception handler included in a program unit. A program unit is either the main program or a procedure. For example, consider the handler:

```
exception
    when data_error => INVALID_DATA_FLAG := 1;
                       ERROR_COUNT := ERROR_COUNT + 1;
    when INVALID_ACCOUNT_NUMBER => output ACCOUNT_NUMBER;
```

When an exception condition is raised, normal execution is suspended. If there is an appropriate handler defined in the program unit that was being executed, the corresponding sequence of statements in the given handler is executed. These statements are executed instead of completing execution of the statement that caused the condition to be raised. After execution of the handler, normal execution of the procedure continues at the statement following the one that raised the condition.

Table 14.2   Predefined Exception Conditions

Condition	Cause
overflow	The absolute value of some quantity exceeds 99999999.
undefined_value	An attempt to obtain the value of a variable to which no value has been assigned.
data_error	The characters read during the execution of an input statement, do not constitute an integer or there is a transmission error due to a hardware malfunction.
subscript_error	The use of an array subscript outside the range 1 through 100.
end_of_input	The execution of an input statement when there is no more data to be read.

If there is no appropriate handler for the exception condition in the program unit, execution of the unit is terminated and the same condition is raised by the call statement that invoked the procedure. This process is continued until either a handler for the condition is executed or the program is terminated. Thus, if the main program does not contain a handler for the condition, the program is terminated.

Consider the simple procedure:

```
procedure INITIALIZE_TABLE:
    END_OF_DATA := 0;
    TABLE_INDEX := 1;
    input X, Y, Z;
    while (END_OF_DATA = 0) loop
        TABLE[TABLE_INDEX] := X + Y + Z;
        TABLE_INDEX        := TABLE_INDEX + 1;
        input X, Y, Z;
    end loop;

exception
    when end_of_input    =>  END_OF_DATA := 1;
    when overflow        =>  TABLE[TABLE_INDEX] := MAX_VALUE;
    when subscript_error =>  output X, Y, Z;
                             TABLE_INDEX := 1;
end;
```

This procedure has handlers for three exception conditions. When the condition for end of input is raised, the value of END_OF_DATA is set to 1. Control then returns to the statement following the input statement that raised the condition. The detection of the end of input is thus used to signal the end of the initialization process. The raising of the overflow condition is assumed to be due to the computation of the value to be inserted in the table. When this happens, the table value is set to the constant value MAX_VALUE defined in the containing program, and execution continues normally.

If the input contains more than 100 sets of values, the *subscript-error* condition will be raised. The handler for this condition prints the set of values last read (and ignored), and resets TABLE_INDEX to 1.

14.2   EXCEPTIONS

There are two broad classes of exceptions:

■   *Domain failure:* The input parameters to the operation do not satisfy the requirements of the operation. In Mini-language Exceptions, the subscripting operation has a domain failure when it is passed a subscript greater than 100.

■   *Range failure:* The operation is unable to produce a result that is in its range. For example, an input statement can encounter an end of file mark instead of a value. As we have seen, this is not necessarily an error; it depends upon the context of the operation. The overflow condition is a kind of range failure.

The exception handling mechanism of the mini-language treats both classes of exceptions in accordance with our definition of an exception. The raising of an exception condition by a statement brings the exception to the notice of the procedure containing the statement. If the procedure does not have a handler, the condition cannot be handled at that level and must be passed higher in the dynamic invocation chain.

Before we discuss the issues in exception handling, we turn to other common means for handling exceptions.

Unusual Return Value

This is the simplest and most primitive method of handling exception conditions. The operation returns an "impossible" value, that is, a value that is established by convention and that lies outside the normal range of the operation.

In its unadorned form, this method has obvious deficiencies. It requires explicit checking after each return from the operation and can destroy the abstraction of the type of the value returned. This can either lead to incomprehensible code that takes advantage of a particular representation for data or it can lead the programmer into spectacular errors.

For example, suppose an operation is defined to calculate the length of some object. Its range is therefore limited to positive values. If the convention is adopted that a specific value (say -1) is used to indicate the detection of an error, the programmer must always be aware that this impossible value may be returned. To forget this is to accept the risk that the value may be used in subsequent arithmetic operations and lead to bizarre results.

The Error Return

This is a mechanism that involves a nonstandard control structure. A call statement passes one or more label parameters designating error returns. These label values mark the beginnings of handlers for various exceptional conditions. For example, consider:

```
GET(I, OVERFLOW, BAD_DATA);
...
OVERFLOW: ...
BAD_DATA: ...
```

The idea is that, if the subroutine detects an exceptional condition, it branches to the label value specified by the appropriate parameter. The use of parameters allows the subroutine to be used in a number of contexts, since it is not tied to specific handlers. This technique imposes little overhead and requires no checking after each return as is required by an unusual return value. However, it does raise serious program structuring issues. In addition, the programmer may have difficulty in knowing where the program is to be resumed after the error has been handled.

In cases where the operation is a block that is internal to the block that invokes it, the label of the handler does not have to be passed as an argument. This makes the program's control structure even more difficult to understand.

Error Routines

In this case, the operation may be invoked with an entry argument specifying the procedure to be invoked by the operation if an exception is detected. For example,

```
GET(I, E)
```

where E is the name of the error handling procedure that is to be invoked if GET wishes to raise a condition.

The exception handler is a procedure and thus returns to its invoker. The structure of the control flow is therefore preserved and the operation that detected the condition is able to respond to any recovery action taken by the handler.

The use of a procedure as an exception handler does not require that the procedure be passed explicitly to the operation. Instead, the handler to be used can be specified implicitly. The handler can be associated with the object being processed or can be dynamically associated with the condition that is detected.

An example of associating the handler with the object would be to specify, as part of the declaration of a file, the procedure to be executed when the end of that file is detected. Thus the handler is associated with the file. As another example, the AED language allows a programmer to divide storage into zones and to associate with each zone a subroutine to be invoked if a subsequent space allocation request for that zone cannot be satisfied.

The dynamic association of a handler with a condition is typified by the PL/I on-unit mechanism. This was perhaps the first attempt to provide an explicit exception condition mechanism in a high level language. It has the disadvantage that, though the handler has many of the attributes of a procedure, there is no parameter passing mechanism. All communication between the operation and the handler must be passed through global variables. This reduces both flexiblilty and clarity.

14.3   ISSUES IN EXCEPTION HANDLING

Is there any real need to worry about exception conditions? Anyone who has ever built a large program that makes any pretense at *robustness* appreciates the problems. As programs grow in size, special cases and unusual circumstances proliferate. Even the performance of a seemingly simple task, like a tape-to-tape copy program, abounds with exception conditions. The end-of-input condition will generally be handled properly since it probably marks the end of the process. However, what can be done about tape label checking and the multitude of possible hardware malfunctions? Exceptions exist in even the simplest task and the complexity that they induce in the program is large. None of the techniques described in the previous section adequately controls this complexity.

It is clear that, for a program to be robust, any exception condition that can arise must be handled. The difficulty is in designing a simple mechanism of sufficient generality to handle all possibilities.

One common method is to make an explicit test for each exception at all possible points of occurrence. This method has the great advantage that no special mechanism is required. In many cases, however, the inclusion of such tests can complicate the structure of the program and hide the algorithm behind a welter of special cases. Thus we need to search for some method that is sufficiently general, has manageable complexity, and yet remains clear enough so that the normal is not obscured by the handling of the exceptional.

In the quest for such a method, there are a variety of issues that must be addressed.

- The specification of a handler

- The use of defaults when the programmer has not provided an explicit handler

- The propagation of conditions outside the program unit in which they are detected

- The resumption of execution following handling

- The possibility of suppressing the detection of conditions

Handler Specification

The basic operation of an exception handler is to perform some diagnostic or repair actions. Frequently, a handler will *take over* when some exception condition is raised. In order to act appropriately, a handler may need access to the environment in which the exception was raised.

One of the critical choices in the design of an exception facility is the method by which the handlers are defined. In Mini-language Exceptions a very simple mechanism is used. A handler may be specified within a procedure. This handler is supposed to *complete* the work of the operation that raised the condition. Because of the simplicity, the mechanism cannot cope with a situation where different handlers are required at different points in a procedure. While the handler has access to the complete environment of the operation, there is no easy way to determine which one of several operations that have the potential for raising the condition actually raised it. For example, if the procedure has several arithmetic expressions, there is no way of telling which operation caused the overflow condition.

Use of Default Handlers

In Mini-language Exceptions, nearly all of the predefined conditions represent error situations. Generally, these error situations have the potential of being raised at many points in the program. This brings up the need for *default* exception handlers.

A default handler is one that is used in the absence of an explicitly defined handler. The Mini-language Exceptions approach defines a single default action for all conditions — program termination.

Termination may not be adequate for many programs. For example, whenever an overflow occurs, we may wish simply to assign the maximum possible number to the offending expression and then resume normal execution. This brings up a number of issues. How does one define a default handler to be used throughout a program? When should a specifically provided handler override the default handler? The question of the resumption of execution will be taken up later in this section.

The conventional response to an error situation in a programming language is a simple abnormal termination of a program, usually with the printing of some diagnostic message. We may view this action itself as simply the default handler provided for the exception situation raised by the error condition. Accordingly, one test of the adequacy of any exception handling mechanism is that it should be possible to define the normal response to errors provided in a programming language. With Mini-language Exceptions, this test is not satisfied.

Propagation of Exceptions

The underlying reason for devising an exception mechanism is the realization that the context in which a condition is detected may not be the proper context in which to process it. For this reason, notice of its detection must be passed to the context where it can be processed. This is generally another procedure at a different level of abstraction. In order to preserve the abstraction, the detecting operation should express the exception condition in terms of the abstraction that it defines.

It may not be possible for the recipient of an exception to process the condition completely. The occurrence of the exception may seriously affect its behavior, forcing it to raise an exception as well. In order to maintain the higher level of abstraction of the recipient, this second exception must be expressed in terms of the abstraction represented by its recipient. In short, it must not simply pass the condition raised by the original operation straight through.

In Chapter 1 we cited the Fortran error message:

```
STATE-ABEND CODE IS: SYSTEM 0200, USER 0000
IO-NONE, SCB=0F10C0, PSW IS 078D2000000A98B7E
```

Here is an example of an exception condition that was originally detected and raised at the level of abstraction of the operating system and passed to the Fortran run time support library. This library represents the change of abstraction level from that of operating system to that of programming language. However, in our example, the condition was not modified at that level to maintain the proper abstraction. Thus the programmer cannot assign any meaning to the message.

This example also illustrates a second problem in design: the unilateral decision by a subroutine to terminate execution rather than to offer the programmer the option of effecting a repair and continuing, or of cleaning up before terminating in an orderly manner. Consider the difficulties that a language module can bring by aborting execution of a data base system instead of propagating the exception upward. Crucial files of the data base may be left in an inconsistent state, potentially causing further erroneous behavior when the data base system is later restored.

A raise statement like that in Mini-language Exceptions provides a simple basis for the propagation of exception conditions while maintaining the proper levels of abstraction. However, because of its extreme simplicity this mechanism does not provide for adequate passage of information from the detecting operation to the handler. There is no way in which variable information can be passed other than through the clumsy use of global variables.

Resuming Program Execution

With most methods of exception handling, the flow of control passes to some remote program text that defines the action to be taken when the exception is raised. Thus the handler may be viewed as a sort of *trap*. One basic question about exception handling is, what happens after handling the exception? This amounts to a question of whether resumption of normal program flow is meaningful.

One view of exception handlers is that they are basically subroutines to which control is automatically passed when the exception is raised. As with all subroutine calls, after completion of the subroutine, control resumes at the statement after the subroutine call. With this view, the notion of a trap is still retained, but resumption of normal program flow is implicit.

A second view is that exceptions represent program errors. This means that when an exception occurs in a given environment, this environment is to be terminated. The primary role of an exception handler is to provide some appropriate clean-up operation before termination. With this view, resumption of normal execution is meaningless. The handler may decide to restore the same sequence of actions under better conditions, but it will do so by a different invocation of these actions, not a simple resumption.

The first view of exception handlers is the one adopted in PL/I. However, the question of resumption was not treated in a consistent manner. In some cases, resumption implies repetition of the action that raised the condition with the presumption that some sort of fix-up has been made in the handler. In other cases, resumption takes place at the statement following the one that raised the condition. For a third class of conditions, no sort of resumption is possible without the use of labels and goto statements.

The second view of exceptions is taken by Ada. It provides for local detection of exceptions, which are synonymous with errors. With this view of exceptions, a handler is part of the program unit in which the exception may be raised. Here, the notion of a trap is perhaps not as appropriate, for the handler takes over in case of a faulty situation within the procedure. In this view, normal program execution resumes at the point in which the procedure is called, just as if there had been no exception raised in the first place.

The view taken by Mini-language Exceptions lies between these two positions. The handler does not really constitute a subroutine, but resumption is possible.

Suppression of Exceptions

It could be said that the detection of exception conditions should never be turned off. There is, however, a counter view to this.

Some exception conditions may be quite inefficient to implement. For example, in a language with arrays whose subscripts are restricted to lie within certain bounds (as is the case with most programming languages), range checks for subscripts may need to be implemented in software. Such checks require an implementation overhead during execution of a program.

In addition, in some languages there are exception conditions that certainly require excess overhead. For example, a language may include the ability for the user to specify assertions that must be true during execution of a program, for example, that the value of one variable must always be greater than the value of another. When assertions are themselves present in a programming language, the validity of each assertion must be checked with the underlying software. Such assertion checks can be quite expensive to implement.

Imagine for the moment that you are sure that the program you have written is correct. That is, assume that you tested it, and that in all conceivable cases the output produced by the program is as desired. While we might argue that a program is never fully certified to be correct, in practice we may want to make this assumption. In these cases, the checking of exception conditions is superfluous. For this reason, we may wish a feature in a programming language to indicate that one or more (or all) exception conditions should not be checked. This gives us the notion of *suppression* of exception conditions.

There seem to be two basic views regarding the suppression of exceptions. On the one hand, perhaps the suppression of exceptions is best indicated by a command given in the environment in which the program is run. Such a feature would not have any direct impact on the programming language itself. On the other hand, we may wish to state the explicit suppression of exceptions within the programming language. This question is not addressed in Mini-language Exceptions.

FURTHER READING

Perhaps the most significant works related to this chapter are the paper [Goodenough 1975] and the thesis [Levin 1977]. These works survey a number of issues regarding exception handling.

An early paper relevant to the discussion here is that by Hill [1971]. A more recent discussion of exception handling is given in [Ichbiah et al. 1979]. Another view of exception handling is that by Parnas and Wurges [1976].

EXERCISES

Exercise 14.1   Programming in Mini-language Exceptions

Write a program in Mini-language Exceptions that will calculate and print the largest integer value supported by the implementation.

Exercise 14.2   Using the Raise Statement

Write a program in Mini-language Exceptions that first reads in a sequence of pairs of integers terminated by a pair of zeros. The first integer of each pair represents a part number and the second, the number of parts in stock. The part numbers should be stored in one array and the quantity on hand in another.

Following the table initialization phase, terminated by the two zeros, another sequence of integer pairs is to be read, this is the sequence terminated by end-of-input. This second sequence represents *additions* to the quantity-on-hand for certain parts in the original sequence. Thus, for each part number in the second sequence, the table must be searched to find the index so that the corresponding quantity on hand can be updated. Finally, the updated table is to be printed out.

During table initialization, the table must be checked for each new part number to ensure that there are no erroneous duplicate entries. During the updating phase, appropriate error action must be taken if a part number that doesn't exist in the table is supplied. Both phases should use the same table search routine, which should report the fact that the searched-for entry does not exist in the table (using a raise statement).

Exercise 14.3   Resumption of Execution after an Exception

There are many points of view on how execution of a program should be resumed after the handling of an exception. In Ada, for example, the action of the handler terminates the execution of the program unit *containing* the statement that raised the exception. Thus execution is resumed after the statement that invoked the unit. Mini-language Exceptions takes the view that the handler terminates the *operation* that raised the exception. In PL/I, the point of resumption depends on the type of exception, and varies from repeating the operation to aborting the program.

An exception may be raised by an operation that has only partially completed and it may be inappropriate or undesirable to return control to the precise point at which the exception was raised. Discuss what might be an appropriate set of return points after the following exceptions:

a. Overflow during integer arithmetic.
b. Subscript range error.

c. End of page after output of the second line of a four-line block of printing.
d. Non-numeric character encountered during conversion of a character string to numeric representation.
e. Insufficient storage during creation of a dynamic data structure.
f. End of file during an input operation.
g. Following the execution of a raise statement.

Exercise 14.4   Handlers with Parameters

Mini-language Exceptions has no provision for the passing of parameters to exception handlers. Suggest modifications to the syntax and semantics of the mini-language that will allow this.

Exercise 14.5   Default Handlers

Mini-language Exceptions defines a single default action for all conditions, program termination. Propose a more useful set of default handlers for the conditions detected in the mini-language.

15
Parallel Processing

We are all familiar with sets of related actions that take place concurrently. The operation of many moving trains on a rail network and the handling of several lines of customers at a bank are typical examples. In contrast, the traditional stored program digital computer has had as its primary objective the sequential execution of the steps forming a single algorithm. As a consequence, most programming languages address only questions of sequence and ignore parallelism.

However, parallelism has had a place in computers. The desire for increased speed has led to overlapping of input and output with computation, arithmetic units that work in parallel, and to multiprogrammed and multiprocessor operating systems. However, this parallelism has generally been hidden from the programmer. In this chapter we examine the programming language implications of specifying independent, but related, tasks that are to be executed concurrently. These are sometimes known as *concurrent processes*. To achieve concurrency in a controlled and reliable manner, the tasks must be able to communicate and synchronize with each other.

It is not necessary that the component steps of the tasks actually take place concurrently. In a multiprogramming, single processor, operating system they may be arbitrarily interleaved. The important point is that the execution of the tasks is only required to be synchronized at specific points specified by the programmer. Thus the requirement for parallel execution poses a new level of discipline on the programming process.

Our discussion here will make frequent use of a single example. We wish to write a program to decode messages. Let us not worry about what the messages mean. They are generated at some remote field station, decoded, and then printed on a line printer. In particular, we wish to define three program units, RECEIVE_CODES, DECODER, and PRINT_MESSAGES:

■ RECEIVE_CODES: This program unit reads encoded data and passes them on, code by code.

■ DECODER: This program unit receives encoded data, decodes them by some method, which does not concern us here, and transmits the decoded characters.

■ PRINT_MESSAGES: This program unit receives characters, and when it obtains a full line of text, prints the line on a line printer.

Both the codes and characters are assumed to be represented by integers.

The important point about our program is that the three program units are conceptually independent and can progress at their own rates. Except for specific points of synchronization, the interleaving in time for executing the individual statements of the three program units is of no concern.

Mini-language Parallel is designed to solve such problems. This mini-language is based on the work of Hoare [1978]; its syntax is inspired by that of Ada.

15.1   MINI-LANGUAGE PARALLEL

As usual, a program consists of a sequence of declarations followed by a sequence of statements, as shown in Table 15.1. Declarations introduce variables whose values are either simple integers or arrays of integers. The bounds of arrays are unspecified. All variables used in a program must be declared exactly once.

The syntax and semantics of the assignment statement are familiar. Addition and subtraction operators may be used in arithmetic expressions.

Table 15.1   Mini-language Parallel

program	::=	program
		    declaration...
		begin
		    statement...
		end;

declaration	::=	declare identifier [, identifier]... [: array];

statement	::=	assignment-statement
		    | start-statement | send-statement
		    | receive-statement | select-statement

assignment-statement	::=	variable := expression ;

start-statement	::=	start tasks
		    task-identifier: statement...
		    [task-identifier: statement...]...
		end tasks;

send-statement	::=	send variable to task-identifier ;
receive-statement	::=	receive variable from task-identifier;

select-statement	::=	select [loop]
		    when guard => statement...
		    [when guard => statement...]...
		end select;

guard	::=	comparison [and comparison]... [and receive-clause] | receive-clause
receive-clause	::=	receive variable from task-identifier
comparison	::=	(operand comparison-operator operand)
expression	::=	[operand +] operand | [operand −] operand
operand	::=	integer | variable | (expression)
variable	::=	identifier | identifier [expression]
task-identifier	::=	identifier
comparison-operator	::=	< | = | ≠ | >

Tasks

A task is a program unit that can be executed concurrently with other tasks. Each task has a name and a body. The body of a task simply consists of a sequence of one or more statements.

A start statement specifies the concurrent execution of one or more tasks. All tasks in a start statement may begin execution simultaneously. A start statement terminates successfully when all named tasks have been successfully completed.

For example, consider the following sketch:

```
start tasks
    RECEIVE_CODES:
        -- statements for obtaining codes

    DECODER:
        -- statements for decoding code values
        -- into character values

    PRINT_MESSAGES:
        -- statements for printing the decoded messages
end tasks;
```

Execution of the start statement results in the parallel execution of the bodies of each named task.

As far as termination is concerned, each task will terminate normally after execution of its last statement. The start statement containing the tasks will terminate when all named tasks have terminated, at which time control continues at the statement following the start statement. In our example above, the start statement will wait at its end for the three tasks named RECEIVE_CODES, DECODER, and PRINT_MESSAGES to terminate. If any of the tasks leads to an execution error, the entire program terminates abnormally.

There is one important requirement on the use of tasks within a start statement. Each of the tasks must be *disjoint* in the sense that a task may not use a variable that occurs as a target variable in one of the other tasks. A *target variable* is a variable that occurs on the left hand side of the assignment statement or a variable that occurs in a receive statement, defined below.

Communications between Tasks

In any system of related tasks, there must be some form of communication. We clearly do not want the trains on a rail network to collide, we may want to ensure that two bank tellers do not make conflicting transactions on the same account, or we may need to coordinate the actions of the devices in a computing system.

In Mini-language Parallel, the basic form of communication between tasks is through send and receive statements. Communication occurs between two tasks whenever:

■ A send statement in one task specifies a value to be transmitted to another task, and

■ A receive statement in the other task specifies a target variable whose value is to be obtained from the sending task.

When these two conditions arise, the two tasks are said to meet in a *rendezvous*:

Consider the statement

```
send NEW_CODE to DECODER;
```

which occurs in the task body for RECEIVE_CODES, and the following clause

```
receive CODE from RECEIVE_CODES;
```

taken from the body of DECODER. There are two possibilities for a rendezvous, according to whether the send statement in the task RECEIVE_CODES is executed before or after the corresponding receive statement is reached by the task DECODER. Whichever gets there first waits for the other. When the rendezvous is achieved, the value of NEW_CODE is passed to the variable CODE, and both tasks again proceed independently.

We thus see the two basic functions achieved with a rendezvous:

1. *Synchronization:* The sending task must execute a send statement naming the receiving task and the receiving task must reach a corresponding receive statement, which names the sending task.

2. *Transmission of information:* The sending task transmits a value to the receiving task.

It should be observed that a receiving task can only handle one send statement at a time. Although not illustrated by our example, there could be several tasks with pending send statements to a single receiving task. The send statements are processed on a first come, first served basis.

Finally, we note that simple integer values and complete arrays may be transmitted during a rendezvous. The type of the value that is sent must match the type of the corresponding receiving variable; otherwise the program is terminated abnormally.

Guarded Statements

A guarded statement (or a guarded sequence of statements) is a statement prefixed by a *guard*, which determines whether or not a statement is to be executed. A guard can contain a sequence of comparisons each separated by and. A guard may also contain a receive clause (defined below). Such a guard may contain only one receive clause, which must appear as the last element of the guard.

Guarded statements form the alternatives of a select statement, as in:

```
select
   when (LINE_POSITION < LINE_SIZE)  =>
      LINE_POSITION := LINE_POSITION + 1;

   when (LINE_POSITION = LINE_SIZE)  =>
      send LINE to OUTPUT_DEVICE;
      LINE_POSITION := 1;
end select;
```

This select statement contains two guarded statements: one for the case when the value of LINE_POSITION is less than LINE_SIZE and the other for when LINE_POSITION equals LINE_SIZE.

Execution of a select statement takes place as follows. First, each of the guards in the select statement is evaluated. If none of the guards evaluates to true, the select statement has no net effect and is equivalent to an empty statement. If exactly one of the guards evaluates to true, then the statement prefixed by this guard is executed. Otherwise, if more than one guard evaluates to true, then a statement with a true guard is selected arbitrarily and executed. In our example above, where line positions are assumed to be integers in a range of 1 through LINE_SIZE, exactly one of the guards will always be true.

It is important to note that when more than one guard evaluates to true, execution of a select statement is nondeterministic. This is in sharp contrast with our other mini-languages, where a program will always execute statements in a determined order. In Mini-language Parallel, it is possible to write select statements with several true guards, and to give different actions for each true guard. The precise effect of such a select statement cannot be predicted.

As mentioned above, a guard may contain a single receive clause. This has the same form as a receive statement but in this context serves the additional function of a guard. For example, consider the following select statement:

```
select
    when receive MESSAGE_CHAR from DECODER   =>
        LINE[LINE_POSITION] := MESSAGE_CHAR;
end select;
```

Here a statement is guarded by a receive clause. A receive clause is said to be:

■ *True* if there is a corresponding send statement that is waiting for its information to be received. In this case, the receive clause performs the function of a receive statement and the information is transferred between the tasks. The statement guarded by the receive clause is then executed.

■ *Pending* if no corresponding send statement has been issued by the task named in the receive clause and that task is still active.

■ *False* if the task named in the receive clause has terminated.

Accordingly, in a select statement, the following cases can arise:

1. One or more guards evaluate to the value true. In this case, one of the guarded statements is executed.

2. All guards evaluate to the value false. In this case, execution of the select statement has no effect.

3. One or more of the guards is pending, and the remaining guards evaluate to false. In this case, the select statement is not executed immediately but must await a corresponding send statement from one of the named tasks. When that send statement is issued, the appropriate guarded statement is executed. If all named tasks terminate without issuing a send statement, the select statement is completed with no net effect.

Thus we see that a select statement may be immediately executed, or may be delayed until a send statement in another task is executed.

Another form of select statement is used to specify loops. This is the select loop statement. For example, consider the following select loop:

```
select loop
   when (COUNT < N)  =>
       COUNT := COUNT + 1;
end select;
```

As long as the variable COUNT remains less than N, the variable COUNT will continue to be incremented by one. The loop will terminate when the value of COUNT is equal to N.

Execution of a select loop is similar to that of a select statement, except that, as long as guards remain true or contain pending receive clauses, the alternatives in the body of the loop will continue to be executed. In particular, execution of a select loop proceeds as follows:

■ If one or more of the guards evaluate to true, one of the corresponding guarded statements is executed, and the select loop is executed again.

■ If none of the guards evaluates to true but one or more of the guards contains a pending receive clause, execution of the loop is suspended. When a corresponding send statement is issued, execution of the loop is continues. If all pending tasks terminate before issuing a send statement, the loop is also terminated.

■ If all of the guards evaluate to false, the loop is terminated.

Predefined Tasks

Two tasks are predefined in Mini-language Parallel. The first is a task named INPUT_DEVICE. This task is assumed to be associated with some input device that sends characters to a program containing a corresponding receive clause. The second is the predefined task named OUTPUT_DEVICE. This task corresponds to some output device that receives lines of text containing 72 characters. Such lines of text are represented as arrays in Mini-language Parallel.

15.2 A FIRST SOLUTION TO THE DECODING PROBLEM

We are now in a position to present a solution to the decoding problem described earlier. This solution is given in Example 15.1.

The program of Example 15.1 essentially consists of three tasks, named: RECEIVE_CODES, DECODER, and PRINT_MESSAGES.

The task RECEIVE_CODES consists of a simple select loop that continues to receive new codes from the input device and transmits these codes to the task named DECODER. Notice that the guard in the select loop for this task consists of a single receive clause. This receive clause continues to wait for values to be transmitted to the target variable NEW_CODE. Notice also that this task may be delayed if no codes are forthcoming for a period of time.

The second task, named DECODER, consists of a simple select loop also, again with a single guarded statement prefixed by a receive clause. When a code is sent from the task RECEIVE_CODES, the value of the code is analyzed and its decoded value is stored in the integer variable named CHAR. Notice here, that in cases where the decoding of codes is somewhat time consuming, this task may operate more slowly than the sending task RECEIVE_CODES. If the data from the input device cannot be delayed, some sort of buffering mechanism will have to be added to RECEIVE_CODES.

Finally, a third task, named PRINT_MESSAGES, again consists of a simple select loop. This loop continues to receive message characters from the task named DECODER, fills an array named LINE with these characters and, when a full line is given, sends the value of LINE to the output device.

The three tasks operate quite independently, but are, of course, synchronized through the corresponding send statements and receive clauses. As given, the three tasks operate forever, and the program never terminates.

15.3 PUTTING A BUFFER IN A TASK

The computation performed on a code by DECODER may not be completed by the time the next code is received by RECEIVE_CODES. Since RECEIVE_CODES cannot receive the next code until the transmission of the previous one has been completed, there may be a loss of input data. Of course, on average, the decoding process must be able to keep pace with the reception of codes, but this may not be true over short bursts of input activity. We would like the reception of codes and their decoding to go on much more independently.

```
program

    declare CODE, NEW_CODE, CHAR, MESSAGE_CHAR,
            LINE_POSITION, LINE_SIZE;
    declare LINE: array;

begin
    start tasks
        RECEIVE_CODES:
            select loop
                when receive NEW_CODE from INPUT_DEVICE  =>
                    send NEW_CODE to DECODER;
            end select;

        DECODER:
            select loop
                when receive CODE from RECEIVE_CODES  =>
                    -- statements for decoding the value of CODE
                    -- and producing the decoded value in CHAR

                    send CHAR to PRINT_MESSAGES;
            end select;

        PRINT_MESSAGES:
            LINE_POSITION := 1;
            LINE_SIZE     := 72;
            select loop
                when receive MESSAGE_CHAR from DECODER  =>
                    LINE[LINE_POSITION] := MESSAGE_CHAR;
                    select
                        when (LINE_POSITION < LINE_SIZE)  =>
                            LINE_POSITION = LINE_POSITION + 1;
                        when (LINE_POSITION = LINE_SIZE)  =>
                            send LINE to OUTPUT_DEVICE;
                            LINE_POSITION := 1;
                    end select;
            end select;

    end tasks;
end;
```

Example 15.1   A solution to the decoding problem

In particular, if our decoding process is slow, we would still like RECEIVE_CODES to accept a burst of new data. For this purpose, we can introduce a storage area for characters in the RECEIVE_CODES task as a buffer. The design must be such that as long as the buffer is neither full nor empty, the task is able to accept requests for both input and output.

To do this, the conditions that guard the alternatives must be such that if there is room in the buffer, a new code can be accepted and, if there are characters to be sent, a send request can be performed. Consider the following outline:

```
select loop
    when (COUNT < STORAGE_SIZE)  =>
        -- what to do if more storage space is available

    when (COUNT > 0)  =>
        -- what to do if the storage area is not empty
end select;
```

Only those statements whose guarding conditions evaluate to true can be executed. Importantly, when both guards are true, either guarded statement can be executed. Thus we have a case of *nondeterminism*, where the choice of actions is not specified by the programmer.

These points are illustrated in Example 15.2. The major change is in the RECEIVE_CODES task where there is an array managed as a circular buffer. That is, whenever the end of the storage area is reached, it is continued again at the beginning. The two indexes, IN_INDEX and OUT_INDEX, are used to denote the elements in the buffer for the next incoming code and the next code for transmission, respectively.

To prevent the RECEIVE_CODES task from being hung up while waiting for the completion of decoding by the DECODER task, the send statement is not executed until a request has been received from DECODER. The request does not have a value that is used, it is merely used as a synchronizing signal.

15.4   INTERRUPTING A TASK

On many systems, we have hardware interrupts that are triggered by certain events. For example, we may wish to install a stop button in our decoding system. If no more codes are to be produced, or if for some reason the user wants the program to terminate, the user can press the stop button. All the tasks must then be brought to an orderly completion with all codes printed.

```
program
    declare CODE, NEW_CODE, CHAR, MESSAGE_CHAR, LINE_POSITION, LINE_SIZE;
    declare COUNT, IN_INDEX,OUT_INDEX, STORAGE_SIZE, REQUEST_Q,REQUEST_A;
    declare LINE, STORAGE_AREA: array;

begin
    start tasks
        RECEIVE_CODES:
            COUNT        :=   0;
            IN_INDEX     :=   1;
            OUT_INDEX    :=   1;
            STORAGE_SIZE := 500;

            select loop
                when (COUNT < STORAGE_SIZE)
                    and receive NEW_CODE from INPUT_DEVICE  =>
                        STORAGE_AREA[IN_INDEX] := NEW_CODE;
                        COUNT                  := COUNT + 1;
                        select
                            when (IN_INDEX < STORAGE_SIZE)   =>
                                IN_INDEX := IN_INDEX + 1;
                            when (IN_INDEX = STORAGE_SIZE)   =>
                                IN_INDEX := 1;
                        end select;
                when (COUNT > 0)
                    and receive REQUEST_A from DECODER       =>
                        send STORAGE_AREA[OUT_INDEX] to DECODER;
                        COUNT := COUNT - 1;
                        select
                            when (OUT_INDEX < STORAGE_SIZE)  =>
                                OUT_INDEX := OUT_INDEX + 1;
                            when (OUT_INDEX = STORAGE_SIZE)  =>
                                OUT_INDEX := 1;
                        end select;
            end select;
        DECODER:
            REQUEST_Q := 1;
            select loop
                when (1 = 1) =>   -- always true
                    send REQUEST_Q to RECEIVE_CODES;
                    receive CODE from RECEIVE_CODES;
                    -- statements for decoding the value of CODE
                    -- and producing the decoded value in CHAR
                    send CHAR to PRINT_MESSAGES;
            end select;
```

Example 15.2   Putting a buffer into the receiving task

```
PRINT_MESSAGES:
   LINE_POSITION := 1;
   LINE_SIZE     := 72;
   select loop
      when receive MESSAGE_CHAR from DECODER  =>
         LINE[LINE_POSITION] := MESSAGE_CHAR;
         select
            when (LINE_POSITION < LINE_SIZE)  =>
               LINE_POSITION := LINE_POSITION + 1;
            when (LINE_POSITION = LINE_SIZE)  =>
               send LINE to OUTPUT_DEVICE;
               LINE_POSITION := 1;
         end select;
      end select;
   end tasks;
end;
```

Example 15.2   continued

Hardware interrupts can be handled in various ways. Conceptually, we can think of the user as another task that transmits a single piece of information, the pressing of the button. This model fits well with the way that we view a task as executing independently except for a particular rendezvous for the purpose of transmitting data.

Example 15.3 shows the complete solution incorporating both the buffering described in the previous section and the provision for a stop button. Note that if the user presses the stop button when the input buffer is full, that is, when

```
(COUNT = STORAGE_SIZE)
```

there is the possibility that one of the input codes will be lost. It seems that in such a situation, shutting down the system should take priority.

15.5   ISSUES IN PARALLEL PROCESSING

Parallel processing brings up a number of new issues with programming languages. Traditionally, we are quite accustomed to the idea of a program as a purely sequential process. After one statement is executed, the next statement to be executed is specified precisely and in a deterministic manner. However, with the advancement of computer technology, systems with multiple processors and multiple devices are

```
program
   declare CODE, NEW_CODE, CHAR, MESSAGE_CHAR, LINE_POSITION, LINE_SIZE;
   declare COUNT, IN_INDEX,OUT_INDEX, STORAGE_SIZE, REQUEST_Q,REQUEST_A;
   declare STOP, STOP_CODE, STOP_FLAG, STOP_DECODING, OFF, ON;
   declare LINE, STORAGE_AREA: array;
begin
   OFF        :=   0;
   ON         :=   1;
   STOP_CODE  := 999;
   start tasks
      RECEIVE_CODES:
         STOP_FLAG    := OFF;
         COUNT        :=   0;
         IN_INDEX     :=   1;
         OUT_INDEX    :=   1;
         STORAGE_SIZE := 500;
         select loop
            when (STOP_FLAG = OFF)
               and receive STOP from USER  =>
                  STOP_FLAG := ON;
                  STORAGE_AREA[IN_INDEX] := STOP_CODE;
                  COUNT                  := COUNT + 1;
            when (STOP_FLAG = OFF) and (COUNT < STORAGE_SIZE)
               and receive NEW_CODE from INPUT_DEVICE =>
                  STORAGE_AREA[IN_INDEX] := NEW_CODE;
                  COUNT                  := COUNT + 1;
                  select
                     when (IN_INDEX < STORAGE_SIZE) =>
                        IN_INDEX := IN_INDEX + 1;
                     when (IN_INDEX = STORAGE_SIZE) =>
                        IN_INDEX := 1;
                  end select;
            when (COUNT > 0)
               and receive REQUEST_A from DECODER =>
                  send STORAGE_AREA[OUT_INDEX] to DECODER;
                  COUNT := COUNT - 1;
                  select
                     when (OUT_INDEX < STORAGE_SIZE) =>
                        OUT_INDEX := OUT_INDEX + 1;
                     when (OUT_INDEX = STORAGE_SIZE)  =>
                        OUT_INDEX := 1;
                  end select;
         end select;
```

Example 15.3   Adding a stop button to the encoding problem

```
DECODER:
    REQUEST_Q := 1;
    STOP_DECODING := OFF;
    select loop
        when (STOP_DECODING = OFF) =>
            send REQUEST_Q to RECEIVE_CODES;
            receive CODE from RECEIVE_CODES;
            select
                when (CODE ≠ STOP_CODE) =>
                    -- statements for decoding values of CODE
                    -- and producing the decoded value in CHAR
                    send CHAR to PRINT MESSAGES;
                when (CODE = STOP_CODE) =>
                    STOP_DECODING := ON;
                    send STOP_CODE to PRINT_MESSAGES;
            end select;
    end select;

PRINT_MESSAGES:
    LINE_POSITION := 1;
    LINE_SIZE     := 72;
    receive MESSAGE_CHAR from DECODER;
    select loop
        when (MESSAGE_CHAR ≠ STOP_CODE) =>
            LINE[LINE_POSITION] := MESSAGE_CHAR;
            select
                when (LINE_POSITION < LINE_SIZE) =>
                    LINE_POSITION := LINE_POSITION + 1;
                when (LINE_POSITION = LINE_SIZE) =>
                    send LINE to OUTPUT_DEVICE;
                    LINE_POSITION := 1;
            end select;
            receive MESSAGE_CHAR from DECODER;
    end select;

    LINE[LINE_POSITION] := STOP_CODE;
    send LINE to OUTPUT_DEVICE;
end tasks;
end;
```

Example 15.3   continued

becoming commonplace. Effective use of these resources demands special constructs for parallel processing.

Concurrency

The fact that different portions of the same program may be executed concurrently can lead to a number of serious problems. These problems arise when two or more tasks have access to the same location. In particular, execution of one of the tasks may update a variable, while another task may not be sure that the value of the variable has been changed. Such a variable is generally called a *shared* variable.

In Mini-language Parallel, this problem is avoided by requiring that each task be disjoint. That is, no task may mention a variable that is updated by another task, and there are thus no shared variables. This restriction clearly simplifies the understanding of concurrently executed tasks. The only means of communication between two tasks is through a rendezvous, as in Ada.

When shared variables are allowed, the construct of a *critical region* is usually introduced, see [Brinch Hansen 1972]. A critical region is a portion of program text for which one or more shared variables are referenced. These variables are protected from use by other tasks during execution of the statements of the critical region.

Critical regions solve the problem of preventing undesired access to shared data; however, shared variables are in a sense global variables and entail some of their complexities. Although Mini-language Parallel was not designed to have the scope of variables limited to tasks in which they are declared, this could have been done. This would have ensured disjointness without hindering communication through a rendezvous. Critical regions do not treat the problem of task synchronization.

Synchronization

The execution of concurrent tasks is not completely independent. A collection of tasks is executed in order to solve some problem. Often one task must complete some computation before another task can complete its own computation. This is the general problem of *synchronization*.

In Mini-language Parallel, the synchronization between tasks is handled by corresponding send and receive statements. Before a task can receive a data item, another task must send the data item to the given task. Thus, even if each task is executed with a given piece of hardware, certain tasks may be suspended during execution. The actual rates at which tasks progress is really a matter for the underlying implementation.

A synchronization primitive available in some languages is the semaphore, introduced by Dijkstra [1968b]. The name semaphore evokes the idea of a signal used on railroads to permit or deny entry of a train to a section of track. A semaphore is a special variable that has an integer associated with it. We might declare a semaphore variable as:

```
declare S: semaphore;
```

The only valid operations on semaphores are P (from the Dutch *passeren* meaning "to pass"), sometimes called WAIT, and V (from the Dutch *vrijgeven* meaning "to release"), sometimes called SIGNAL. The two semaphore operations allow a process to cause itself to wait for a certain event and then to be awakened by another process when the event occurs. P and V have the following meaning:

P(S): Wait until the value of S > 0 and then subtract one from S and continue execution.

V(S): Add 1 to S. This will allow a process that is waiting because it executed P(S) to continue.

Both P and V must be performed indivisibly. That is, there can be no partial completion of the operation while something else takes place. On some machines, the equivalent of these operations is implemented as a hardware instruction.

An example of how these might be used to communicate between tasks is shown in Example 15.4. The difficulty with semaphores is that they are not associated with the shared variable except by a programmer convention. The compiler is thus not able to check that the semaphore is being used to ensure mutual exclusion of the tasks whenever the value of the variable is changed. As a programming language mechanism they are therefore, unreliable.

Communication

In addition to synchronizing their behavior, tasks must also be able to exchange information. In Mini-language Parallel, synchronization of tasks and exchange of information are inseparable. These two requirements are embraced by the concept of a rendezvous. During the rendezvous, the value of an expression is passed to a target variable in another task.

A rendezvous has several strong advantages in the writing of concurrent programs. For one, it allows interactions between tasks to be clearly defined and isolated. Furthermore, there is a pleasant symmetry

```
program
    declare COUNT;  -- used to pass information between tasks
    declare S: semaphore;
begin
    COUNT := 0;
    start tasks
        SENDER:
            select loop
                when (1 = 1) =>
                -- code to observe an event
                P(S);        -- prepare to change COUNT
                COUNT := COUNT + 1;
                V(S);        -- signal that COUNT is available
            end select;
        RECEIVER:
            select loop
                when (1 = 1) =>
                    P(S);    -- prepare to read COUNT and reset it
                    print COUNT;
                    COUNT := 0;
                    V(S);    -- signal that COUNT is available
            end select;
    end tasks;
end;
```

Example 15.4   Use of semaphores

between send and receive statements. The symmetry helps make the behavior of the tasks quite explicit. Most importantly, aside from a rendezvous, we may view the operation of each task independently from the others.

In Mini-language Parallel, the sending task must name the task to which information is sent, and the receiving task must mention the sending task. In certain circumstances, this symmetry may have drawbacks. In particular, it is difficult to describe the behavior of a task that can accept information from several other tasks, independently of the origin of the information. In the programming language Ada, only the sending task can name the destination to which information is sent. From the receiver's point of view, the information received is anonymous.

Scheduling

In most applications of concurrent processing, there will be senders and receivers of information. In particular, a request to receive information may have been preceded by numerous requests to send the information, presumably from different tasks. In Mini-language Parallel, when this case arises, the requests to send information are presumed to be processed on a first come, first served basis. This brings up the notion of *scheduling*.

The problem with this method of scheduling is that a first come, first served basis may not always be desirable. In particular, there may be certain tasks whose urgency is far greater than that of other tasks. In some languages, tasks can be assigned a *priority*, and tasks with a more higher priority are processed first.

It is possible to express the notion of urgency entirely within Mini-language Parallel. This can be accomplished by the suitable use of select statements, where outer level guards can be used to handle urgent requests and nested guards can be used to handle less urgent requests. While this kind of solution may appear to be somewhat awkward, it may, in fact, express the desired urgency in an appropriate manner. A final resolution to this matter is not clear.

Deadlock

Imagine for the moment a task named TASK_A and one named TASK_B, which contain the following statements:

```
start tasks
   TASK_A:
      receive VALUE_A from TASK_B;
      send (VALUE_A + 1) to TASK_B;

   TASK_B:
      receive VALUE_B from TASK_A;
      send (VALUE_B - 1) to TASK_A;
end tasks;
```

When these two tasks are initiated, they will immediately *deadlock*. That is, TASK_A will await a value from TASK_B, and TASK_B will await a value from TASK_A. Since neither value has been sent, both receive statements will be suspended, in this case indefinitely.

The deadlock problem for concurrent tasks is as difficult to avoid as the writing of infinite loops in a sequential language and the detection of deadlocks is just as difficult. Only the care of the programmer can prevent this circumstance from happening.

Nondeterminism

In the select statement of Mini-language Parallel, more than one guard may evaluate to true. In this case, one of the corresponding guarded statements is executed. The choice among the guarded statements whose guards evaluate to true is arbitrary. In this sense, the execution of the select statement is *nondeterministic*.

This is consistent with much of concurrent processing. Frequently, a task is used to control a mechanical device that has a timing variance that is much larger than the machine instruction time. Thus, when an execution of the task is repeated, it will be impossible to obtain synchronization without using special synchronizing constructs. Programmers who are used to repeatability in the execution of simple sequential programs find it difficult to become accustomed to the nondeterminancy of concurrent programming.

The application of nondeterminism is not limited to concurrent processes. An elegant solution based on nondeterminism to the problem of providing control structures in a programming language has been proposed in [Dijkstra 1975]. There, the conditional and iterative structures are of similar form to the select statement of Mini-language Parallel. Indeed, its use of guarded commands comes from Dijkstra's work by way of Ada. In the conditional statement, one of the guards *must* be true, otherwise the statement terminates abnormally. In the iterative form, the iteration continues as long as there exists a true guard. In both cases, if more than one guard is true, the statement sequence to be executed is selected nondeterministically. This has the potential of permitting certain optimizations to be effected by the compiler while allowing the programmer to retain determinancy by specifying that no two guards are ever true concurrently.

Concurrent processing does not necessarily imply a mechanism with nondeterministic behavior, although such is the case in Mini-language Parallel, the proposal by Hoare [1978], and Ada.

Comments on Parallel Processing

As with most of the topics treated in the Mini-languages, a full discussion of all the attendant issues is difficult, and as usual, we make no pretense of treating these areas completely.

Two general remarks seem to be in order. Parallel processing is important, and in many application areas it is essential.

Second, while it may seem superfluous to say, we believe strongly that extreme care is required in the design of any linguistic facility to handle parallel processing. When tasks operate in parallel, the potential chaos to the average programmer is enormous. No expense should be spared to make the facility in a programming language as clear as possible. Any such facility should be designed with a careful eye towards making it one that can be programmed with ease and with clarity.

FURTHER READING

The basis for this chapter, as mentioned earlier, to the work of Hoare [1978]. Certainly, this work deserves reading for a further examination of the issues discussed here.

An early survey of parallel processing is presented in [Brinch Hansen 1972]. A further work [Brinch Hansen 1977] describes the actual concepts used to define a version of Pascal that includes parallel processing.

Often, concepts are developed that later turn out to be somewhat minor variations of concepts introduced much earlier. Such is the case with the parallel processing facilities introduced in Mini-language Parallel. Here we have in mind the very early work of Conway [1963], which introduces the idea of a *coroutine*. It is here that the notion of a *rendezvous* is introduced.

The application of guarded commands to sequential programming languages is described in [Dijkstra 1975].

EXERCISES

Exercise 15.1   Terminology for Parallel Processing

In a difficult area like parallel processing, it is all the more important to define the terminology precisely. Write a one to four sentence definition of each of the following terms:

Task	Critical Region
Synchronization	Deadlock
Rendezvous	Delay
Guard	Semaphore

Exercise 15.2   Programming in Mini-language Parallel

Modify the program in Example 15.3 so that there are two separate RECEIVE_CODES tasks, named RECEIVE_CODES_A and RECEIVE_CODES_B, which obtain data from different sources, and feed their buffered input to DECODER. Each one of them is able to receive a stop signal from its own user. Receipt of a stop signal by either task shuts down the entire program, including the other receiving task, in an orderly manner.

Exercise 15.3   Mutual Exclusion

One method of implementing process waiting is through a loop that repeatedly tests the condition for the termination of the wait. The body of the loop is empty. This technique is known as *busy waiting*, since the processor is executing constantly during the waiting period.

Consider the following two implementations of the P and V semaphore operations through busy waiting. Supposing that busy waiting is acceptable and that there are two tasks that use the constants THIS and OTHER to distinguish them, determine whether the implementations are correct. The first is:

```
P(S):
   S[THIS] := true;
   while (S[OTHER] = true) loop
   end loop;

V(S):
   S[THIS] := false;
```

The second is:

```
P(S):
   S[THIS] := true;
   while (S[OTHER] = true) loop
     S[THIS] := false;
     while (S[OTHER] = true) loop
     end loop;
     S[THIS] := true;
   end loop;

V(S):
   S[THIS] := false;
```

If either, or both, of these implementations is incorrect, explain.

Exercise 15.4   Semaphores

Consider a variant of Mini-language Parallel that does not have the send and receive mechanism defined in Section 15.1 but instead allows the declaration of semaphore variables as described in Section 15.5. Rewrite the program in Example 15.2 using this variant of the mini-language.

Exercise 15.5   Guarded Commands

Consider a variant of Mini-language D where the if statement and loop statement are described by the syntax:

```
if-statement        ::=    if
                               when guard => statement...
                               [ when guard => statement... ]...
                           end if;

loop-statement      ::=    loop
                               when guard => statement...
                               [ when guard => statement... ]...
                           end loop;

guard               ::=    condition-expression
```

During execution of the if statement, the statement sequence corresponding to an arbitrarily chosen true guard (at least one of the guards must be true, otherwise the program terminates abnormally) is executed. Execution of the loop statement takes place in the same way except that, if no guard is true, no action is performed and the loop is terminated. Execution of the the loop statement is repeated until none of the guards is true.

Rewrite the program in Example 5.1 using this version of Mini-language D with guards.

The Landscape Re-examined

16
The Swamp of Complexity

Notation to be effective
1. Economy
2. Subordinate Detail

A programming language is a notation and, as such, serves to record and assist the development of human thought in a particular direction — the formulation of processes to be carried out on a computer. For a notation to be effective, it must have, among other properties, economy and the ability to subordinate detail. In a programming language, by *economy* we mean that a wide range of programs can be expressed naturally using a relatively small vocabulary and simple grammatical rules.

economy

subordinate detail

The ability to subordinate detail, often called abstraction, leads to a reduction in programming complexity. The power of a language to provide abstraction is the source of its usefulness to the programmer. It allows the programmer to concentrate on the problem being solved without having to worry about the very detailed stream of instructions that must be given to the machine.

Although the mini-languages presented here are all small, they nevertheless show complexities, for example, the dereferencing rules in Mini-language Ref, and the intricacies of scope rules. Real programming languages are many times more complex than any of the mini-languages. It is this complexity that seriously restricts their effectiveness as an adequate notation.

16.1 THE FORMS OF COMPLEXITY

There are many forms that complexity takes in a language. All too frequently, a language designer pays only token homage to simplicity, without really making the underlying design simple. Although simplicity may be attempted by building the language from the simplest elements, there is no guarantee that these can be combined clearly to form a coherent whole. In this section, we follow the general organization of the book in examining the forms of complexity.

Complexity Due to Scale

Probably the greatest single symptom of complexity is the scale of the language. Generally size comes through an attempt to meet the demands of would-be users, who want to see special additions to make their own applications easier. The two largest languages are at the moment, and we hope that this will remain true, PL/I and Ada. In both cases, much of their size has come about through the attempt to meet many isolated special demands.

The design goal for PL/I was a language that would satisfy the needs of scientific, commercial, and special purpose users. Following the release of the initial version of the design, there started a dialogue between the designers and the future users of the language. This dialogue continued up to the production of the ANSI Standard for PL/I. During this period, far more has been added than has been deleted. As a result, using the language has been likened to "flying a plane with 7,000 buttons, switches, and handles to manipulate in the cockpit" [Dijkstra 1972b].

Ada was designed to meet specifications produced by the Department of Defense, see [Whitaker 1978], for a language to be used throughout the Department and the military services. The specifications were drawn up by taking requests for facilities from potential users of the language. These requirements were used by its designers, who in turn, had their own requirements to satisfy as well. Further adding to the cacophony of advice were the many consultants and hundreds of critics. The objective was, of course, to amalgamate all these requirements into a coherent whole. This process has been described as like trying to commission a symphony for an orchestra by constructing it from a few bars each contributed by a large number of individual composers.

In both PL/I and Ada, the size and complexity of the languages go to the limits of the user's intellectual control. These languages, which were designed by what amounts to very large committees, may be compared to languages that were designed by individuals or small committees, for example, Algol 60, Algol 68, Pascal, and APL. Although they may have other problems, they do not suffer to the same degree from complexity due to absolute size.

A language may be small and yet suffer from complexity due to scale. This can come about through the addition of features that are beyond the scope of the language. Pascal was designed primarily as a language to be used in teaching. Admittedly Pascal has achieved a popularity beyond that for teaching, but as a pedagogic language, it is extremely large. For example, we question the need for the proposed complicated rules for file types [Addyman et al. 1980], record variants (hardly an introductory topic), the rather elaborate scope rules, the goto statement (of questionable value in a language with many one-in, one-out structures), set types (of limited use as defined), and so forth.

Pascal Summary Critic

Almost every programming language suffers in some way from excessive complexity, either in size, compression of language forms, or special cases. There are several consequences of such complexity:

Complexity Consequences

■ Potential and beginning users feel threatened by the magnitude of the language.

■ Writing comprehensible tutorial documents becomes almost impossible. As a result, teaching the language becomes very difficult.

■ Implementation is error prone and inefficient, with diagnostic messages that are difficult to interpret.

■ Language forms become overloaded so that subtle and often treacherous distinctions must be made by the user.

■ It becomes more difficult for the user to develop a simple set of rules for using the language. Thus the number of errors made increases.

Syntax

What is needed above all is that the high level syntax should be simple. Consider, for example, the Pascal declaration section. Here everything is static and there is reasonable consistency.

Pascal Compliment

Each statement of the language should have a meaning that matches its intuitive meaning for the user; that is, there should be no nasty surprises. An example of this kind of surprise is to be found in APL. Throughout our early mathematical education we became familiary with the precedence of multiplication and division over addition and subtraction. In APL, operator precedence runs strictly from right to left. For example, the value of the APL expression (36 / 4 + 5) is 4,

Intuitive Intuitive Meaning

not 13, as we would expect from our mathematical experience. It might well be that the APL rule is the best one and traditional mathematics is wrong in its approach. That is beside the point — the APL expression has a different meaning from the intuitive one of most of us.

English-like constructs

In keeping with the idea of relying on the user's intuitive feeling for the meaning of the forms in the language, the use of English-like constructs helps the English-speaking user. With reservations, we support the direction taken by Cobol. Unfortunately, the form of Cobol is flawed by a lack of clear structure. This makes Cobol programs difficult to understand despite their resemblance to natural language. Following the usage in English, Cobol uses the period to end complete sentences. Unfortunately, the omission of a period is easy to overlook, and this can change the meaning of a program without any warning. For example in

```
IF TYPE-CODE IS EQUAL TO 'A'
    PERFORM SCALE THROUGH EXIT-SCALE
    ADD 1 TO TITLE-COUNT
ELSE
    PERFORM TITLE-PRINT
    MOVE 1 TO TITLE-COUNT
MOVE BLANK TO TYPE-CODE.
```

the indentation is misleading. The absence of a period at the end of the next-to-last line includes the final line as part of the else clause. BLANK is only moved to TYPE-CODE if TYPE-CODE is not 'A' .

Syntax uniform in constructs

Finally, the syntax should be uniform in its use of constructs. That is, the form of a particular construct should be independent of the context of its use. Consider the punctuation in the two Fortran statements:

```
READ (5) A, B, C, D
GO TO K, (10, 20, 30, 40)
```

In one case there is a comma, in the other none. In one case, the list is in parentheses, in the other, the single item.

Semantics

Side-Effects

Probably the greatest contribution to semantic complexity comes from side-effects. In various places in this book we have shown how side-effects can lead to loss of clarity. A classic case is a function subprogram that can change the values of its arguments or of global variables in addition to returning a value to the invoker. This can lead to programs that are almost impossible to understand. Indeed, their precise meaning can depend upon some quirks of a particular implementation rather than a designed feature of the language.

Functions, although the most commonly mentioned, are not the only sources of side-effects in programming languages. In Example 4.2 we saw how the assignment

    REF_INT_C := INT_B;

where ??

can affect the outcome of the assignment

    INT_A := REF_REF_INT_E;

pg 362

even though the two statements do not explicitly reference any common variables. A similar situation arises with lists in Section 13.2. Side-effects are the root of the problems with aliasing. *< (207) (216) 243 since location (value) can be accessed by more / more*

However, it is important to remember that side-effects are really endemic to procedural languages since they depend on the side-effect of changing the computer store in an assignment. This is the basic principle of programs that is descended directly from the original von Neumann design of a computer. Functional languages like Mini-language Apply have no side-effects. Indeed, some contend, particularly [Backus 1978], that the continued reliance on the von Neumann model of computation has limited the proper development of funtional languages, which are conceptually much simpler.

Control Structures

In Chapter 9, we examine the question of the kinds of control statements that should be available in a programming language. Our conclusion is that the matter reduced to a balance of complexity. On the one hand, a possible reduction of programming effort may be obtained by adding higher level control structures such as exit and cycle; on the other an increased complexity of the language is caused by additional statements.

M. Conclusion

We believe that the case for these higher level control structures has yet to be proven. This is not, by any means, a universally held belief. The disigners of the language Bliss felt that each specific control environment required its own escape mechanism. Each escape scheme causes control to leave a specific control environment. This seems to us to be an excessive burden of complexity for a single semantic pattern.

Types

One of the problems with the term *type* is that it tends to be overused. PL/I has subsumed the notion of type into the more general one of *attribute*, which includes the ideas of scope and storage management. Our concept of type is limited to the specification of the set of values that may be taken by an object and the class of operations that manipulate the objects.

In languages where the choice of type is limited to those fixed in the language initially, the concept remains fairly simple except for the question of conversion from one type to another. Where there are many built-in types, the number of possible conversions is large. Most of these occur between various forms of numeric representation.

A great deal of complexity is added to a language by the many possible conversions, especially if they can occur implicitly, as in PL/I. The addition of the attribute complex doubled the number of potential conversions without adding an adequate return on this investment in complication. By requiring that conversions be mentioned explicitly, some of the complexity is reduced. However there remains an inescapable residue of complexity due to the variety of numeric representations that are forced on the language designer by the realities of hardware. This is really due to the mapping of the real world's infinite domain of numbers onto the computer's finite one.

Composite data types bring complexities of their own. First, there is the question of operations on composite values. Even such an apparently simple operation as assignment can be anything but simple. For arrays, questions of bounds arise, and for records, there are such fundamental issues as how much alike must two records have to be in order to be assignable. If the question of variant records is added, the problem becomes even more difficult. Indeed, the inclusion of variant records of the form described in Section 6.5 adds considerable complexity to the language.

An interesting example of the question of balance between complexity and utility is that of character strings. As discussed in Chapter 6, there are two fundamentally different views of character strings: either as an array of the primitive type character, or as a primitive type in their own right. Making them a part of the already existing array construct would seem at first to be a simplification. However, the need to handle varying length character strings either requires flexible array bounds, an added complication of both the language and the implementation, or puts considerable extra detail into programs, which degrades the utility of the language. On balance, the provision of the character string as a primitive type certainly seems to provide the simpler solution.

Procedures and Parameters

Procedures provide a form of packaging. They simplify programs by allowing details that are not germane at the level of the caller to be replaced by a call statement. The argument-parameter correspondences provides generality so that a single procedure can be used in a variety of contexts.

In order that the full effects of this simplification can be realized, the interface between the caller and the subroutine must be kept as simple as possible. That is to say, the boundary around the procedure should have only one passage for data, the argument-parameter transmission. Any others, such as the use of globals, necessarily weaken the integrity of the structure and reduce its effectiveness as an abstraction. *One passage of data*

As discussed in Chapter 7, there are many ways in which the argument-parameter transmission can be defined. Again, simplicity is the criterion. Passing by reference is certainly the simplest; however great care is required to avoid the complexities of aliasing. *Simplicity*

While procedures act as statements, functions act as expressions. If clarity is to be preserved, functions must not have side-effects as this inevitably brings questions of order of evaluation and a host of rules that hinder more than they help. *pg. 299*

Mini-language Apply is a pure function language where there is no possibility of side-effects. When this principle is used in procedural languages, some questions arise. If a function can have no side-effects, then it can cause no change of state, and therefore input-output transmission cannot be permitted. It is not clear at this stage how this question can be resolved. Lisp originally started as a pure applicative language, but later versions included the use of global variables. It is not obvious that this added complexity was exchanged for a corresponding simplification in programming.

Scope

The original intent of scope rules was to allow localization of names and to permit the reuse of names from in other contexts. Thus the rules of scope define the set of names that may be used at a given point in a program. From the relatively simple concept of block structure many more complicated schemes have been developed, each ramification being rationalized as rectifying some previous deficiency. Each ramification has also added its quota of complexity. Ada provides an example of how scope rules can become greatly complicated, as is attested by the fact that the reference manual devotes an entire chapter to the subject.

The entire issue of scope itself needs to be questioned. Fortran has seldom been criticized on scope grounds, yet the scope rules are simple. Although COMMON variables complicate matters, the underlying idea is simple — nesting is not allowed and everything is local. The Cobol model is also simple, but just the opposite — everything is global.

Input and Output

Generally, the area of input and output has been one of the most complex features of programming languages. While some of the complexity is due to the nature of the problem being solved, much is due to the way in which the approach has evolved. Solutions have tended to be ad hoc without a proper high level treatment.

Exceptions and Parallelism

At this state in the development of programming languages, progress in these areas has only occurred recently. Thus, while the earlier attempts at the problem, *fork*, *join*, and *semaphores* for example, had much complexity, there seems to be good progress in the direction of simplification.

16.2   ESCAPING FROM THE SWAMP

A discussion of the languages PL/I, Ada, and Algol 68 is instructive. One of the design goals of Algol 68 was minimization of the number of independent primitive concepts. Power and breadth was obtained by combining these concepts uniformly. A construct that can be used in one context can be used in any other context where there is no semantic ambiguity. Since the primitive concepts are independent, duplication of function is avoided. Both PL/I and Ada lack this uniformity. Although PL/I allows user defined functions as objects that can be assigned, the built-in functions cannot be used in this way. Ada has task *types*, but no objects or operations that belong to this type.

The mechanism for defining new types and operators allows a language to be extended to suit a particular application. In Algol 68 this mechanism has been used to keep the core of the language very small. All the operators and some types like complex numbers are defined through this mechanism in a *standard prologue*. Conceptually, an implementation of Algol 68 could be realized with a relatively simple compiler for the core language and processing the text of the standard prologue before each source program. This would not be an efficient method from the point of view of the user.

Much of PL/I's size is due to its attempt to cater, without the benefit of extensibility, to a large community of users. Ada, on the other hand, has been able to take advantage of the technology of extensibility. However the basis for the extension is a very large language in its own right; many times larger than the core of Algol 68. The core of Ada was designed to economize on concepts and yet meets its many requirements. As a result, many of its elegant features, for example, the type model, packages, and one-in, one-out control structures, are obscured.

While the design of Algol 68 is elegant in its basis, its external appearance is not. The definition of the language is forbidding with much new terminology for old concepts. The syntax seems often to have been designed to save keystrokes rather than to promote readability, and the same symbol often serves many purposes, depending on the context.

Nevertheless, the message seems clear. The way to escape the dangers of complexity and yet provide a powerful programming language must be based on:

■   a minimum of independent concepts combined in a uniform manner.

■   a comprehensive definition mechanism to provide the breadth.

■   a small core language on which the extensions are based.

■   a syntax that is chosen for its readability.

The problems that must be solved by today's languages are not simple. It is important that the programmer's task not be compounded by an additional layer of complexity from the very tool that is being used to solve the problem.

EXERCISES

Note: All of the following exercises are difficult, and could be used for term projects.

Exercise 16.1   Implementing a Mini-language

Language implementations are a popular exercise, and for good reason. By the time you are done, you will have a much deeper knowledge of the language and an appreciation of the difficulty of what first appears to be an easy task. The difficulty of the task is most evident by the many implementations that are never finished.

Your task is to implement *one* of the mini-languages. Obviously, some are more difficult than others. Mini-language Core is probably a good representative language. Mini-language Typedef is quite difficult, and Mini-language Parallel even more so.

There are many characteristics of a good implementation:

1. *Completeness.* The implementation should adhere exactly to the definition.

2. *Correctness.* All difficult cases should be tested. Boundary cases (for example, a program with no variables or with arithmetic over large numbers) should also be tested.

3. *Response to Errors.* This area is always difficult. The implementation should try to give good feedback to a user who makes an error. If a program contains many errors, the implementation should not get completely lost, but should try to recover and go on.

4. *Human Engineering.* The listings provided for the user should be clean and readable. Printing all kinds of diagnostic information may be a poor idea.

5. *Documentation.* The implementation, test cases, summary of its behavior, and performance data should be presented clearly and crisply.

A common complaint in many efforts of this sort is low quality work resulting from an overly optimistic and ambitious effort. Another complaint is a lack of concern for the user [see Ledgard et al. 1981]. So don't be afraid to limit the scope of the task. Put your emphasis on the quality of the result.

Exercise 16.2   Error Assistance

The possibilities for errors in programs are endless. Often the manual is of little help.

Your task here is to provide a document to be used with one of the mini-languages, your choice. The document is intended to provide as much help as possible to a programmer who has made an error. The following points are important.

1. *Coverage.* You should attempt to cover all possible errors in both syntax and semantics. The errors will range from simple spelling or punctuation mistakes, to input-output errors, to various ways in which a program will give rise to an infinite loop.

2. *Examples.* You should give examples of each kind of error. The examples should be short and to the point.

3. *Organization.* The organization of the document should allow the programmer with a specific error to get help without wading through each case.

A good place to start this exercise is with a written list of all conceivable cases that could arise. For Mini-language Core, a good document will probably require twenty or more pages.

As samples of such errors, a programmer might write

```
A1 := A1 + 1;
```

instead of

```
A1 := A2 + 1;
```

or might input three values in the wrong order, or might forget to test for a case that leads to division by 0.

Exercise 16.3   Designing a Mini-language

The teaching of widely-used programming languages is in part difficult because of the larger scale and complexity of the language. One technique to alleviate this problem is to teach only a small (but useful) fragment of the language first. Such a fragment would need its own documentation and its own examples. It would become a "mini-language" in the same sense as those of previous chapters.

Your task is to choose a language you know well, and from it prepare a mini-language subset that would be suitable for teaching. The result of your effort will be a document describing the mini-language. Your mini-language must be small. It should be useful enough that it could be used for several weeks of teaching.

Exercise 16.4   Literature Review

Almost any topic in this text is treated, directly or indirectly, by articles in the literature. Subjects like semantics, control structures, or parallelism are heavily treated, while topics like human engineering or scale have been given less attention.

Choose a topic taken from the index of this text and attempt to find at least ten works relevant to the subject. Prepare a report on the topic. The report should discuss the relevance of the topic, debatable concerns, unresolved issues, ramifications in existing languages, and questions of scale and complexity. Your report should clearly state at least one conclusion of your own.

Exercise 16.5   Language Critique

When a new book is published, it is common to see book reviews commenting on its significance, its weakness, its bias, and so forth.

Your task here is to do the same for a programming language that is unfamiliar to you. In particular, you are to prepare a twenty to thirty page report treating the major issues in its design. You may wish to discuss:

1. The justification for the language
2. The clarity of syntax
3. The documentation
4. Areas in need of more work
5. Constructs that are difficult to use
6. Human engineering of the effort
7. Features that could be deleted.

Ada and Algol 68 are two good general choices. If you wish to try something different, pick a special-purpose language like Snobol or Apt. If you are not familiar with some of the older classics, try Basic or Fortran.

Exercise 16.6   Detailed Paper Review

Developing a critical perspective of papers in the literature is certainly a strong asset. Each of the following papers is in some way important to the study of programming languages.

[Backus 1978]   [Hoare 1973]
[Beech 1970]   [Knuth 1974]
[Bliss 1971]   [Ledgard 1977]
[Gannon and Horning 1975]   [Liskov and Zilles 1974]
[Haberman 1973]   [Tannenbaum 1976]

Your task is to select one of these papers and to provide a *detailed* technical review (10 or 15 pages). Your review should summarize the work, point out its strengths and weaknesses, its clarity, and any other aspect you wish.

References

[Ada]
Reference Manual for the ADA Programming Language
U.S. Department of Defense, July 1980
(Also to be published by Springer-Verlag, New York, Spring 1981)

[Addyman et al. 1979]
A. M. Addyman et al.
A Draft Description of Pascal   *Pascal*
Software Practice and Experience, May 1979

[AED]
Softech Inc.
Introduction to AED Programming, 4-th Edition
Softech Inc., Waltham, Massachusetts, 1973

[Aho and Johnson 1974]
Alfred V. Aho and Stephen C. Johnson
LR Parsing
Computing Surveys, June 1974

[Aho and Ullman 1977]
Alfred V. Aho and Jeffrey D. Ullman
Principles of Compiler Design
Addison-Wesley, Reading, Massachusetts, 1977

[Algol 60]
Peter Naur, Editor
Revised report on the Algorithmic Language Algol 60
Communications of the ACM, January 1963

[Algol 60]
Edsger W. Dijkstra
A Primer of Algol 60 Programming
Academic Press, New York 1960

[Algol 68]
Aard van Wijngaarden et al.
Revised Report on the Algorithmic Language Algol 68
Acta Informatica, Vol.5, 1975,
(also reproduced in Sigplan Notices, May 1977)

[Algol 68]
Charles Lindsey and S. G. van der Meulen
Informal Introduction to Algol 68
North-Holland Publishing Company, Amsterdam 1975

[Algol W]
Niklaus Wirth and C.A.R. Hoare
A Contribution to the Development of Algol
Communications of the ACM, June 1966

[Alphard]
William A. Wulf, Ralph L. London, and Mary Shaw
Abstraction and Verification in Alphard: Introduction to Language and Methodology,
USC Information Science Technical Report, University of Southern California, Los Angeles, 1976

[APL]
APL Language
Form No. GC26-3847-4, IBM Data Processing Division, White Plains, NY

[APL]
Kenneth E. Iverson
A Programming Language
John Wiley and Sons, 1962

[Apt]
Apt Part Programming
McGraw-Hill Book Company, New York 1970

[Arsac 1979]
Jacques J. Arsac
Syntactic Source to Source Transforms and Program Manipulation
Communications of the ACM, January 1979

[Backus 1978]
John Backus
Can Programming be Liberated from the von Newmann Style?
Communications of the ACM, August 1978

[Barron 1977]
David W. Barron
An Introduction to the Study of Programming Languages
Cambridge University Press, 1977

[BCPL]
Martin Richards
BCPL: A Tool for Compiler Writing and System Programming
Proceedings of Spring Joint Computer Conference, 1969

[Beech 1970]
David Beech
A Structural View of PL/I
Computing Surveys, March 1970

[Bliss]
William A. Wulf, D.B. Russel, and A. Nico Habermann
Bliss: A Language for Systems Programming   *BLISS*
Communications of the ACM, December 1971

[Boehm and Jacopini 1966]
Corrado Boehm and Giuseppi Jacopini
Flow Diagrams, Turing Machines, and Languages with Only Two Formation Rules
Communications of the ACM, May 1966

[Brinch Hansen 1972]
Per Brinch Hansen
Concurrent Programming Concepts
Computing Surveys, June 1972

[Brinch Hansen 1977]
Per Brinch Hansen   *Pascal*
The Programming Language Concurrent Pascal
IEEE Transactions on Software Engineering, June 1975

[Brosgol 1977]
Benjamin Brosgol
Some Issues in Data Types and Type Checking
in *Design and Implementation of Programming Languages*
Springer-Verlag, New York, 1977

[Bruno and Steiglitz 1972]
J. Bruno and K. Steiglitz
The Expression of Algorithms by Charts
Journal of the ACM, July 1972

[Burge 1975]
William H. Burge
Recursive Programming Techniques
Addison-Wesley, Reading, Massachusetts 1975

[Church 1941]
Alonzo Church
The Calculi of Lambda-conversion
Annals of Mathematic Studies, No. 6, Princeton University Press, 1941

[Clark 1973]
R. Lawrence Clark
A Linguistic Contribution to Goto-less Programming
Datamation, December 1973

[Cleaveland and Uzgalis 1976]
James C. Cleaveland and Robert C. Uzgalis
Grammars for Programming Languages: What Every Programmer Should Know about Grammar
American Elsevier Publishing Company, New York, 1976

[Clu]
Barbara Liskov et al
Clu Reference Manual
Massachusetts Institute of Technology
MIT/LCS/TR-225, Cambridge, Massachusetts 1979

[Cobol]
American National Standard Programming Language Cobol,
ANSI X3.23-1974, American National Standards Institute, New York, 1974

[Conway 1963]
Melvin E. Conway
Design of a Separable Transition-Diagram Compiler
Communications of the ACM, July 1963

[Cooper 1967]
David C. Cooper
Bohm and Jacopini's Reduction of Flow Charts
Letter to the Editor, Communications of the ACM, August 1967

[Curry and Feys 1958]
Haskell B. Curry and Robert Feys
Combinatory Logic, Vol. 1
North-Holland Publication Company, Amsterdam, 1958

[Demers et al 1977]
Alan Demers, James Donahue, Ray Teitelbaum, and John Williams
Encapsulated Data Types and Generic Procedures
in *Design and Implementation of Programming Languages*
Lecture Notes in Computer Science, Springer-Verlag, New York, 1977

[Dijkstra 1968a]
Edsger W. Dijkstra
Goto Statement Considered Harmful
Letter to the Editor, Communications of the ACM, March 1968

[Dijkstra 1968b]
Edsger W. Dijkstra
Cooperating Sequential Processes
in *Programming Languages* (F. Genuys, editor)
Academic Press, New York 1968

[Dijkstra 1972a]
Edsger W. Dijkstra
Notes on Structured Programming
in *Structured Programming* by Dahl, Dijkstra, and Hoare
Academic Press, New York 1972

[Dijkstra 1972b]
Edsger W. Dijkstra
The Humble Programmer
Communications of the ACM, October 1972

[Dijkstra 1975]
Edsger W. Dijkstra
Guarded Commands, Nondeterminancy, and Formal Derivation of Programs
Communications of the ACM, August 1975

[Donahue 1976]
James E. Donahue
Complementary Definitions of Programming Language Semantics
Lecture Notes in Computer Science, Springer-Verlag, New York, 1976

[Elgot and Robinson 1964]
Calvin C. Elgot and Abraham Robinson
Random Access Stored-program Machines: An Approach to Programming Languages
Journal of the ACM, October 1964

[Elson 1973]
Mark Elson
Concepts of Programming Languages
Science Research Associates, Chicago, 1973

[Euclid]
Butler W. Lampson, et al,
Report on the Programming Language Euclid
Sigplan Notices, February 1977

[Floyd 1967]
Robert W. Floyd
Assigning Meaning to Programs
Proceedings of Symposia in Applied Mathematics Vol. 19
Mathematical Aspects of Computer Science, 1967

[Fortran]
Ansi Standard Fortran
American National Standards Institute, New York, 1966

[Fortran 77]
Draft Proposed ANS Fortran
American National Standards Committee X3J3
Sigplan Notices, March 1976

[Gannon and Horning 1975]
John D. Gannon and James J. Horning
Language Design for Programming Reliability
IEEE Transactions on Software Engineering, June 1975

[Garwick 1963]
Jan V. Garwick
The Definition of Programming Languages
in *Formal Language Description Languages*, (T. B. Steel, editor)
North-Holland Publication Company, Amsterdam 1963

[Goodenough 1975]
John B. Goodenough
Exception Handling: Issues and A Proposed Notation
Communications of the ACM, December 1975

[Gordon 1979]
Michael J. C. Gordon
The Denotational Description of Programming Languages: An Introduction
Springer-Verlag, New York 1979

[Gries and Gehani 1977]
David Gries and Nargain Gehani
Some Ideas on Data Types in High-Level Languages
Communications of the ACM, June 1977

[Guttag 1977]
John Guttag
Abstract Data Types and the Development of Data Structures
Communications of the ACM, June 1977

[Haberman 1973]
A. Nico Haberman
Critical Comments on the Programming Language Pascal
Acta Informatica 3, 1973,

Pascal

[Harel 1980]
David Harel
On Folk Theorems
Communications of the ACM, July 1980

[Henderson 1980]
Peter Henderson
Functional Programming Application and Implementation
Prentice-Hall International, London, 1980

[Hill 1971]
I. D. Hill
Faults in Functions in Algol and Fortran
Computer Journal, August 1971

[Hoare 1969]
C. A. R. Hoare
An Axiomatic Approach to Computer Programming
Communications of the ACM, October 1969

[Hoare 1972]
C. A. R. Hoare
Notes on Data Structuring
in *Structured Programming* by Dahl, Dijkstra, and Hoare
Academic Press, New York, 1972

[Hoare 1973]
C. A. R. Hoare
Hints on Programming Language Design
Computer Science Department, Technical Report STAN-CS-73-403, Stanford
University, California, December 1973
(also in Computer Systems Reliability, Infotech State of the Art Report No. 20,
1974)

[Hoare 1978]
C. A. R. Hoare
Communicating Sequential Processes
Communications of the ACM, August 1978

[Hoare and Wirth 1973]
C. A. R. Hoare and Niklaus Wirth
An Axiomatic Definition of the Programming Language Pascal
Acta Information 2, 1973

[Hofstadter 1979]
Douglas R. Hofstadter
Godel, Escher, Bach: An Eternal Golden Braid
Basic Books, Inc., New York 1979

[Ichbiah et al. 1979]
Jean Ichbiah et al.
Rationale for the Design of the Ada Programming Language
Sigplan Notices, June 1979

[Johnston 1971]
John B. Johnston
The Contour Model of Block Structured Processes
Sigplan Notices, February 1971

[Jones and Muchnick 1978]
N.D.Jones and S.S. Muchnick
Tempo: A Unified Treatment of Binding Times and Parameter Passing Concepts in Programming Languages
Lecture Notes in Computer Science, Springer-Verlag, New York 1978

[Knuth 1967]
Donald E. Knuth
Remaining Trouble Spots in Algol 60
Communications of the ACM, October 1967

[Knuth 1969]
Donald E. Knuth
The Art of Computer Programming, Vol 2.
Addison-Wesley, Reading, Massachusetts 1969

[Knuth 1974]
Donald E. Knuth
Structured Programming with Goto Statements
Computing Surveys, December 1974

[Kosaraju 1974]
Rao Kosaraju
Analysis of Structured Programs
Journal of Computers and System Science, December 1974

[Landin 1964]
Peter J. Landin
The Mechanical Evaluation of Expressions
Computer Journal, Vol. 6(4), 1963

[Landin 1965]
Peter J. Landin
A Correspondence between Algol 60 and Church's Lambda-Notation
Communications of the ACM, February 1965

[Ledgard 1971]
Henry F. Ledgard
Ten Mini-languages: A Study of Topical Issues in Programming Languages
Computing Surveys, September 1971

[Ledgard 1977]
Henry F. Ledgard
Production Systems: A Notation for Defining Syntax and Translation of Programming Languages
IEEE Transactions on Software Engineering, April 1977

[Ledgard et al. 1981]
Henry F. Ledgard, Andrew Singer, and John Whiteside
Directions in Human Factors for Interactive Systems
Lecture Notes in Computer Science, Springer-Verlag, New York, 1981

[Ledgard and Marcotty 1975]
Henry F. Ledgard and Michael Marcotty
A Genealogy of Control Structures
Communications of the ACM, November 1975

[Lee 1972]
J.A.N. Lee
Computer Semantics
Van Nostrand Reinhold, New York, 1972

[Levin 1977]
Roy Levin
Program Structures for Exceptional Condition Handling
Ph.D. Thesis, Computer Science Department, Carnegie Mellon University, 1977

[Lisp 1.5]
John McCarthy et al.
Lisp 1.5 Programmer's Manual
MIT Press, Cambridge Massachusetts, 1962

[Liskov and Zilles 1976]
Barbara Liskov and Stephen Zilles
Specification Techniques for Data Abstractions
Sigplan Notices, June 1976

[Lucas and Walk 1969]
Peter Lucas and Kurt Walk
On the Formal Definition of PL/I
Annual Review in Automatic Programming, Vol. 6 Pergamon Press, 1969

[MacLaren 1970]
M. Donald MacLaren
Data Matching, Data Alignment, and Structure Mapping in PL/I
Sigplan Notices, December 1970

[Mailloux and Peck 1968]
Barry J. Mailloux and John E.C. Peck
Algol 68 as an Extensible Language
Sigplan Notices, May 1969

442 References

[Marcotty et al. 1976]
Michael Marcotty, Henry F. Ledgard, and Gregor Bochmann
A Sampler of Formal Definitions
Computing Surveys, June 1976

[Markov 1954]
Andrei A. Markov
A Theory of Algorithms
(Russian) Academy of Sciences of USSR, Moscow 1954
English translation by Israel Program for Scientific Translations

[McCabe 1976]
Thomas J. McCabe
A Complexity Measure
IEEE Transactions in Software Engineering, December 1976

[McCarthy 1960]
John McCarthy
Recursive Functions of Symbolic Expressions and Their Computation by Machine
Communications of the ACM, April 1960

[McCarthy 1962]
John McCarthy
Towards a Mathematical Theory of Computation
Proceedings of IFIP Congress 1962, North-Holland, Amsterdam 1962

[Mills 1972]
Harlan D. Mills
Mathematical Foundations for Structured Programming
IBM Corporation Report FSC 71-6012, Gaithersburg Maryland, February 1972

[Morris 1973]
James H. Morris
Types are Not Sets
Proceedings of Sigplan/Sigact Symposium on Programming Languages, Boston, 1973

[Nicholls 1975]
John E. Nicholls
The Structure and Design of Programming Languages
Addison-Wesley, Reading Massachusetts, 1975

[Organick et al. 1978]
Elliott I. Organick, Alexandra I. Forsythe, and Robert P. Plummer
Programming Language Structures
Academic Press, New York, 1978

[Pal]
Arthur Evans, Jr.
Pal: A Language Designed for Teaching Programming Language Linguistics
Proceedings ACM National Conference, 1968

[Parnas and Wurges 1976]
David L. Parnas and H. Wurges
Response to Undesired Events in Software Systems Proceedings
Second International Conference on Software Engineering, 1976

[Pascal]
Kathleen Jensen and Niklaus Wirth
Pascal User Manual and Report
Springer-Verlag, New York, 1975

[Pascal]
Niklaus Wirth
The Programming Language Pascal
Acta Informatica, Vol. 1, 1971

[Peterson et al. 1973]
W. Peterson, T. Kasami, and N. Tokura
On the Capabilities of While, Repeat, and Exit Statements
Communications of the ACM, August 1973

[PL/I]
American National Standard Programming Language PL/I
ANSI X3.53-1976 American National Standards Institute, New York, 1976

[Pratt 1975]
Terrance Pratt
Programming Languages: Design and Implementation
Prentice-Hall, Englewood Cliffs New Jersey, 1975

[Richard and Ledgard 1977]
Frederic Richard and Henry F. Ledgard
A Reminder for Language Designers
Sigplan Notices, December 1977

[Rutishauser 1967]
H. Rutishauser
Description of Algol 60
Springer-Verlag, New York, 1967

[Sammet 1969]
Jean E. Sammet
Programming Languages: History and Fundamentals
Prentice-Hall, Englewood Cliffs New Jersey, 1969

[Sammet 1978]
Jean E. Sammet
The Early History of Cobol
Sigplan Notices, August 1978

[Schwenke 1978]
Robert Schwenke
Survey of Scope Issues in Programming Languages
Computer Science Department, Technical Report CMU-CS-78-131, Carnegie Mellon University, Pittsburgh, 1978

[Scott 1970]
Dana Scott
Outline of a Mathematical Theory of Computation
Proceedings 4th Annual Princeton Conference on Information Sciences and Systems; (also Technical Monograph PRG-2, Oxford University Computing Laboratory, Programming Research Group, Oxford 1970

[Scott and Strachey 1972]
Dana Scott and Christopher Strachey
Toward a Mathematical Semantics for Computer Languages
in *Computers and Automata*
John Wiley and Sons, New York, 1972

[SETL]
Jacob Schwartz
The SETL Language and Examples of its Use
Computer Science Department, Courant Institute of Mathematical Sciences, New York 1971

[Simula 67]
O. J. Dahl, B. Myhrhaug, and U. Nygaard
The Simula 67 Common Base Language
Norwegian Computing Center, Oslo, 1968

[Snobol]
R. Griswold, J. Poage, and I. Polansky
The Snobol 4 Programming Language
Prentice-Hall, Englewood Cliffs New Jersey, 1971

[Stoy 1977]
Joseph Stoy
Denotational Semantics
MIT Press, Cambridge, Massachusetts, 1977

[Strachey 1966]
Christopher Strachey
Towards a Formal Semantics
in *Formal Description Languages for Computer Programming* (T. B. Steel, editor)
North-Holland Publishing Company, Amsterdam, 1966

[Strachey 1967]
Christopher Strachey
Fundamental Concepts in Programming Languages
International Summer School in Computer Programming, 1967

[Strachey 1972]
Christopher Strachey
Varieties of Programming Languages
Technical monograph PRG-10, Oxford University Computing Laboratory,
Programming Research Group, September 1972

[Tannenbaum 1976]
Andrew S. Tannenbaum
A Tutorial on Algol 68
Computing Surveys, June 1976

[Tennent 1976]
Richard D. Tennent
The Denotational Semantics of Programming Languages
Communications of the ACM, August 1976

[Weil 1965]
Roman L. Weil, Jr.
*Testing the Understanding of the Difference Between Call By Name and
Call By Value in Algol 60*
Communications of the ACM, June 1965

[Whitaker 1978]
William A. Whitaker
The US Department of Defense Common High Order Language Effort
Sigplan Notices, February 1978

[Whitehead 1911]
Alfred North Whitehead
An Introduction to Mathematics
Oxford University Press, Oxford 1911

[Wirth 1971]
Niklaus Wirth
Program Development by Stepwise Refinement
Communications of the ACM, April 1971

[Wirth 1973]
Niklaus Wirth
Systematic Programming: An Introduction
Prentice-Hall, Englewood Cliffs New Jersey, 1973

[Wirth 1974]
Niklaus Wirth
On the Design of Programming Languages
in *Information Processing 74*, Jack L. Rosenfeld, Ed.,
North-Holland, Amsterdam, 1974, pp. 386-393

[Wirth 1976]
Niklaus Wirth
Programming Languages: What to Demand and How to Assess Them, and Professor Cleverbyte's Visit to Heaven
E.T.H. Institute fuer Informatik, Technical Report 17, Munich, March 1978

[Whorf 1956]
Benjamin Whorf
Language Thought and Reality
MIT Press, Cambridge Massachusetts, 1956

[Wulf and Shaw 1973]
William Wulf and Mary Shaw
Global Variable Considered Harmful
Sigplan Notices, August 1973

Index